MODERN HUMANITIES RESEARCH ASSOCIATION

CRITICAL TEXTS

VOLUME 16

Editor
BRIAN RICHARDSON
(*Italian*)

ANGELO BEOLCO (IL RUZANTE)
LA PRIMA ORATIONE

ANGELO BEOLCO (IL RUZANTE)
LA PRIMA ORATIONE

Edited by

Linda L. Carroll

MODERN HUMANITIES RESEARCH ASSOCIATION
2009

Published by

The Modern Humanities Research Association
1 Carlton House Terrace
London SW1Y 5AF

© The Modern Humanities Research Association, 2009

Linda L. Carroll has asserted her right under the Copyright, Designs and Patents Act 1988 to be identified as the author of this work.

Parts of this work may be reproduced as permitted under legal provisions for fair dealing (or fair use) for the purposes of research, private study, criticism, or review, or when a relevant collective licensing agreement is in place. All other reproduction requires the written permission of the copyright holder who may be contacted at rights@mhra.org.uk.

First published 2009

ISBN 978-0-947623-79-1

ISSN 1746-1642

Copies may be ordered from www.criticaltexts.mhra.org.uk

Table of Contents

Preface	1
Acknowledgements ....……....................................	3
Abbreviations	4
Introduction: 'New Law and Statutes': Playwright, Peasants, and *Papalisti*..	5
La prima oration, VR 36 and Translation…...........................	78
La prima oration, VR 1636...	103
La prima oration, BMV, Ital. XI 66..	115
Bibliography	127
Index ………...	143

Preface

This volume contains the first full transcription of all three known manuscript versions of the *Prima oration* (*Prima oratione, First Oration*) of Angelo Beolco, who is better known by the name of his peasant character Ruzante, and the first translation into English of any version. The oration was delivered to Cardinal Marco Cornaro on the occasion of his assumption of the bishopric of Padua. The best-known version is found in a large miscellany, Venice, Biblioteca Nazionale Marciana, MS Ital. XI 66 (=6730), which contains the greatest number of Beolco texts and whose compilation was concluded shortly after 1530. The other two versions are found in two manuscripts of the Biblioteca Civica of Verona, 36 and 1636, both produced in that or a nearby city in the middle or later 1530s. Both of these manuscripts contain other works by Beolco, as well as works by other authors. The oration was first printed in Venice by Stefano Alessi in 1551. It has been edited most recently by Ludovico Zorzi (Turin: Einaudi, 1967) and Giorgio Padoan (Padua: Antenore, 1978), accompanied by a translation into standard Italian. Zorzi based his edition on a combination of the XI 66 text and the first printed version. Padoan drew on the manuscripts and early printed versions to reconstruct portions of the text missing from some of the manuscripts and relied on XI 66 for language forms ('Nota ai testi', p. 56). In both cases, uneven note was taken of the textual variants.

The present edition's scholarly apparatus draws on a more extensive base of sixteenth-century materials than that of earlier editions, including many new sources, and this provides evidence for a new dating scheme and the elucidation of numerous enigmatic passages. Cornaro's official episcopal entrance having occurred in 1521, the oration has been universally ascribed to that year. However, the present edition will provide evidence that the first version of the text, represented by VR 36, was written in the summer of 1518, the year of Cornaro's elevation and of his visit to the family estate in Asolo near Treviso where, according to this manuscript, it was performed. Evidence will also be provided that a second performance, based on a distinct version (VR 1636), was presented in September 1518 in Venice at a party that Cornaro organized for his fellow cardinals Innocenzo Cibo and a Salviati cousin, nephews of the pope who were visiting from Rome. A hypothesis will be presented concerning the identity of the associates of Beolco's who assembled VR 1636 (or the archetype on which it was based) and who worked on, and conveyed to Venice, the third version and some of the other texts that were copied into XI 66. An extensive discussion of contemporary historical events and of the domestic and foreign policies of the Venetian Republic will allow numerous of the oration's passages to be better understood and the variants distinguishing the three versions to be better appreciated. With the referents more fully explained, the oration may be understood as a serious social and economic programme, and the full complexity and merit of Beolco as a thinker and orator valued.

The present edition is based on a new transcription of the texts made by the editor. The translation aims to present the text in an English version that preserves the liveliness of the rural Paduan dialect original and the multi-layered referentiality of a text that only appears to be naive. The Zorzi and Padoan Italian translations were helpful on numerous points but also presented some errors and misreadings that are corrected here.

Acknowledgements

Thanks are due to many individuals whose assistance and support helped bring this book to fruition. I am particularly grateful to Brian Richardson, Italian Editor of the Critical Texts series, for his invaluable advice. The late Prof. Giovanni Battista Pellegrini of the University of Padua gave unstintingly of his philological and cultural expertise over many years. The late Prof. Kenneth Setton of the Institute for Advanced Study, Princeton, contributed in important ways to the understanding of the historical context. The wonderfully eclectic conferences organized by the late Prof. Giovanni Calendoli of the University of Padua, in uniting a wide range of scholars from many fields, stimulated many new hypotheses. Dr Marino Zorzi, director of the Biblioteca Nazionale Marciana, provided numerous insights into Venetian patrician culture. He also graciously gave direct access to manuscript materials and permission to publish them, as did Dr Agostino Contò of the Biblioteca Civica, Verona. The director of the Archivio di Stato, Padua, Dott.sa Francesca Fantini D'Onofrio, and numerous staff members provided expert assistance with materials. At the Archivio di Stato, Venice, Dott.sa Michela Dal Borgo and Dott.sa Alessandra Sambo were especially helpful. Thanks go also to the personnel of the Archivio di Stato, Modena, especially the former director Dr Angelo Spaggiari, the Archivio di Stato, Mantua, and Státní Oblastní Archiv, Brno (Czech Republic). Expert assistance was provided by the personnel of the Biblioteca del Museo Correr (Venice), the Biblioteca Civica (Padua) and the Biblioteca Capitolare della Curia Vescovile di Padova. As always, any errors are my responsibility alone. I am grateful to the American Philosophical Society for a grant supporting the transcription of the texts and to Tulane University for a Phase II Research Enhancement Fund grant supporting part of the research and a Weiss Presidential Fellowship supporting part of the editorial work. Finally, special thanks go to Bruce Boyd Raeburn, both for his personal support and for his knowledge of jazz and its role in New Orleans culture and society, which provided an always stimulating point of comparison with Ruzante's improvisation and its role in the culture and society of Venice and northeastern Italy in the early sixteenth century.

Abbreviations

The following abbreviations are used in the present volume (full references for published works can be found in the Bibliography):

ASMn	Archivio di Stato, Mantua
ASMo	Archivio di Stato, Modena
ASP	Archivio di Stato, Padua
ASV	Archivio di Stato, Venice
BCP	Biblioteca Civica, Padua
BCV	Biblioteca del Museo Correr, Venice
BMV	Biblioteca Nazionale Marciana, Venice
DBI	*Dizionario biografico degli italiani*
GDLI	*Grande dizionario della lingua italiana*
Sanuto	Marino Sanuto (Marin Sanudo), *I diarii*, ed. by Rinaldo Fulin and others

Introduction

'New Law and Statutes': Playwright, Peasants, and Papalisti

1. The Author

Born in Padua around 1496 or somewhat before, Angelo Beolco was the natural son of Gian Francesco Beolco, whose noble Lombard father Lazzaro, during the lengthy peace of the latter fifteenth century, had advanced his business activities along the Po Valley. Lazzaro became a citizen of Vicenza and set himself up in the cloth business in Padua with the assistance of his in-laws, who originated in the cloth-making town of Pernumia; he also made frequent trips to Venice. He soon become involved in the book trade, which had a steady market in the students and faculty of the University of Padua and the prosperous city of Venice.[1]

Gian Francesco attended the University of Padua, where he met numerous Venetian patricians, it being the only one they were permitted to attend. Joining the faculty, he completed a second degree in medicine and was elected prior. The family acquired property in various locales of the Pavan (the countryside around Padua), including Pernumia, Montagnana, and Arquà, the elegant village that was the preferred home and final resting place of Petrarch. Historian Paolo Sambin discovered documents suggesting that Angelo's mother was a household servant whose family had come from one of the 'borghi' (faubourgs) of Padua where rural families often settled upon their arrival, one adjacent to the Euganean Hills. On the basis of another document, Sambin deduced that Angelo was probably born in 1496. The servant's contract, which expired in 1497, was not renewed, which would have resulted in her departure from the household (Sambin,

---

[1] The material in this section summarizes Carroll, *Angelo Beolco*, esp. Chapter One, which synthesizes research by Emilio Lovarini, Emilio Menegazzo, Paolo Sambin, Antonio Bonardi, Giorgio Padoan and others, cited in detail there.

'Lazzaro', pp. 133, 163-65). Shortly thereafter Gian Francesco married a woman from a prosperous Montagnana family that had long been members of the Paduan wool guild and that provided soldiers to Venice (Lazara, unnumbered fol. but 18^v; Sanuto, XXV, 535, XXXIV, 261). When Padua took advantage of Venice's defeat in 1509 at Agnadello by the League of Cambrai to offer itself to its traditional overlord the Holy Roman Emperor (then Maximilian I), Angelo's paternal uncles participated on the imperial side. Their ardour was signalled by the name given to a cousin born then, Imperio, the partisans' battlecry. When Venice retook the city two months later, the uncles were arrested and sent to Venice. The war dragged on for eight years, with Padua, the bastion of Venice's mainland state, often its centrepiece (Polano). In 1517, as the war ended, Beolco's father began to withdraw to the peace of Pernumia, leaving the tending of his agricultural properties and the peasants who cultivated them to his eldest son.

Possibly beginning even before the war, Angelo developed a theatrical career as a peasant character in rustic comedies of his own composition in Padua and its countryside, and perhaps Ferrara (Carroll, '"Fools"', pp. 63-67). It eventually involved performances for patricians in Venice, documented from 1520 to 1526; they generally occurred during Carnival but one celebrated (and scandalized) a May wedding in the Ducal Palace. After an especially raucous episode in 1526, Ruzante's name disappears from Venetian records but occurs in those of Padua and Ferrara, where he led a comic troupe. He developed a patronage relationship with Alvise Cornaro (apparently no relation to Cardinal Marco), a Venetian transplanted to Padua who built a fortune in agricultural land in the Pavan. At his father's death in the early 1520s, Beolco moved from his household to Cornaro's. He may have served as a soldier during the first years of the new round of warfare that followed the formation of the League of Cognac, 1526-27 (Menegazzo, 'Stato', p. 164 n. 76). In the final years of the decade, during a time of severe famine, he served as Cornaro's agent in buying land from desperately impoverished peasants. While his early plays (*Prima oratione, Pastoral, Betia*) reflect the buoyant relief characteristic of the first postwar period, the works of the late 1520s (*Seconda oratione, Dialogo facetissimo, Reduce*,

Bilora, Moscheta, Fiorina) echo their exhaustion and despair.[2] The final works (*Piovana, Vaccaria, Anconitana*), which follow the Roman tradition much more closely than the others, embrace the peace resulting from Charles V's virtual conquest of the Italian peninsula, though showing reluctant resignation to the social stasis that accompanied it. His last known work (a version of the *Lettera all'Alvarotto*) dates to 1536 (or, if dated in the Venetian style, 1537); the final phase of his life was absorbed by the management of the farm properties of others. He died in 1542 while rehearsing Sperone Speroni's tragedy *Canace*.

2. *Padua, Venice and the Papacy (1509-1517)*

An extraordinary text, Angelo Beolco's *First Oration* (entitled in the manuscripts *Prima oration*, in Italian *Prima orazione*, with the blended form *Prima oratione* also commonly used) celebrated an extraordinary occasion, the assumption of the bishopric of Padua by Venetian patrician Marco Cornaro (Corner), which restored the important and wealthy diocese to Venetian hands after exclusive papal control. Given its caption in VR 36, 'Oration de Ruzante recitata al Cardinal Cornaro al barcho soto Asolo in Trivisana' (An oration of Ruzante's recited to Cardinal Cornaro at his barn below Asolo in the Trevisan countryside), the oration has been associated exclusively with a performance at the Cornaro family villa near Asolo presumed to have taken place in 1521 after the cardinal's formal episcopal entry. While the present work accepts such a performance as likely, it will explore neglected indications that multiple performances occurred beginning in 1518 for audiences with whom Beolco was deeply familiar, that the text refers in a meaningful way to numerous and repeated contemporary events important to those audiences, and that the manuscript variants reflect the author's presentation of his philosophy to three audience types (compare Turner).

The return of the wealthy bishopric to a Venetian patrician represented Venice's political renewal. Pope Julius II, the head of the anti-Venetian League of Cambrai, had taken it over in May 1509 after the battle of Agnadello, naming as its holder his nephew

---

[2] The chronology of Beolco's plays is too vexed a question to treat here, especially as many of them appear to have been rewritten multiple times (see e.g. Carroll, 'Dating'). The present list is provided for ease of reference only.

Sisto Gara della Rovere (Dondi Dall'Orologio, *Dissertazioni*, IX, 88-98). By July, Venice had retaken Padua's civil government, but Julius proved a more formidable opponent. Further Venetian defeats the following year allowed him to extract a variety of ecclesiastical and financial privileges (Setton, III, 77-78; compare Gilbert). Gara della Rovere never made his entrance into Padua; illiterate and uninterested in church affairs, he spent much of his time in the country or at the baths. By the time of his death in March 1517, the papacy had passed to Leo X (Giovanni de' Medici).

Leo announced his choice of successor from his hunting lodge at La Magnana, where he was vacationing with Cornaro and other favourites (Sanuto, XXIV, 51-52, 94). Both Leo and Cornaro wrote to the Venetian government requesting Cornaro's 'possesso' (physical possession). Cornaro promised to put the bishopric and his life to the service of the Republic to overcome patrician suspicions that as a 'papalista' (patrician with ecclesiastical ties) he would put the (political) good of the Church before that of the Republic (Sanuto, XXIV, 58, 60, 150; for 'papalisti', see Cozzi, 'Stato'). Despite foreign competitors and the claims of the Venetian patrician Dandolo family, the Senate responded with an overwhelmingly affirmative vote. Within days, Cardinal Marco's brother Zuan took possession of the episcopal palace and even suggested himself as suffragan despite being married. The cathedral canons sent their archdeacon, apostolic protonotary Hironimo Giustinian qu. Unfredo of the distinguished Venetian patrician family, to speak to Padua's Venetian governors about the continuation of the bishop's alms to the poor. They were apparently worried that the notoriously acquisitive Corner would utilize diocesan revenues for private purposes rather than follow the saintly path of an earlier bishop, Pietro Barozzi.[3]

In appointing Cornaro, Leo gained an envoy whose family occupied the innermost circle of Venetian power, its prestige bolstered by descent in the maternal line from the Byzantine

---

[3] da Corte, fol. 104ʳ. When a given Venetian patrician name and surname are borne by more than one individual, the bearers will be distinguished by patronym preceded by 'di' (a living father) or 'qu.' (a deceased one).

imperial Comneno family.[4] The Cornaro were also possessed of the wealth becoming ever more essential to maintaining power (Finlay, *Politics*, esp. pp. 159-60; Gilbert, pp. 43-48, 103-07). The family fortune was based on vast holdings on the Greek islands that provided staple products including sugar and wine to Venice's Western or Flanders galleys (Brown, II, 46-49 n. 2), which conveyed them to northern Europe. Overlooked by scholars are the family's equally strong ties to Padua, which began with the fourteenth-century marriage of future doge Marco Cornaro (Bishop Marco's great-great-great grandfather) to Giovanna Scrovegni, daughter of Enrico Scrovegni, whose fabled chapel had been frescoed by Giotto (Kohl, pp. 80-81, 174-75). The Corner owned property in the parish of S. Zuan in Verdara to which Beolco's uncle and grandfather were linked (*Estimo*, reg. 351 [352], fol. 241^r; Sambin, 'Lazzaro', pp. 151-52, 159-61). Cardinal Marco's mother's family, the Morosini, owned large amounts of property in Padua, Piove, and Montagnana (*Estimo*, reg. 351 [352], fols 134^r, 242^v). Corner family members, including Bishop Marco's father Zorzi (Giorgio), had served as 'podestà' (civil governor) of Padua four times (Gloria, IV, 274, 278, 279). Cardinal Marco had studied at the arts faculty there while Beolco's father was its prior (Dorighello, fols 393^v-94^r). One of the Republic's wealthiest and most influential patricians, Zorzi held many other high offices and was considered a leading candidate to succeed the elderly doge Leonardo Loredan. His sister Caterina, after a brief reign as queen of Cyprus, had been withdrawn by the Republic to a dignified retirement at her small but 'glittering court' near Asolo, in the foothills of the Alps (Grubb, p. 171). It had served as the backdrop to the *Asolani* of Venetian patrician and man of letters Pietro Bembo.

Such a well-connected bishop could draw Venice toward Leo's political and religious purposes, especially his effort to unite Christian leaders in a war against the Turk. Venice was particularly difficult to enlist because its maritime empire and trade were connected with areas ruled by the Turks, who in 1516 and 1517 conquered Mamluk Syria and Egypt with their key Venetian

---

[4] Sanuto, XVI, 152-54; information on Corner in this paragraph from Giuseppe Gullino, 'Corner, Giorgio', 'Corner, Giorgio', 'Corner, Marco', 'Corner, Marco', 'Corner, Marco', *DBI*; Sanuto, XXIX, 210-16, 251-57, XXIII, 362

trading cities of Damascus and Alexandria, cutting off Venice's silk supply (Molà, p. 57).

Already in 1514, Leo had deployed Cornaro and Bembo, then his secretary, to persuade Florence and Venice to his pro-Spanish position.[5] Leo's 1514 strategy may also have included imperialist relatives of Beolco's stage partner Marc'Aurelio Alvarotto, Giacomo and Francesco, who in that year petitioned the Venetian government to be pardoned for their role in the 1509 dedition and to reclaim their Paduan properties (Sanuto, XVIII, 232; Bonardi, pp. 434-35). Their father Conte, a respected professor and imperialist leader, had died in Venice's notorious 'cages', which were actual cages set up in the granary to handle treasonous political prisoners in wartime, where they were exposed to harsh physical conditions and ridicule (Scarabello, p. 6). While Francesco Alvarotto remained confined to Venice, Giacomo was apparently allowed to return to Padua. An accomplished jurist, he left to establish himself elsewhere. In 1511, along with numerous other Paduan imperialists, he was present in the Gonzaga entourage accompanying imperial ambassador and bishop of Gurck Matteo Lang to a meeting with Julius II in Bologna. There Lang unsuccessfully advanced Maximilian's proposal to reconstitute the League of Cambrai in order to reclaim Padua and other imperial lands taken by Venice (Sanuto, XII, 117-18). Marco Cornaro also attended the meeting, his bad humour perhaps attributable to Lang's purpose. Shortly thereafter, Giacomo Alvarotto found employment in Florence as a member of a judicial commission, first under the republican government and then under the Medici, after their restoration with the support of Ferdinand of Aragon. The Alvarotto brothers' 1514 petition was supported by a large payment and an offer of the good offices with the pope of another brother, Alvarotto, and a nephew, who held important appointments at the papal court. It was granted, although with the proviso that in wartime they obtain permission to go to Padua and its territory. When Giacomo appeared before Venice's Collegio (war committee) in July to express his loyalty, he brought a letter of thanks from Giuliano de' Medici, with whom Francesco was staying. Giuliano, the son of Lorenzo il Magnifico and brother of Leo, had made many friends while in Venice during the Medici

---

[5] Sanuto, XIX, 306, 308, 309, 311, 312, 313, 316, 319, 320-21, 322, 323, 326, 327, 336, 338-39, 340, 353, 359, 362, 369, 374-75; Giannetto, p. 265.

exile that had ended two years before.[6] Such a congeries of facts raises the suspicion that the Alvarotto too were serving to bring Leo's Spanish programme to Venice and its imperial-leaning dominion.

Shortly after the petition was granted, Giacomo joined the service of Alfonso I d'Este, Duke of Ferrara, and would represent him on diplomatic missions to the pope, the emperor, and the Republic. In the same year, Leo allowed Alvarotto Alvarotto to assign his nephew his Paduan canonicate but Alvarotto, excommunicated for debt in 1517, apparently (re)assigned it to the son of patrician Troian Bolani, probably for a sum. After Alvarotto's death in 1518, Leo, at the behest of Cardinal Marco, conferred it upon Andrea Mercadelli, raising protests from Antonio Grimani on behalf of Bolani. Indications point to this as one episode in the ecclesiastical competition between the Cornaro and the Grimani, leading 'papalista' families. Numerous Bolani family members had houses and businesses in Padua and in Pernumia, Montagnana, and Piove.[7]

Venice itself had relied on Cardinal Marco to represent its interests in Rome. Immediately after Agnadello, he and Cardinal Domenico Grimani had attempted to persuade Julius II to lift his excommunication of the Republic (Sanuto, VIII, 389, 502). In 1515, during a time of delicate negotiations with Leo over a land exchange with the Swiss allotting the formerly Venetian cities of Brescia and Bergamo to Giuliano de' Medici, Cornaro assumed the Venetian ambassador's duties when he fell ill (Sanuto, XIX, 27, 196, 362-63, 367). He also served as the ambassador's intermediary with the pope (Sanuto, XX, 175, 329, 537, XXI, 135, 257, XXII, 18-19, 559, 606, XXIII, 39-40, XXIV, 13, 51, 94). Frequently accompanying Leo, including at the lodge where political discussions were conducted as well as hunting (Sanuto, XV, 389, XIX, 109, 390, 450, XXII, 6, XXIII, 144, XXIV, 51), Cornaro supplied the Venetian government with a steady stream of

---

[6] Sanuto, XVIII, 381; Dondi dall'Orologio, *Dissertazioni*, IX, 11, 13; Lovarini, 'Ruzzante a Venezia', pp. 81-107, 98-99.

[7] da Corte, fol. 108^v; Dondi dall'Orologio, *Dissertazioni*, IX, 11, 13; Sanuto, XXVI, 125, 201-02; Bembo also competed for the benefice: *Lettere*, II, 297 lett. 597, 305 lett. 607, 311 lett. 614, 330 lett. 637. Bollani: *Estimo*, reg. 351 (352), fols 115^r-116^r, 144^r, 164^r, 186^r, 192^v-193^r, 299^v, 333^r, 339^v; Lazara, unnumbered folio but 1485. Beolco's *Piovana* is set in Piove.

fresh news, some of it exclusive (Sanuto, XX, 70, 129, 526-27, 586, XXI, 115). Leo was aware of Cornaro's communications: when he was making plans contrary to Venetian policy, Cornaro was excluded (Sanuto, XX, 193, 375, XXII, 524). A turning point came in September 1515 with the Battle of Marignano. A decisive French victory resulting in their capture of Milan and the withdrawal from Italy of the Swiss, the mainstay of the papal army, Marignano demonstrated the superiority of Venice's French affiliation over Leo's with Ferdinand and his in-law Maximilian.

3. Marco Cornaro, Bishop of Padua, Visits Asolo and Venice (1517-1518)

It was in this context that Leo named Cornaro to the bishopric of Padua in 1517. Some months later, he planned a campaign to unite Europe in a crusade against the powerful and aggressive Turkish sultan Selim the Grim, who had recently conquered the southeast rim of the Mediterranean. The commission of cardinals named to assist him, which included Cornaro, recommended that Venice contribute twice as many galleys as France or Spain, an unlikely outcome given Venice's preference for peaceful relations with the Turks. In March 1518, Leo announced his plan for a five-year truce among Christian rulers, a necessary preliminary to the crusade. As Kenneth Setton explains, 'None of the major monarchs would venture into the East unless his fellows joined him. He would not leave his enemies behind to attack his lands in his absence. He would not spend his money on a crusade unless his rivals employed all their available resources in the same cause' (Setton, III, 173-85 (p. 181)). Following his announcement, the pope sent an eminent cardinal to each of the four major courts (the empire, Spain, France, and England) to persuade them to convert vague words of support into ratification of the peace.

While Marco Cornaro, unlike his confrères, was not a papal legate, he journeyed to Venetian territory in June 1518. Venetian diarist Marin Sanudo (Marino Sanuto) noted that, having arrived in the seaport of Chioggia, Cornaro avoided the expense of a visit to Venice or his new see by proceeding directly to Asolo.[8]

---

[8] The state had apparently sold the holding to the Cornaro: Sanuto, XXV, 461, XX, 446.

During his sojourn, his brother Francesco, the Venetian ambassador to Spain, sent a letter to Bernardo Loredan, the doge's son, which was read by the Council of Ten. In it Francesco described a festivity conducted by the new king Charles presenting him to the people and foreign ambassadors dressed in dazzling garments and surrounded by nobles. It concluded with war games. Francesco Corner, clearly seeing the ceremony as being of urgent state concern, instructed that the letter be taken immediately to Asolo to his uncle Polo Capello, a member and former head of the Council of Ten, and to Cardinal Marco (Sanuto, XXV, 538-40).

That Charles and Francis I were headed to war for the dominance of Italy was becoming ever clearer. To provide defence funding, the Venetian government decided to conduct a new *estimo* (calculation of taxes on mainland property) to update its ownership records. The updating had been sought by the city of Padua to reapportion the tax burden on the extensive amount of its land that had passed into Venetian hands and the many exemptions achieved by Venetians. In April 1518 Padua sent university-trained orator Gaspare Orsato to renew its request. Francesco Pesaro, a member of the mainland governance commission, introduced an alternative bill with some terms favoured by the Paduans. Pesaro's bill was defeated by the main bill requiring less taxation of Venetians.[9]

The papal legates succeeded in generating some interest in Leo's crusade, in part because Selim planned an assault on Europe in August. Francis had additional reasons for agreeing: his plans with Venice to bring the pope into a Franco-Venetian league to induce the pope to invest him with Naples, of which the pope was liege lord. Francis would thus garner a base from which to drive Charles from Italy and a period of peace in which to renew his coffers, drained by the preceding war and offerings to the electors for the imperial crown that by July had secured a majority of their votes. Venice, anxious to retain the support of the monarch viewed as most favourable to the Republic's interests, conceded Francis's preferences on point after point. For example, while their original position was that mainland imperialist rebels should remain in prison, they agreed under pressure from Francis to allow them back into the dominion, though not near borders with the empire. By August, the Senate approved the truce, though publicly claiming

---

[9] Favaretto, *L'istituzione*, esp. pp. 129-96; Sanuto, XXV, 367, 471, 503; ASV, Senato, *Secreta*, reg. 47, fol. 140^{r-v}.

that their ambassador to France, Antonio Giustinian, had accepted it without their permission.[10]

During Cornaro's Asolo sojourn, the Paduan cathedral canons sent him a delegation, who reported with joy the results of their discussions. It again was headed by Hieronimo Giustinian qu. Unfredo, the brother-in-law of both Nicolò Dolfin di Pietro, who in 1516 had published Boccaccio's *Decameron* (Richardson, p. 60), and of Andrea Magno, whose son Stefano in 1521 would make the only known manuscript copy of Beolco's *Pastoral* (Padoan, 'Fortuna', p. 203; Sanuto, XXXVII, 22). Hieronimo's brother, the procurator Andrea, and his kinsman the procurator Hironimo qu. Antonio in 1525 would attend the rehearsal of a Ruzante play drawing so many high-ranking patricians that it emptied the Senate chamber. It also caused such scandal that it was substituted before opening night (Sanuto, XXXVII, 559-60). During the canons' visit to Asolo, the truce, which at last included Maximilian, was reported in Padua, especially its provision allowing the city's exiles to return (da Corte, fol. 115^v).

Maximilian's consent had been wrung from him with the promise of Venice's payment of 20,000 of the agreed-to 100,000 ducats of war reparations on 1 September. He was shorter of funds than usual because, driven by his wish to have his grandson Charles succeed him and alarmed at Francis's efforts, he was expending exorbitant sums to bring a majority of electors to his will. The Venetian Senate voted on 18 August that payment to Maximilian would be remitted by Alvise Pisani, head of Venice's largest bank, to be repaid out of revenues from Venice's mainland state (Sanuto, XXV, 581-82, 592, 596, 598). On 19 August, a report reached Venice that Maximilian had captured sufficient votes to ensure Charles's election, the electors' commitment sealed in writing before Francis could counter it. The rabidly pro-French Pisani retracted his offer, refusing to act as the government's banker until his accounts with the state had been reviewed.[11]

---

[10] Setton, III, 180-86; Knecht, pp. 82-85; Moncallero, 'La politica', esp. pp. 75-83; R. Zago, 'Antonio Giustinian', *DBI*; Senato, *Secreta*, reg. 47, fols 112^v-13^r, 113^r-14^v, 119^v-20^r, 130^v, 142^r-50^v; text of the truce: Sanuto, XXV, 673-79.

[11] Sanuto, XXV, 600, 601, 611-12, compare XXVI, 7; Moncallero, *Bibbiena*, pp. 75-81; Knecht, pp.165-67. Pisani died participating in the 1528 French siege of Naples.

INTRODUCTION

The Signoria then turned to bankers Antonio Capello and Luca Vendramin. The Capello, one of Venice's most prominent banking families, had long-standing commercial ties to England, the empire and the papacy (Angelo Ventura, 'Cappello, Paolo', *DBI*; Sanuto, XXXV, 388; Lane, 'News', p. 8; Gilbert). The war having damaged their extensive mainland property and reduced its income (Varanini, pp. 807-79; Sanuto, XIII, 174-75, XXIV, 251, 352), the Capello were concerned to maintain peace with the empire. This was especially true of Antonio, who during the war had served as proveditor (civilian overseer of the army) and in Venice's relations with the papacy, in which he practiced even-handed pragmatism.[12] The Vendramin also had extensive mainland holdings, principally in the Friuli, where the empire repeatedly stressed its strong claims in the early sixteenth century. Luca had property near Padua that he was augmenting, in some cases jointly with Antonio Capello.[13] Moreover, the Vendramin had ecclesiastical ambitions.

On 8 September, Marco slipped into Venice for a secret twenty-day visit (Sanuto, XXVI, 20). While there he conferred with the doge and hosted a lavish banquet for eleven leading patricians: his father Zorzi Corner, procurator and knight; his uncle Polo Capello, knight; the doge's son Lorenzo Loredan, procurator; Domenego Trevisan, procurator and knight; Andrea Gritti, procurator; Hironimo Giustinian qu. Antonio, procurator; Alvise Pisani, procurator; Lunardo Mocenigo, son of the late doge Zuan; Zorzi Pisani, university laureate, knight, and member of the commission instituted to oversee the University of Padua because of the role of German students in ceding the city to the emperor; Andrea Trevisan, knight; and Michiel Salamon, a head of the Council of Ten (Sanuto, XXVI, 20, 44-45).

The Corner and most of the guests figured among the small group of patricians occupying what could be termed a hinge

---

[12] Angelo Ventura, 'Cappello, Paolo', *DBI*; see also Antonio Capello qu. Batista (Sanuto, XXIII, 312, 313, XXIV, 250-51), who sought election to the governorship of the strategic fortified town of Legnago, for which Mallett and Hale, pp. 264, 299, 389, 391, 410-11, 414, 425; Concina, pp. 6, 8-9, 19.

[13] Zamperetti, *I piccoli principi*, pp. 212, 222, 280; Cozzi and Knapton, p. 210; Luca Vendramin: *Estimo*, reg. 351 (352), fols 203^v, unnumbered but 203bis, 341^v; Antonio Cappello: *Estimo*, reg. 351 (352), fol. unnumbered but 203bis, reg. 352 (353), fol. 37^r; da Corte, fols 119^v-20^r; Cestaro.

position concerning Venetian external affairs, a position that had become more critical with the electors' commitment to Charles. They believed that good relations with Spain and the empire were vital to the survival of the Republic, which would allow it to pursue preferred pro-French policies under more favourable conditions. The group consisted of families whose positions at the ends of the politico-economic spectrum left them most affected by the influence of Spain, the empire and the papacy on recent adverse economic circumstances. Very wealthy families such as the Corner and Pisani needed to protect their struggling commercial fortunes and growing mainland 'latifondi', as well as their exalted political and ecclesiastical ambitions, while hard-pressed families, frequently clients of the wealthier ones, clung to low-level benefices, small agricultural holdings, and modest state posts (Carroll, 'Venetian Attitudes').

Venice then faced dual economic adversities. In the eastern Mediterranean, the Turks threatened Venetian commerce in goods including wine, sugar and textiles. The Portuguese, meanwhile, stymied Venice's Asian commerce at its source in the Indian port of Colacut, where their caravels often loaded the entire supply of spices and jewels and, bypassing the Mediterranean, took them directly to Lisbon and then on to northern Europe (Finlay, 'Crisis'; Brown, II, 82 n. 6, 76 n. 1; Sanuto, XXV, 203). As reported in the summer of 1518 by Francesco Corner, the Portuguese also aimed to control the Mediterranean route by creating a small ship that could sail from India through the Red Sea (Sanuto, XXV, 444-45). Even greater competition was taking shape in the Spanish effort to dominate the spice trade, which culminated in Charles's financing of Magellan's expedition, negotiations for which began in late 1517 (Kellenbenz).

Venice's merchants were particularly concerned with trade in this period because of the resumption of the Flanders galleys, state-sponsored ships carrying Asian and Mediterranean goods to northern Europe, that had ceased sailing during the War of the League of Cambrai (Carroll, 'Venetian Attitudes'). Charles, who through his inheritance of Spain and Flanders already controlled much of the litoral along which the Flanders galleys sailed (Lane, p. 341, map 9), would as emperor assume control of central Europe, which had formerly traded precious metals for Eastern goods in Venice but which had followed trade to Lisbon. Moreover, the empire laid claim to much of the mainland farm property to which, under the leadership of the Cornaro and others

(Beltrami, p. 46), patricians were increasingly turning as a substitute investment. Maximilian's efforts to activate such claims had turned the mainland state into a battlefield for eight years, ravaging agricultural and industrial resources. The mainland's rich ecclesiastical benefices, the other sought-after source of patrician income, had also suffered from the war; moreover, the papacy was increasingly usurping local authority over them (Cestaro).

A few details will indicate how active the families of Cardinal Marco's dinner guests had been in each of these arenas. Hironimo Giustinian qu. Antonio, member of a ducal family that began acquiring mainland property before 1200 and continued in the fifteenth century with mills, farmland, and a castle, held extensive property with his wife Agnesina Badoer (Ling, p. 308 n. 17; Varanini, pp. 820, 834, 839; Lewis, pp. 12-13). He strongly supported the Alexandria galleys that traded Asian goods in the Egyptian entrepôt (Sanuto, XXI, 35). Trevisan holdings around Padua were so extensive in the Carrara period that they were exempt from taxes (Gloria, III, 245; Calore, p. 22; Ling, p. 312; Varanini, pp. 814-15). The Corner's acquisition of land, which began before Venice took control of Padua in the early fifteenth century, continued thereafter with both farmland and mills.[14] As the Venetian state expanded, it confiscated the holdings of former mainland 'signori' and 'condottieri', which, to meet war expenses, were sold into private hands. The Pisani thus assembled vast urban, agricultural and industrial holdings in the late fifteenth and early sixteenth centuries.[15] The bulk of Capello acquisitions consisted of farmland near Verona, confiscated properties of the Scaligero and dal Verme; the importance of their rents is demonstrated by the zeal with which, at the end of the war, family members set about collecting the eight years' worth owed them (Sanuto, XXIV, 250-51, 352). Polo Capello's holdings near Bassano, whose wood and minerals provided lucrative returns, had been occupied and his house burned by the enemy (Sanuto, XIII, 174-75; Varanini, pp. 811, 849-50, 853; Cozzi and Knapton, p. 127).

---

[14] Beltrami, p. 46; ASV, *Archivio Grimani Santa Maria Formosa*, busta 3 labelled *Acquisti di folli C[arta]*, fol. 1^r, copy of document of 12 September 1406; Lazzarini, 'Possessi', pp. 213-14, 217; Lazzarini, 'L'industria', p. 56; Varanini, p. 836.

[15] Sanuto, III, 46-47; Lazzarini, 'Beni', p. 277; Menegazzo, p. 181 n. 1; Fasullo, 'Livelli', p. 118; Varanini, pp. 832, 849-50.

The defence needs created by the mainland state divided the patriciate into two opposing groups, with the guest families providing leaders for each. Doge Tommaso Mocenigo, who had served as 'vice-podestà' of Padua early in the fifteenth century, emphasized in a famous speech that the wars required to defend the mainland caused heavy expenditures and reduced income (Lane, *Venice*, pp. 228-29). His caution prompted a curious pattern of response among his descendants, who included another doge, guest Lunardo's father. While few Mocenigo owned mainland property, (Varanini, pp. 811-12 but compare Sanuto, XXIV, 352) some married into proportied families and even into the feudal nobility, increasingly so as the fifteenth century drew to a close. Lucia Mocenigo, wife of Antonio III of the powerful Counts of Collalto, was even sent to the imperial court in 1510 (Rambaldo, fol. $16^{r\text{-}v}$; Sanuto, IX, 326), while Lunardo's cousin Bianca married into the Martinengo family.[16] Such connections parallelled the family's accelerating involvement in mainland defence. By 1518 Mocenigo kinsmen had occupied the offices of 'podestà' and 'capitanio' (military governor) of Padua eight additional times (Gloria, I, 272-83). During the 1509 siege of Padua, Alvise was elected proveditor general in Treviso (Sanuto, IX, 153-54, 155), his duties including relations with the Collalto (Sanuto, X, 612, 633). Lunardo offered himself and eight men for the defence of Padua and Treviso in 1513 (Sanuto, XVII, 247). During repeated terms as 'savio' (the 'savi' were an important government commission), he demonstrated a lively interest in mainland defence and governance, including the hiring of Gianfrancesco Gonzaga as captain general of the army (Sanuto, X, 185, 199-200, 211-12) and the critical fortress of Legnago. Lying south of Verona and near the border with Mantua, Legnago guarded Padua and the Polesine (a rich agricultural area between the Adige and Po rivers that Venice had taken from Ferrara through war in the late fifteenth century) and was located close to Capello lands. Antonio Capello was elected to its command in late 1516 (del Torre, p. 187).

The other point of view was given voice by humanist Bernardo Giustinian in his funeral oration for Doge Francesco Foscari, against whose aggressively acquisitive approach Mocenigo had spoken. Typifying the link between humanism and

---

[16] BCP, C.M. 894, *Albero genealogico della Nobile Veneta Famiglia dei Mocenigo dall'anno 1195 all'anno 1773*, unnumbered folio.

mainland dominion, he expressed his pride in the mainland state and exhorted his fellow patricians to its preservation (King, esp. pp. 381-83; Mallett, p. 252). The Foscari-Giustinian approach prevailed, its adherents including most of the families represented at the 1518 banquet, many of whose members shouldered the burden of defence staffing and financing predicted by Mocenigo. Domenico Trevisan and Zorzi Corner had served as 'podestà' of Padua (Gloria, I, 279; Giuseppe Gullino, 'Corner, Giorgio', *DBI*). Trevisan's expertise in defence resulted in his election as proveditor of the army in Padua in 1514; though refusing the post (Sanuto, XVII, 498, 500, 501), he influenced mainland policy in the Senate (e.g. del Torre, p. 187; Sanuto, XXIV, 218-19). Earlier in the war years, Trevisan and five others, including Polo Capello, had been sent as ambassadors to Julius II for delicate negotiations over territorial and benefice issues (Seneca, pp. 133-34). Capello, the husband of Zorzi Corner's sister, had also served as proveditor of the army during the Cambrai war. He was responsible for the Ferrara front, where Venetian efforts were coordinated with those of the papacy (Gilbert, p. 30-34). The positions that he subsequently espoused in the Senate showed a healthy respect for Spanish military prowess (Sanuto, XVIII, 270-71), perhaps based on a familiarity acquired when he was ambassador to King Ferdinand of Naples.

Zorzi Corner and Andrea Gritti had held numerous governance posts on the mainland and served as co-proveditors general at the outset of the Cambrai war, although their roles subsequently diverged. Shortly before the battle of Agnadello, Corner left the front without authorization. Despite his protestations of illness, he was blamed for the defeat, relieved of his post, and threatened with state prosecution (Sanuto, VIII, 422, 427). Cardinal Marco was accused of consorting with enemy cardinals in Rome and Caterina of treasonous dealings with imperial agents to protect their holding in Asolo (Sanuto, VIII, 429-30, IX, 7). When Padua was again threatened several years later, Zorzi and his son Zuan offered twenty-five men for its defence (Sanuto, XVII, 247). Andrea Gritti had been born on a holding near Verona formerly belonging to the dal Verme, and his family had grown wealthy from importing grain from the eastern Mediterranean (Varanini, pp. 849-50). Raised in Venice by his naval hero grandfather, Andrea displayed a unique zeal in the defence of the mainland state, permanently capturing the city's respect with his bold and successful plan to retake it, beginning with Padua (Finlay, 'Fabius'). The plan was drawn up in consultation with patricians including Andrea Trevisan (Concina, pp. 5, 7), whose military and governance talents were employed in Venice's campaign to retake Brescia and reestablish its government.[17] His preference for imperial affiliation emerged in debates over candidates for the governorship of the army (Sanuto, XII, 276, 421).

Corner's and Capello's leadership extended to war finances; when loans were required to meet expenditures, both responded generously. In Capello's case, the response was both personal and through his family's bank, which required surety in the form of state revenues.[18] Both also were elected to high office during the war and after. As has been seen, the bank of guest Alvise Pisani also served the state, which by 1519 owed it 150,000 ducats for functions chiefly related to war finances, also to be repaid with state revenues. Pisani's endeavours had been rewarded the previous year with a procuratorship, his election assisted by an enormous loan to the state and the marriage of his daughter, with a dowry of 10,000 ducats, to Zorzi Corner's son Zuan.[19] In that same year he purchased a cardinalate for his son Francesco (Carroll, 'Dating'). Zorzi Pisani, elected shortly before to the Council of Ten (Sanuto, XXVI, 16), was kinsman to Alvise and to the Corner, his mother from a branch that had bought confiscated Carrara mills.[20] His university study at Padua equipped him with the prerequisite to a diplomatic career, the university degree in law allowing him to deal with other European states that, unlike Venice, followed Roman law (Grubb, esp. pp. 28-46). His service as ambassador to Alexander VI and to Ferdinand of Naples was followed, in 1509,

---

[17] Sanuto, XXII, 270; del Torre, pp. 233, 230-31; and see Sanuto, XVII, 252 for his participation in the defence of Padua and Treviso.

[18] For Corner loans see e.g. Sanuto, XIX, 153, XX, 448 and for office XXV, 615; for Capello loans, Gilbert, pp. 34-35 and e.g. Sanuto, XII, 433 and for office Giuseppe Gullino, 'Corner, Giorgio', *DBI*; on war loans and public office in general, see Finlay, *Politics*, pp. 163-96.

[19] Finlay, *Politics*, pp. 158-61; Lane, 'Venetian Bankers', pp. 82-83; for examples of his role Sanuto, X, 334, XIII, 433, 452, XVII, 249, XVIII, 417, XIX, 153, XX, 129, 448, XXII, 507, 508-09.

[20] Barbaro, VI, 138: his mother was Franceschina Corner di Fr[ances]co qu. Ferigo; ASV, *Archivio Grimani Santa Maria Formosa*, busta 3, file labelled *Acquisti di folli C [Carta]*, fol. 1^r copy of document of 12 September 1406.

by a mission to Julius II concerning the League of Cambrai. During the war he served as a 'savio', offered to defend Padua or Treviso, and contributed funds to the state (Sanuto, XII, 283, XVII, 247, XXII, 511, 675, XXIII, 306). At its close, he was elected to the commission to reopen and oversee the University of Padua, which recommended a papal contribution of 10,000 ducats (Sanuto, XXIV, 680). Smaller but still generous war loans had been offered by procurator Hironimo Giustinian, who had served on the mainland defence council, the 'savi a terraferma' (Sanuto, XVII, 249, XIX, 153, XX, 448). His kinsman Antonio Giustinian, prior to his service as ambassador to France, had served as ambassador to Julius and Maximilian during their period of enmity to Venice. Proveditor of the army during the Venetian alliance with the papacy and Spain, Hironimo Giustinian, along with Andrea Gritti, had been captured by the French when they took Brescia in 1512; after his release he conveyed their offer of alliance to Venice (Seneca, pp. 32-33, 45, 156, 162).

Although another guest, Lorenzo Loredan, had been among the 'hawks' whose aggressive stance on mainland expansion had provoked Julius II into forming the League of Cambrai (Seneca, pp. 26-27, 135) and his family had large mainland holdings (Varanini, pp. 820, 822, 834), neither he nor his family boasted a distinguished defence career. During the war, his father, doge Leonardo, had resisted calls to go to the front and rally the forces, though he had responded generously to his own calls for loans (Sanuto, XIII, 452, XIX, 153, XX, 129, 448) and promised two sons to the defence of Padua and Treviso (Sanuto, XVII, 247).

Least prominent yet still distinguished was the elderly Michiel Salamon. Nominated to the Council of Ten in April 1518 by a former 'podestà' of Padua, Salamon had immediately been elected one of its three Heads, replacing Polo Capello, whose election as 'savio' required his resignation. Salamon was re-elected head for July and September (Sanuto, XXV, 340, 341, 510, 687). Perhaps issues of mainland defence figured in his selection: he had served as 'podestà e capitanio' in Treviso in 1502 and his success as grain minister in provisioning Venice during the war under the most difficult conditions was recognized with a plaque in the Ducal Palace (Sanuto, IV, 283, 504, 838, XII, 266, 385, XV, 348).

Additional reasons for preoccupation with the mainland were developing among guest families. The year before the banquet, Andrea Trevisan had purchased a farm confiscated from a Paduan rebel, an early instance of what would soon become a broad-based state sale. In January 1519, under the leadership of Domenego Trevisan and Zorzi Corner, a group of patricians would successfully sponsor a bill to pay off the Monte Nuovo, the funded war debt initiated in 1482 for the war with Ferrara that had suspended payments for many years (Lane, 'Funded Debt', pp. 79-80). Payments would be made through the sale of state properties, including some confiscated from Paduan rebels (del Torre, p. 155). The families of the guests, already well represented among the purchasers of rebel holdings, would be important participants in the Monte Nuovo sales. Among the first was Zorzi Corner, in association with his son-in-law Zuan Francesco Loredan and Lorenzo Loredan (Rigobello, 'Modi', pp. 22, 24, 26; Sanuto, XIII, 423). Alvise Pisani would add many prize properties to those already accumulated. Domenego Trevisan was elected to conduct the sales.[21]

That the families of two of Venice's three cardinals were involved with the dinner indicates the intentness with which the hinge group sought Church benefices and offices (Carroll, 'Venetian Attitudes'; Carroll, '"I have"'). Members of the Trevisan and Giustinian families had held numerous influential church offices in Padua, Venice, and the Venetian state and had been influential in papal courts (Dondi Dall'Orologio, *Serie*, pp. 94-95, 208; Sanuto, VIII, 502). The synergetic interaction of benefices and public office is illustrated by the mainland governance positions that family members had also held and even more clearly in Bishop Bortolo Trevisan's greeting Maximilian in Feltre as its civic head during the emperor's triumphal visit after Venice had lost dominion of the region.

While in Venice, Cardinal Marco received a letter from fellow cardinal Innocenzo Cibo, then in Ferrara, who wished to visit Venice with his Salviati cousin (Sanuto, XXVI, 50). A nephew of the pope, Cibo was en route to Florence to celebrate the wedding of another cousin, Lorenzo di Piero di Lorenzo de'

---

[21] Sanuto, III, 46-47; Lazzarini, 'Beni', p. 277; Menegazzo, 'Ricerche', p. 181 n. 1; Fasullo, p. 118; Varanini, pp. 832, 849-50; Bonardi, pp. 576, 577, 579, 581; ASV, *Ufficiali alle Rason Vecchie*, reg. 48, fol. 1[bis]^v; specifically for the purchase of state properties: Pisani: fols 5^v-8^r [for Crivello properties going to Pisani: Bonardi, p. 579], 13^r-14^r, 15^v-16^r, 20^r, 27^v-28^r, 41^v-42^r, 46^v-47^r; Trevisan: fols 11^v-12^r; Loredan: fols 17^v-18^r, 50^v-51^r, 51^v-52^r, 54^v-55^r; Gritti: fols 23^v-24^r, 49^r; Domenego Trevisan: del Torre, pp. 151-77; Loredan: Varanini, pp. 820, 835; Lazzarini, 'Beni', pp. 284-85.

Medici, to Madeleine de la Tour d'Auvergne. The groom had been made duke of Urbino by Leo, who had confiscated that state from his general Francesco Maria della Rovere after accusing him of insubordination; the bride had connections to the French royal house. The marriage, the fruit of a lengthy search that had included important prospects in Navarre and Spain, reflected the French affiliation preferred by the family of Lorenzo's mother Alfonsina Orsini. Arranged early in the year as Leo initiated efforts to unite the Christian princes against the Turk with whom France normally allied, it also served Leo's policy of engaging simultaneously in multiple, even conflicting, affiliations.[22]

Corner responded by hosting them at his father's luxurious home, throwing a lavish party for them attended by other ecclesiastics as well as women guests and their husbands (Sanuto, XXVI, 53-54). The ecclesiastics included his brother-in-law Cardinal Francesco Pisani and the bishops of Corfù, Candia, Baffo (Paphos) and Famagosta. The bishop of Corfù, Cristoforo Marcello, a humanist, had begun his ecclesiastical career as the protégé of the saintly Bishop Barozzi and shared his concern for the poor. He joined the papal court in 1508, serving as a secret Venetian agent during the difficult moments after Agnadello (Logan, pp. 120-21, 146-490). Jacopo Pesaro, the bishop of Baffo, had a complicated history with the papacy. Admiral of the papal fleet and hero of the wars against the Turks early in the century (Ballarin, pp. 316-17), Pesaro was then hosting Cardinal Adriano Castellesi, whose flight from Leo's accusations of an assassination plot had cut short his long diplomatic service to the pope in England. According to Sebastian Giustinian, the Venetian ambassador to the English crown, Castellesi had recently been entrusted by Henry with conveying to Leo for his adherence the text of a league uniting England, Spain and the empire (Gigliola Fragnito, 'Castellesi, Adriano', *DBI*; Sanuto, XXIV, 395, XXV, 33). The only non-Venetian ecclesiastic to attend the dinner party was the bishop of Famagosta, Valerio Boni, a member of an important noble family of Brescia, where Zorzi Corner had been 'provveditore in campo' (field overseer) before Agnadello. Wealthy and bounding the Venetian state on the west, Brescia contributed significantly to its defence through large tributes and

---

[22] Sanuto, XXV, 197, 205, 211, 223, XXVI, 19; Carroll, 'Dating', esp. pp. 970-72; Cummings, *Politicized Muse*, pp. 99-114.

'condottieri' such as the Martinengo, who, although employed by Venice, were nobles enfeuded to the emperor. Within the month, Cardinal Marco made Boni 'locumtenens' of his bishoprics of Padua and Verona (da Corte, fol. 117^{r-v}). Shortly thereafter Boni was dispatched by the Venetian government to supervise ecclesiastical witch trials of rural women near Brescia being conducted with excessive zeal and cruelty (Sanuto, XXV, 609-10, XXVI, 23).

At the party, the cardinals were called onto the dance floor for the 'ballo del cappello' (hat dance), considered licentious because its premise was for women to ask men to dance (Sanuto, XXVI, 53-54; Lovarini, 'Aggiunte', pp. 204-06). Particular sensitivity to female beauty in the guests' circles may be indicated by the possession of Giorgione's *Dresden Venus* by the brother of one of them, as documented by the art historian Marc'Antonio Michiel, who the following week accompanied the two Venetian cardinals on their return to Rome ([Michiel], p. 105). The day before, Cardinals Cibo and Salviati had left for Padua and Mantua and, ultimately, Florence and Rome (Sanuto, XXVI, 69).

4. War Approaches (1518-1521)

In the period following Cornaro's return to Rome, official and personal relations between the Venetians and Paduans connected with Ruzante intertwined with events on a larger scale. Their shared concerns over mainland defence, relations with other Italian states especially Mantua and Ferrara, and relations with the empire became increasingly apparent. On 27 January 1519, the heads of an impressive bag hunted in Ferrarese territory by a group of young patricians were displayed near Rialto (Sanuto, XXVI, 397). Led by Cardinal Marco's brother-in-law Zuan Pisani, whose father Alvise, as has been noted, was one of the largest Venetian landowners in Padua and its territory (*Estimo*, reg. 351 [352], fols 95^{r-v}, 269^{r}-71^{v}), the group was composed chiefly of members of the 'compagnia della calza' Immortali.[23] The father of one who

---

[23] The 'compagnie della calza' were associations of young Venetian patricians who organized private and semi-public festivities (Muir, pp. 167-73; Labalme, Sanguinetti White, and Carroll, Chapters VI and IX). The two 'compagnie' inviting Beolco for his early performances were the Immortali (the Immortals; see Carroll, 'Shepherd') and the Ortolani (the Farmers; see Carroll, '"I have"'). While the Immortali tended toward pro-French families willing to accommodate to the

was not, Alvise Donado, was the outgoing 'podestà' of Padua, against whom University officials had lodged complaints of neglect with the Venetian Collegio the previous August (Sanuto, XXV, 584; Gloria, I, 280). Accompanying the group were Alvise and Giacomo Cornaro, whose names lack the patrician patronym; given that the bag was exhibited the following day in Padua by the Alvise Cornaro who lived near the Basilica of St Anthony (da Corte, fol. 121^r), who had a brother Giacomo and who was or would soon become Ruzante's patron, it is virtually certain that it was he with the group. A further attestation of Cornaro's close, ongoing relationship with the group is the signature 'Alovise Chornero' on a petition addressed to Federico Gonzaga by the Immortali in June 1520 (ASMn, *Archivio Gonzaga*, busta 1454, fol. 326^v).

Cardinal Marco's brother Jacomo travelled to Rome to visit him that spring, along with the Immortale Marco Contarini, and Pietro Trevisan, son of the procurator Domenego. During the visit, Cardinal Marco divided some of his benefices among his nephews, the sons of Jacomo and Francesco (Sanuto, XXVII, 323). The following month, the Cardinal's father and brothers lodged in the Paduan bishop's palace at the expense of the poor fund (da Corte, fol. 124^r). Marc'Antonio Loredan, father of Immortale Zuan Francesco, completed his term as military governor of Padua in August, accompanied on his return to Venice by Zorzi Corner, Alvise Pisani, and Domenego Trevisan (Sanuto, XXVII, 574). He was replaced by Alvise Contarini, possibly the brother of Immortale Ambrosio (da Corte, fol. 125^r).

In June Charles was officially elected emperor, the wealth and extent of his dominions making him 'il primo re del mondo' (the top-ranking king in the world), as Gabriel Moro warned his fellow patricians (Sanuto, XXVII, 455). Moro, whose brother had just been chosen captain of the Flanders galleys (Sanuto, XXV, 580, 612, XXVI, 46-47, 48, 52, 495), had good reason to know and

---

empire and centred on the Corner and several other families, the Ortolani tended to families whose pro-imperial leanings were stronger and were led by the Grimani, the Giustinian, and several other families. The highest-ranked families of both 'compagnie' tended to maintain a presence in the 'rival' group with a member of a cadet branch. Families represented in both 'compagnie' vigorously sought benefices (Carroll, 'Venetian Attitudes'; Carroll, '"I have"').

be concerned. A relative by marriage of the Martinengo (Sanuto, XX, 373), Moro was also first cousin to the Veronese noble Nogarola, such strong imperial partisans that they remained unforgiven by Venice (Sanuto, XXVIII, 203). Moro held agricultural property in the Pavan, (*Estimo*, reg. 351 [352], fols 134^v-35^r) as did his kinsman Cristoforo, a former 'podestà' of Padua. Cristoforo's holding bounded those of a Zacaroto (*Estimo*, reg. 25 [26], fol. 178^v), whose kinsman Giacomo was a member of Beolco's Paduan theatre group.

On 4 January 1520, the Republic signed an agreement with the empire concerning possession of some Friulan towns taken by the empire during the war, and Loredan returned to Padua to accompany Janus da Campofregoso to Mass in the cathedral. Campofregoso, the former doge of Genoa and an important figure in Venice's defence, was being courted by imperial officials to influence Venetian policy (Sanuto, XXVIII, 248-49; da Corte, fol. 128^r).

A month later, in a festivity with imperial overtones, Ruzante had his first recorded performance in Venice. Hosting him were the Immortali, whose number included Cardinal Marco's brother Zuan and two other Corner. A 'festa belissima et abondante, che in memoria di homeni vivi la più bella non è stà fata in questa terra' (very beautiful and abundant festivity, that in living memory is the most beautiful one ever held in this city), it celebrated the induction of Federico II Gonzaga and the Venetian patricians Stefano Querini and Ferigo Priuli (Sanuto, XXVIII, 253-56 (255)). Gonzaga, the new marquis of Mantua, had unsuccessfully sought a 'condotta' in the Venetian army, while Querini's father had met in 1518 at Abano with the duke of Ferrara about state boundaries and their effect on his farm holdings.[24] Priuli's brother Francesco would become procurator and 'capitanio' of Vicenza within two years (Sanuto, XXVIII, 253-56, XXXIII, 344; Rylands, pp. 18-19). While brandishing war implements, the Immortale festivities signalled the potential of peaceful co-existence with the empire by displaying the Trojan iconography it favoured (Carroll, 'Venetian Attitudes'; Carroll, '*Charles V*'). They concluded with a 'comedia a la vilanescha' (country comedy) by Ruzante, who three days later performed

---

[24] For further information about the meeting and its significance, see below p. 43.

semi-privately for procurator Domenego Trevisan (Sanuto, XXVIII, 264). A month before, the Venetian ambassador to Rome had warned his government of a possible imperial campaign in Italy and of the pope's advice to fortify the mainland cities and to bring Federico to their side as a bulwark against an imperial march through his strategically-located state. The lavish festivities demonstrate the extent to which Venice followed his advice (Sanuto, XXVIII, 152-53; Rodriguez-Salgado).

Selim the Grim died, succeeded by the peaceful Suleiman. With this concern removed, the drift toward war in Europe accelerated, bringing to the fore in Venetian government councils the question of receiving official investiture of mainland holdings from the emperor, liege lord of much of it. Francesco Contarini, recently elected ambassador to the emperor and brother of a participant in the Ferrarese hunt, urged the Senate in August 1520 to complete the work of their ancestors, including his father, in obtaining investiture by persuading Charles that they were already invested. His principal reason was the protection it offered in time of war, an important consideration for his branch of the Contarini, whose descent in the maternal line from the Carrara had brought immense landed wealth in Padua and the Pavan.[25] (Contarini had a brother each in the Ortolani and the Immortali [Sanuto, XXIX, 119].) Support was also expressed by the procurator Antonio Grimani, who declared that 'la Germania è il late di questa terra' (Germany is the [mother's] milk of this city); the knight Alvise Mocenigo joined him the following day. Serious preparations for war began in summer 1520, including a review of troops by Valerio Marcello, a member of the mainland governance commission and relative of an Immortale. The officer presenting troops on the western frontier near Brescia was Marc'Antonio Martinengo (Sanuto, XXIX, 120; Senato, *Secreta*, reg. 48, fol. 159$^{r\text{-}v}$; ASMn, *Archivio Gonzaga*, busta 1454, fol. 513$^{r\text{-}v}$).

In January 1521, the new Prince of Bisignano, Pier Antonio di Sanseverino, travelled from Charles's court, where he had been a favourite, to his lands in the kingdom of Naples, an important source of troops employed against Venice. He stopped in Padua where, on instructions of Francesco Corner and at the purse

---

[25] Sanuto, XXIX, 119-20, 121; *Estimo*, reg. 351 (352), fol. 134^v, reg. 357 (358), fols 2^r, 204^v, 206$^{r\text{-}v}$, 207$^{r\text{-}v}$, 210^r; BMC, P.D. c 2650/4, fols 110^r-12^r; BMC, P.D. c 2650/1, fols 110$^{r\text{-}v}$, 111^r.

of Zuan Corner, he was lodged in the bishop's palace (da Corte, fol. 140^r; Sanuto, XXIX, 534). In Venice he was fêted by the Ortolani, including the newest member, Marc'Antonio Martinengo, who conceived a wish to join the group at the wedding of Ortolano Pietro Grimani and the daughter of Hironimo Pesaro. A member of the 'da Londra' branch, so named because they had built their fortune on trade with London, Hironimo had had the frustrating experience some years before of arriving in Falmouth only to see 'as many as five Portuguese barks in the Thames, with 380 tons of spices from Colocut' (Brown, II, 76 n. 1). Undaunted, he was deeply involved in the revival of the northern galleys at the end of the Cambrai War, successfully proposing that they stop in England only and not go on to Flanders. The captain chosen was his kinsman Alessandro (Carroll, 'Venetian Attitudes', pp. 35, 38-39). Shortly thereafter he married his daughter to the son of the rich spice merchant Francesco Grimani. Pesaro was also involved with mainland defence, having served on a commission to inspect Padua's walls the previous year (Sanuto, XXIX, 9, 45).

Martinengo's request to join the Ortolani was granted (although his petition to add the strategic castle of Sirmione to his 'condotta' of fifty cavalry and 100 crossbowmen was denied). To thank them, he offered a 'cena sontuosa' (sumptuous supper), at which 'fu recità una bela et nova comedia per Ruzante et Menato padoani' (there was the performance of a lovely and new comedy by Ruzante and Menato the Paduans). The host was Piero Pesaro da San Beneto. His extensive mainland holdings included a house in Padua in the same quarter as Marc'Aurelio's branch of the Alvarotto and land held jointly with Hironimo in Este near Alvise Cornaro's (Sanuto, XXIX, 429, 536, 567 (429); *Estimo*, reg. 351 [352], fols 303^{r-v}, 315^{r-v}). His connections included at least one mainland rebel (Sanuto, XXVII, 427, compare XXVIII, 203). Also a member of the 'da Londra' branch, he exported arms (bows) and wine to England (Sanuto, XI, 508, XII, 162). As member of the mainland governance commission in the preceding period, he had proposed numerous measures to regularize military finances and improve preparedness to fight (Sanuto, XXVII, 14-16, 63, 76, 229, 255, 256, XXVII, 260, 433-35, XXVIII, 44, 222-23, 234, 265-66, 355, 359, 498, 510, 516, 642). These led to his nominations as 'podestà' of Brescia and reviewer of troops, which he declined (Sanuto, XXIX, 51, 53).

Martinengo came armed to a second 1521 Ortolano party because of the vituperative words said to him by some members.

Although swords were drawn by his men and a number of others, including Zuan Cosaza who had led the 1520 Immortale cortège in armour, no one was hurt. On 1 February, the Heads of the Ten banned comedies in the city (Sanuto, XXIX, 606).

By the end of the month, Andrea Magno had taken up his post as military governor of Padua, where one of his most important duties was the continued fortification of the walls (Sanuto, XXIX, 642) and where his son would make the only known copy of Ruzante's *Pastoral*.

During spring and early summer 1521, the French continued to solicit Venetian involvement in war preparations and a finalization of their alliance. Although at first many leading Venetians preferred a peace-seeking approach to prevent Charles from invading the peninsula, they soon gravitated toward the French, stranding Antonio Grimani in the earlier position (Sanuto, XXX, 16, 23-24). Leo, hardening his stance against Luther, issued a bull excommunicating anyone possessing his works, which the Venetian government had read in all churches except St Mark's (Sanuto, XXX, 72, 73, 74). In April, Venice allied with France, while in mid-May concluding a peace with Charles ending the war of Cambrai, after which Francesco Corner returned from his ambassadorship.

Francis and Leo moved to a war footing, ending hopes of a papal-French-Venetian entente and setting Venice against Leo (Setton, III, 194; Senato, *Secreta*, reg. 48, fol. 190^{r-v}). Shortly thereafter, Hironimo Pesaro, who had served as proveditor of Treviso in 1514 and 'capitanio' of Padua from 1515 to 1517, was elected to the newly-created office of proveditor general. He stopped in Padua on 11 August on his way to the battlefield (Sanuto, *ad indicem*, XVII, XVIII [but with incorrect patronym], XXVI, XX, XXI, XXXI, 159; da Corte, fol. 145^r). Zorzi Corner, Andrea Gritti and Lunardo Mocenigo met in Padua to inspect Padua's water defences, lodging in the bishop's palace (da Corte, fol. 143^r; Sanuto, XXX, 166, 171, 178, 183, 184, 186). Gritti held a supper for the army high command after Cornaro's departure. When the Germans won a significant victory over the French in Lombardy (Pavia) in late June, Leo and Charles consolidated their accord to take Milan from the French for Charles and Ferrara from the Este for Leo. Leo recruited soldiers in the Romagna, to which he would add Spanish troops, and began pressuring Venice to change sides (Sanuto, XXX, 410, 416, 418, 464, 465, 468, XXXI, 147). A muster of Venetian troops under Babon di Naldo of

Brisighella was held in Padua (Sanuto, XXXI, 131).

5. The Episcopal Entrance (1521)

In June 1521, as Doge Lorenzo Loredan lay dying and Cardinal Marco's father was cited as wishing to purchase election as his successor, Cardinal Marco requested papal permission to leave Rome to claim his Paduan bishopric (Sanuto, XXX, 351). The election of the new doge occurred in early July, the leading contenders being Domenego Trevisan and Antonio Grimani. Although vehemently opposed by Zorzi Corner and Alvise Priuli, who spoke against electing a 'papalista', Grimani emerged triumphant (Sanuto, XXX, 475-76).

As was the custom, orators were sent by other civic entities to congratulate him. The duke of Ferrara sent three, including Giacomo Alvarotto. While there, they demonstrated to the Heads of the Ten that Leo was preparing to assault Ferrara, probably a bid to dissuade Venice from joining him (Sanuto, XXXI, 78-79, 82, 84, 97). Padua sent a delegation consisting largely of imperial nobles and university affiliates. In their speech they proposed peaceful coexistence, noting that both cities honour Antenor. They praised Venice for having fought off Spain, France, Germany, Liguria, Tuscany, and Rome in the recent war (compare *Oration*, par. 11) and having defended Padua from siege (not acknowledged as imperial) as Furius Camillus had defended Rome from the Gallic siege. They implored Grimani to repair the war's damage, including the burned villages and the farmhouses seized by barbarians (Sanuto, XXXI, 147-53). Having expressed their hope that his son (Cardinal Domenico) would soon become pope, they swore their fidelity to him. Some days later Marino Becichemo made a long Latin oration on behalf of the arts students, eliciting an expression of support for the University from Grimani (Sanuto, XXXI, 199).

Leo and Charles declared war on Francis on 1 August.

Journeying to Padua from Verona where he had stopped to visit his bishopric, Cardinal Marco received a delegation of the cathedral chapter, possibly at the abbey of Praglia (where there was an Alvarotto friar). After a short oration from the delegation, the details of the ceremonies were decided, with the feast of the Assumption (15 August) chosen for the formal entrance (da Corte, fol. 142^v; *Acta Capitularia*, XIII, fol. 43^r). On that day, accompanied by 'podestà' Marin Zorzi and 'capitanio' Andrea

Magno, the bishop entered the city and was offered an oration and skits with images of justice (da Corte, fol. 146^v). After tribute ceremonies that were disturbed by a skirmish between the Brisighellese infantry and some others, he entered the cathedral, where his father and sixty of the most prominent Venetian patricians awaited him. That almost all of them wore plain black silk rather than the honoured and celebratory scarlet is a strong indication of the conflict they felt with a church whose leader's politics were on a collision course with theirs.

Having delivered an oration, Cardinal Marco withdrew to the bishop's palace. It had been richly adorned for a supper which he offered to prelates and patricians and after which, according to contemporary biographer Bernardino Scardeone, Ruzante delivered an oration. Although Scardeone's statement is well known to scholars, it has been dismissed as the product of a faulty memory, largely on the basis of Ruzante's declaration in the *Prima oration* (par. 1) that he does not want to give his speech in Padua.[26] However, the question deserves revisiting because of supporting information provided by two other sources and a reference in VR 1636 (par. 13) to another cardinal who was 'chive a Pava' (here in Padua). Francesco Scipione Dondi Dall'Orologio (*Dissertazioni*, IX, 100) states that on August 15 Cornaro heard orations by canon Vincenzo Dolce 'ed altri che gli recitò a nome dei Collegj Angelo Beolco, detto Ruzante' (and others that Angelo Beolco, called Ruzante, recited to him in the name of the 'Collegj').[27] Dondi Dall'Orologio does not cite his source, which is likely to be a fourth record, as Scardeone does not name Dolce and da Corte records his speech as occurring on August 16; there may also be confusion of Ruzante's oration with that of Jeronymo dal Mullo, given on August 19 'in collegij deli rectori et medici' (in the convocations of the rectors and the doctors; da Corte, fol. 147^r). The second source, da Corte (fol. 146^v, for location and guests), records Cornaro's supper and orations but not one specifically by Ruzante. The omission of this detail is not surprising, as the pious priest, despite being an intimate of Beolco's half-brother,

---

[26] See e.g. Zorzi, 'Note', pp. 1554-55 n. 1, quoting the Scardeone passage.

[27] The term is left in the original as it is not clear if the eighteenth-century author used it with the same meaning as local sixteenth-century sources, i.e. the university faculties, e.g. 'lo collegio di doctori legisti', 'colegij deli rectori et medici' (da Corte, fol. 147^r).

assiduously avoided mention of the playwright even while recording events at which he probably performed (da Corte, fol. 262^v; Carroll, '"I have'") In the present author's view, it is likely that Ruzante delivered an oration on 15 August after Cardinal Marco's supper as entertainment at the end of a long day, a common practice of Cornaro's circle.

The next day, Cardinal Marco celebrated High Mass, after which another oration was given. He then hosted a large group of ecclesiastics at a dinner, followed by a further oration, after which many high-ranking Venetians returned home. Although the archpriest of Verona left on 17 August, warned by the fleeing Vicentines that the Germans might take his city, most attendees remained an additional day for a further oration on behalf of the law faculty, after which the majority of the remaining Venetians departed. The medical faculty's oration occurred a day later, as did a further one by Marino Becichemo, subsequent to which Cardinal Marco's mother and her daughters-in-law left for Venice. The archdeacon Giustinian presented a gift of silver plate to Cardinal Marco who, unlike his Foscari predecessor, did not give it to the cathedral but kept it for himself. Andrea Gritti, on his way with the artillery to Vicenza where he would be 'provedador in campo', stopped in Padua to talk with Cardinal Marco and archdeacon Giustinian, after which Cardinal Marco and Andrea Magno toured the city's fortifications with a group of prelates and local nobles.

His exhausting responsibilities concluded, Cardinal Marco indulged in a variety of relaxing activities. After spending 26 August to 2 September at his hunting lodge ('barcho dela caza'), presumably the 'barco' at Asolo, recorded in VR 36 as the locus of a recitation of the *Prima oration*, he went to Luvigliano (where a bishop's villa would later be built). There, for enjoyment and to keep them from idleness, he took his dogs and hunters for a hunt in the Ferrarese, whose bag he gave to the important rather than to charity (da Corte, fols 148^r, 149^r). In late November, shortly after the imperial capture of Milan, Cardinal Marco returned to Rome. His offer to obey any Venetian government commission to speak with the pope was curtly rejected (Sanuto, XXXII, 164). The faithful ecclesiastical diarist da Corte sourly observed that the bishop had given little and caused much expenditure on the part of church and community (fol. 150^v).

Beolco continued to perform annually at Carnival in Venice and even once for the wedding of Doge Antonio Grimani's grandson in the Ducal Palace. Months after his last documented performance in Venice at a 1526 Carnival banquet at which the French king, then imprisoned in Spain by Charles V, was mocked with a plucked rooster (Sanuto, XL, 789-90), the Venetian Republic officially joined France, the papacy, and other allies in the anti-imperial League of Cognac. Days later, Beolco may have assumed a role in the Venetian army, perhaps associated with the light cavalry company of Giacomo Vicoaro.[28] These Albanian forces, termed 'stradioti', were employed by the Republic in swift and ruthless attacks. Vicoaro had served late in the war of the League of Cambrai near Vicenza and Verona (Sanuto, XX, 546-47, XXI, 129, 434, 462, XXII, 309; XXIII, 263, 273, 333, 565, XXIV, 261, 263, 273, 332-33, 565). In the early 1520s his commission was increased and he was sent to the western border near Brescia in preparation for war.[29] During the war, his company worked at various times under Piero Pesaro as proveditor general, Janus da Campofregoso, Marc'Antonio Martinengo (charged with the defence of Cremona and Brescia), Roberto da Sanseverino Count of Caiazo, Alessandro Donà Count of Pandin,[30] and Toso da Collalto (Sanuto, XXXVII, 287, 301, 552, XL, 136, 141, 163, 588, XLII, 151, 225-27, 298, 483, 525, XLV, 243, 404, 432, 516, 519-20, 545, 574, XLVI, 428, 509, 527, XLVII, 13, 302). They fought alongside the great south German social reformer Michael Gaismair (Carroll, 'Nontheistic', pp. 887-90), whose anger at

---

[28] The 1526 document recording Beolco's extravagant expenditure for a horse (ASP, *Archivio Notarile*, reg. 5031, fol. 202; Sambin, 'Altre testimonianze', pp. 223, 240) refers to him as 'strenuus', a term, as Menegazzo observed ('Stato economico-sociale', p. 104 n. 76), signifying soldier, which Menegazzo hypothesized Beolco to have been in the years 1526-27. The document immediately preceding it (fol. 201^r-02^r) documents the purchase of a horse by the standard-bearer of Vicoaro's company.

[29] Sanuto, XXI, 180, 232, 334, 345, 410, XXXII, 49, 64, 118, XXXIII, 395, XXXVII 55, 268, 552; Senato, *Secreta*, reg. 49, fol. 38^r; ASV, Capi del Consiglio di Dieci, *Lettere di Condottieri di gente d'armi*, busta P.V. 307, letters of Camillo Orsini of 21 January 1524.

[30] One of a number of contemporary Venetian patricians who were professional soldiers (Sanuto, XXXVI, 477, 625), Donà was married to a mainland noblewoman (Sanuto, XLI, 145-46); he predicted that lack of Venetian support would result in the loss of Pavia (Sanuto, XXXVII, 301). A reference in the prologue of Beolco's *Vaccaria* to the 'Conte di Pandin' as a source of easy money may refer to Donà's relationship with the papal banker Agostino Chigi, who had loaned Venice an enormous sum during the darkest days of the Cambrai war (Sanuto, XVI, 317).

Charles and Ferdinand's rejection of his programme resulted in his bringing the feared German 'Landsknechte' to the Cognac cause (Sanuto, XLIII, 153). As imperial troops increased, Vicoaro's company was sent to defend Pavia, crucial to the Lombard campaign. When it was taken by imperial forces after Cesare Martinengo defied an order to double the guard, the company suffered devastating losses including the death of Vicoaro (Sanuto, XLVII, 315, 355, 445, 447, 478, 548, XLIX, 54, 203-06).

In the Veneto in 1528, Beolco delivered his *Second Oration* to Francesco Cornaro, who had taken the place of his now-deceased brother in the College of Cardinals. The war dragged on as the Cognac allies attempted to enforce a united front while privately seeking separate peaces with Charles. After the horrifying 1527 Sack of Rome, intellectuals of the papal circle sought refuge in northern Italy; the Venetian dominion was especially appealing because of the Republic's success in keeping the fighting outside its borders. One of these was Francesco Berni, a Tuscan comic writer who lived for periods in Verona and Padua (Virgili, esp. pp. 252-53; Reynolds, pp. 49-51). He was associated with Giovan Matteo Giberti, who succeeded Cornaro as bishop of Verona and who in 1528 invited Venetian printers to found a press there, and he received a 'privilegio' (an early form of copyright) from the Venetian government in 1531 for an edition of Boiardo's *Orlando innamorato* (which was never published; Reynolds, pp. 47-48, 78). In a letter to Cardinal Marco's nephew, also named Marco, that is undated but probably of early 1533, he expressed his admiration for Beolco, spelling his name in the Tuscan way, 'Ruzzante' (Berni, pp. 305-07 Lettera IX; Virgili, pp. 252-53).

Beolco, who by then was a member of the extended household of Alvise Cornaro, was likely to have also frequented the literary circle of Janus da Campofregoso, which often met at his villa near Lake Garda not far from Verona. A long-term member of the circle was Matteo Bandello, and Berni joined it later for a time (Virgili, pp. 416-17). During the final phase of the war, Campofregoso was finally accorded the honour of being named governor general of the Venetian army, the commanding officer of the infantry. Within months of reporting to the front, he died and was buried in Verona. The delegate to the ceremony honouring him in Venice was a Father M. Bandello, probably the great short-story writer (Carroll, "'I have'").

Several features of the plays as they appear in XI 66 suggest hypotheses. These aspects include Beolco's apparent reworking of them with the assistance of a man of literary rather than theatrical experience, the Tuscanization of numerous morphological features especially in the unfinished *Betia* (for both see Paccagnella, pp. 186-88), the simultaneous increase of characteristic Pavan linguistic features (see Section 8 below, especially p. 59), and the specific order in which the works were copied into the miscellany. These features suggest that Beolco worked extensively on the plays, especially the *Prima oration* and the *Betia*, in connection with repeated performances on the mainland, that at least the work of the *Betia* (which is contained in separate fascicles: Paccagnella, pp. 186-88) was assisted by Berni and the texts copied under his direction, and that the texts were brought to Venice by Bandello to be copied into the great miscellany connected with the chancellery (Carroll, "'I have'"). Given that Beolco showed no interest in publishing his own works and that 'Ruzzante' was spelled in the Tuscan way on his 1533 petition to the Venetian government for a 'privilegio' to publish two of them (which in fact were never published), Berni may have been been the force behind the petition rather than Beolco.[31]

6. The First Performance in Asolo, 1518: VR 36

Thus far neglected, the variants in the *Oration*'s three known manuscripts yield valuable information, including evidence of three different performances. That evidence begins with the statement heading the VR 36 version that it was given to Cardinal Cornaro at the Barco at Asolo in the Trevisan countryside, as the only texts of Beolco's headed with designations of the place of performance were ones performed in multiple locations (e.g. the *Betia*, with distinct prologues for performances in Padua and Venice). Although VR 36's date of composition has invariably been assumed to be 1521, a correlation of its variants with the historical context points to the summer of 1518, with a possible second performance in 1521.[32]

---

[31] In the many archival documents viewed by the present author which the playwright signed with his sobriquet, he always used a single *z*, never *zz*.

[32] The openness of Nino Borsellino in the question of the dating of the plays in general and his sensitivity to textual nuances facilitated the present probing of evidence.

Given the links between Beolco and the cathedral chapter, he may have accompanied their delegation to Asolo or visited at the same time. The leader of the 1518 group, Hironimo Giustinian qu. Unfredo, as has been noted, was the uncle of both Stefano Magno and the Ortolano Dolfin Dolfin, and his close relatives would attend Ruzante's 1525 performance. The canons' concern with episcopal services to the poor correlates with Ruzante's opening request (par. 2), which capitalizes on the favourable attitude of Venetians toward the peasants for their role in saving the mainland state (Baratto; Menegazzo, 'Stato'). With the linguistic deformation of his opening gambit (his hallmark *s*-prefix), Ruzante puts Cornaro on his own revolutionary footing.

An apparently visiting delegation of university 'literati' is viciously critiqued: 'those clap-creaking favour-hounds who sit on the sliterary shit-thrones' (par. 1). The absence of the detail 'of/from Padua' would be explained by its exclusively Paduan professorial composition, also implied by its singularity relative to the other versions' two groups (favour-hounds and occupiers of shit-thrones). Alluding to the contemporary association of syphilis, recently arrived in Italy, with love and thus with cultivators of Arcadian literary conventions (such as those in Beolco's *Pastoral*), Ruzante implies that Cornaro shared his disdain.

Venice's 1518 decision to update the Estimo seems of particular relevance to the serious disadvantages faced by the rural 'Territorio' relative to the cities, decried by Ruzante (par. 1). As has brilliantly been delineated by Lorena Favaretto, the review was 'la più importante dell'età moderna' (the most important of the modern era) because, beyond being the last time that Venetian-held properties were registered, it brought to light and into conflict the various privileges and exemptions claimed by classes of property holders, thus affecting the political and cultural climate of the 1520s. The cities were absorbing immigrants from the country, who took their tax contributions with them without diminishing the tax obligations to their former homes. Moreover, Venetians had vastly increased their property holdings in Padua and the Territorio, thus subtracting their contribution toward the tax burden, again without reducing the burden itself. Venetian landholding, as Favaretto has noted, participated both in the trend away from trade and toward a landed aristocracy and gave value to agricultural production. Other factors were the damage or destruction of many properties during the war and their 'affrancazione', in which a large payment freed the owner permanently from a portion of the tax burden. Increasingly utilized to raise funds needed for military expenditures, 'affrancazione' favoured wealthy urban dwellers, principally Venetians whose commercial and banking activities provided large amounts of liquid capital (*L'istituzione*, pp. 149, 150, 163).

Rural dwellers attempted to balance the equation by utilizing the civic structures developed over the fifteenth century as their fiscal and military importance grew. Their strategy was to convince the Venetian government that the important support that they had given the Republic during the war should be recognized through their equalization in civic status with cities and towns, particularly regarding tax and work obligations (Favaretto, 'La richiesta'; Zamperetti, p. 260; Olivieri, 'Riforma', pp. 2, 109-48). Already in late 1515, the small communities in the Pavan had sent delegates to Venice to convince the government to exempt them from consumption taxes aggravating the deep poverty inflicted by the lengthy war fought on their soil. They were apparently granted a suspension that expired two years later, when the Venetian government reimposed the taxes to finance the reopening of the University of Padua. Resistance by the rural communities proved vain. To achieve their goals, they would have to act through their unifying civic entity, the Territorio (Favaretto).

By the autumn of 1517, tax issues were also becoming compelling for Paduans, as more attention was focused on the repair and maintenance of the mainland defence system to be financed with the 'dadia', paid only by citydwellers and the clergy. Venice's orders to them to present property declarations in October 1517 resulted in little action, probably because Paduans were concerned that the massive Venetian acquisition of immobile properties in their city and Territorio be recorded and tax obligations redistributed accordingly. Padua sent an orator to Venice to appeal their position to the Collegio in April 1518. He was opposed by a group of Venetians owning property in the Pavan (including the sons of Zacaria Contarini) led by Marino Zorzi, recently returned from a lengthy ambassadorship to the papal court. Sanudo drily records that nothing was decided.[33] In June, declaring that it could no longer defer the request, the Senate passed a bill requiring the new registration of properties by both Paduans and

---

[33] This paragraph depends on Favaretto, *L'istituzione*, Chapters VI and VII, especially pp. 129, 130, 150; Sanuto, XXV, 367

Venetians, and elected the necessary officials. The VR 36 version of the *Oration* thus could be read as an immediate countermove to the Paduans' successful request. Beolco may have held out particular hope for his appeal because of Cardinal Marco's position as Padua's religious authority, outside the university and therefore lacking the financial stake in the taxing of the rural population of the professors whose salaries derived from it.

Beolco's fondness for ribbing people to their faces emerges in the Territorio's eschewal of priestly representatives (par. 2), which in addition offered a protective distance to ecclesiastical supporters. It may also reflect Cornaro's feeling of being importuned by the canons, who not only wished to condition episcopal finances but were led by a prominent member of a family associated with his learned rival Grimani (Sanuto, XXIX, 441). Ruzante's play on the lawyers' titles ('dotori' or 'do tori': the first the Paduan version of 'dottori', the plural of the title granted holders of university degrees, and the second Paduan for 'two towers') and his proud contrast to his own three towers may be understood on several levels. The most immediate is youthful virility mixed with rebellion against a father with two university degrees and a predeliction for Tuscan, an example of the sexual drive serving both rebellion and separation from the parent (Monga, pp. 43-44, 120 n. 18; Halberstadt-Freud). On the mythical level, it was a sign of the devil, in keeping with Ruzante's Harlequinesque aspects and possibly alluding to the ecclesiastical inquisition against witches of concern to the new bishop, which included accusations of sleeping with multi-membered demons (Sanuto, XXV, 609-10, XXVI, 23). The historical context offers several other possibilities. A castle with three towers was the insignia of Pernumia (Zorzi, 'Note', p. 1556, n. 7). Given that Beolco family friend and Evangelical reformer Anton Francesco de' Dottori built a chapel there (Lovarini, 'Notizie', p. 42) and that the three towers surviving Jerusalem's destruction became its emblem, Pernumia may be being cast thereby as the new Jerusalem, as the Pavan will shortly be declared the earthly paradise. Another possible referent is the della Torre family associated with the University of Padua: Girolamo had been a member of Beolco's father's graduation committee, his son Marc'Antonio had worked with Leonardo da Vinci, and a second son belonged to a literary circle around law professor Francesco Alvarotto (Sambin, 'Lazzaro', p. 157; Laurenza, pp. 76-77; Carroll, 'Shepherd').

Ruzante's rejection of Florentine (par. 2) expresses resentment felt at its growing use throughout the peninsula (see Sabbatino), the result of factors that included its promotion as part of a programme of political and cultural hegemony by the Medici (Ferroni, p. 98; Cruciani, pp. xii-xxxiv). Leo X led that effort, utilizing the talents of his Venetian patrician secretary Pietro Bembo, whose 1505 *Asolani*, while set at the Cornaro court at Asolo, was written in Trecento Tuscan; scholars have often seen the *Prima oration* as a kind of anti-*Asolani*. In 1518 Bembo was composing one of the first Tuscan grammars, the *Prose della volgar lingua*. His devotion to Petrarchan poetry was foundational to one of the most influential movements of the Italian Renaissance, which, in contributing importantly to the spread of Tuscan as a supraregional language, was causing writers to abandon their own tongues, as Ruzante notes ruefully in the *Intermedio d'una comedia de Ruzante alla Pavana* also contained in VR 1636 (see below). This context explains his gleeful underlining of Petrarch's preference for the Pavan village of Arquà (par. 3) over his native Tuscany when the poet was able to choose where to live and be buried.

The success of the Medici programme co-occurring with the papacy's undermining of Venice's power in other spheres, resentment of it was particularly strong in Venice and augmented by defence of the city's own linguistic and literary accomplishments. Bembo's furtherance of it being perceived as a betrayal, his diplomatic visit to Venice in 1514 ended his father's political career (Giannetto, p. 256). Florentine merchants' usurping of Venetian commerce by developing the port of Ancona and working with the Portuguese (Earle) may have made Ruzante's anti-Florentine sentiments particularly welcome to Venetian patricians including Cornaro, despite his closeness to Leo.

Ruzante's refusal to have been born in 'Egypt of Bethlehem, where Jesus God was' (par. 2), rather than signalling peasant ignorance, may refer to the recent Turkish conquest of Egypt and Syria (which included the Holy Land), alarm at which caused Venetian authorities to divert mainland defence funds to the Arsenal (Sanuto, XXV, 119, 598). By coupling his allusion to this new threat with one to the Pavan's superiority, he encouraged Cardinal Cornaro and other powerful audience members to turn their attention away from foreign regions receding from their control and toward the local peasants. Similarly, his boasted ability to speak Florentine as well as a Politan from Robbing (Neapolitan from Urbino) may be a sly reference to Neapolitan political and military support for Leo's robbing Francesco Maria della Rovere of Urbino (Sanuto, XXIV, 610, 641). Leo started his war against della Rovere for the latter's failure to pursue Leo's anti-French campaign despite the fact that Leo himself secretly signed pacts with the French. Moreover, Leo's real purpose in taking Urbino was to provide his nephew with a state (Setton, III, 165-66; Verstegen).

Ruzante's reference to Antenor as founder of Padua (par. 4) subverts the learned tradition by reminding the audience that his homeland is now Turkey (whose enmity to Venice is underlined later in the oration). It also exploits the learned tradition to win the contemporary competition for primacy of origin and thus primacy *tout court* by flaunting the Pavan's precedence of Padua and therefore, implicitly, also of Rome and Venice (compare Speroni, *Apologia*, I, 351; Muir, pp. 66-68; Brown, p. 25).

The allusion to swallows' origin 'from beyond Colecut and even from beyond the sun's den' requires decoding. Swallows pass through the Pavan not on their way from Colecut, the major port and marketplace on India's western coast, but on their migration between transalpine countries and Africa (Berthold, pp. 57-58). This would have been common knowledge among peasants, including Ruzante.[34] Instead, what had gone beyond Colecut were German finances supporting both the Portuguese who had recently penetrated China and the Spanish who were undertaking the western route to Asia that would prove the roundness of the world.[35] That the swallows may be read as a personified metaphor, common at the time (compare Erasmus's *Praise of Folly*), is supported by a similar metaphor's overt explication in the *Seconda oratione* (*Second Oration*) delivered to Cardinal Marco's brother Francesco, in which Ruzante disparages the indulgences that have drawn German soldiers over the mountains as grapes do flocks of starlings.[36]

---

[34] For Ruzante's knowledge of the habits of other birds, see *La pastoral*, 'Proemio a la villana', vv. 1-5 and Scene 12, vv. 10-18, in *Teatro*, pp. 7, 57-59.

[35] Brown, II, 76 n. 1; 'coato' (den) corrects the mistranscription 'coaro' (cover) of the Zorzi edition: *Teatro*, p. 1187.

[36] *Seconda Oratione*, in *Teatro*, pp. 1207-21, p. 1215, par. 15. For contemporary staging of metaphors, see Sanuto, VIII, 500 for a rooster (France) picking at the

INTRODUCTION

Colecut (Calicut, Colocut; the source of the name 'calico') had attracted German merchants, principally the Fuggers, after the discovery of the African cape route. Maximilian I pretended the extension of his empire to India and had Indians from Colecut included in various artworks, including as his troops in a contemporary series of woodcut triumphs (Burgkmair and others, pp. 18-19 n. 71). German efforts to secure a trade monopoly were stopped by the Portuguese king, also intent on obtaining the monopoly and assisted by the pope (Mathew, p. 21). However, the king soon discovered that his resources were insufficient and, to attract essential German and (non-Venetian) Italian investment, offered special privileges that were so advantageous that many German merchants transferred their Asian business to Lisbon, closing their Venice offices (Mathew, pp. 7-8).

Among German merchants, the Fuggers offered the Portuguese a unique advantage through their virtual monopoly on copper, one of the few commodities of interest to Asian merchants.[37] The firm acquired mines put up as collateral by Frederick III and Maximilian I for loans they could not repay, including for Maximilian's wars against Venice. The Fuggers extended their clientele to the Catholic Church, handling the sale of indulgences and financing the Swiss Guard, for the latter of which the pope granted them the concession of his mint. They next induced the Church to moderate its prohibition on lending at interest, providing an alternative to dwindling income from Portugal. In 1514, as the Portuguese were supplanting the Fuggers in commerce to northern Europe with a Portuguese agent, a theologian sponsored by the German banking firm advanced the case for moderate interest, with which the University of Bologna (in papal territory) concurred immediately but the universities of Vienna and Leipzig only after imperial intervention. The next year a family member established himself at Leo's court, developing

---

eyes of a lion (of St Mark, Venice) to symbolize the victory of French over Venetian influence in Milan.

[37] The account given in the next few paragraphs synthesizes the material presented in Kellenbenz and Mathew, esp. Chapters 1, 4, and 5. I am grateful to my Tulane University colleague Elio Brancaforte for the numerous speakers on the topic of relations between Europe and India invited to his Colloquium 401 'New Worlds, Old Worlds' in Spring 2008.

close relations with cardinals and becoming deeply involved in papal finances, including the sale of indulgences.

When Charles became ruler of the Netherlands, he provided a new source of income to the Fuggers, continuing his dealings with them as king of Spain after 1516. He began planning a western route to the Spanish portion of the Spice Islands in 1517, an endeavour in which the Fuggers were principal collaborators. Their *coup de grace* was the financing of his election to the imperial crown. In 1518, Maximilian's poor health presaging his death, Francis promised the electors half of his annual income. Upon their response that the Fuggers' promises were the only ones they trusted, Francis made the German bankers a lucrative offer. Unflaggingly loyal to the empire and bolstered by other Germans, the Fuggers resisted and, after Maximilian's death, assembled for Charles the astounding sum of 543,000 florins from their own resources and those of the Welsers and of Genoese and Florentine bankers (Mathew). In spring of the same year, they handled Leo's new campaign of indulgence sales, which included the Pavan.

The 'swallows' therefore represent German financial interests, which had formerly gone to India and beyond but which in 1518, with the indulgence campaign, migrated to the Pavan (Setton, III, 174-85; Mathew, p. 111). There they bore 'furti', a play on 'fruti' (children or offspring and interest or income), but also on 'furti' (thefts), drawing Cornaro's attention to exploitation of peasant religious sentiment. Venetian views of the Fuggers may be gauged by the fact that when in 1517 the papal treasurer through either insolence or ignorance offered Fugger services to Venice in conveying the sum of the Republic's treaty obligations to Maximilian, he was rebuffed in favour of Venice's own banks (Sanuto, XXIV, 527-28). Nonetheless, Ruzante's promise to Cardinal Marco at the conclusion of the oration (par. 22) that he will receive as many benefits as he gives seems to echo the Fugger maxim 'do ut des'.

The oration goes on to describe other birds that also seem emblematic of Germans, especially the troops whose likelihood of return to the Pavan increased with the competition between Francis and Charles. During the Cambrai wars German soldiers had been called birds by Paduan peasants because of the imperial eagles on their banners; they came to plunder, i.e. feed off of, the Pavan but at least some of them were themselves the objects of peasants' profiteering.[38] Their fattening on local grain found a parallel in 1518, when German purchase of grain in the Venetian mainland was so extensive that it was depriving local populations, prompting the Council of Ten to forbid it (Sanuto, XXV, 391, 575-76). The reopening of the University of Padua would also attract German students, one of its largest contingents, who contributed to the local economy both directly and through consumption taxes (Sanuto, XXV, 30) and who were famous for their drinking songs and seducing of local girls.

Ruzante's observation (par. 5) that one cannot go from Treviso to Rome without passing through the Pavan pokes fun at Cornaro for having done precisely that (in reverse) in 1518 to avoid the expense of the episcopal entrance (Sanuto, XXV, 461). The baths of Abano so ambiguously praised attracted an unusual group of clients in 1518. On 27 April, the Venetian government granted Alfonso d'Este permission to visit them in May (Sanuto, XXV, 367). Three days later, a visit was permitted to Apollonia Lang, the sister of imperial supporter Cardinal Lang, then in Venice to assist her husband, Cristoforo Frangipani, an imperial officer still imprisoned in the Ducal Palace for the severe harm he had inflicted on Venice during the war (Sanuto, XXV, 369, 674). By May 7, the Council of Ten allowed its member Piero Querini to visit Alfonso in Abano as a private citizen and dispatched as its own representative Francesco Donà, probably the same one who would be addressed in Beolco's 1524 *Lettera giocosa* (*Playful Letter*) (Sanuto, XXV, 387, 400, 417-18). It was reported by governmental secretary Hironimo di la Vedoa (son of Gaspare di la Vedoa, both possibly important in the compilation of XI 66) that the duke's colour was bad and that he had no appetite. The reason was doubtless Leo's intent to add Ferrara to the state that he was building for his nephew Lorenzo by attacking from his port of Ancona, as was reported by the Venetian ambassador (Sanuto, XXV, 342). Venice's representative was sent to convert this fear into a reason to ally with itself and France (ASV, Senato, *Secreta* reg. 47, fol. 132^r).

The reference to Loreto (in the dialect form 'Loreo', par. 5) seems oddly placed, as there is no obvious connection between

---

[38] Compare the characters Ruzante, Betia and Tonin in Beolco's *Moscheta*, one version of whose prologue (the *Intermedio*) is contained in VR 1636, for which see below.

Abano and Loreto, a town in the Marches that was the site of a popular cult centring on a house believed to be that of the Virgin Mary. If the visits to Abano represented a tug-of-war between imperial and French partisans for Alfonso's loyalty, the connection may have been a 1514 pilgrimage taken to the Loreto in the Marches by Bembo and papal favourite Bibbiena (Bernardo Dovizi) during which Bibbiena reportedly persuaded Bembo to abandon his French sympathies for Leo's imperial ones. It was in consequence of that change that Bembo was sent to Venice on his failed mission to effect a similar change there (Moncallero, pp. 383-87). Pilgrimages to Loreto were apparently routinely utilized as excuses for politically-motivated excursions to Venice. In March of 1518, the former Spanish ambassador to the papal court, a wealthy prelate, did so. At Cardinal Marco's request, he was the honoured guest of his father Zorzi; departing from Venice, he went on to visit the Collalto (Sanuto, XXV, 288-89, 294). Two months later, a group of French dignitaries who had been to Loreto stopped in Venice for the feast of the Ascension; they dined in the Ducal Palace, though the doge was absent, probably an expression of political detachment (Sanuto, XXV, 398).

Another possible connection was the homonymous town of Loreo near the River Po, where Querini owned considerable farmland, under Alfonso's rule since the Ferrarese 1509 victory over Venice in which Alfonso's son Cardinal Ippolito had played such an important role that Maximilian promised him the governorship of Padua. The official enfeudment of the region, including Loreto (Loreo), was negotiated with the emperor in 1510 by Alfonso with the assistance of Cardinal Lang, then at Maximilian's court.[39] Several years later, Querini concluded negotiations with Alfonso to receive the income from the farms (Sanuto, XVI, 208, 407, 452) and, immediately the nearby town of Adria returned to Venetian hands in late 1517 (Sanuto, XXV, 115), agitated with Alfonso to agree that his land was under its jurisdiction.[40] It is likely that his visit to Alfonso at the baths had the same purpose. 'Podestà' of Padua from 1514 to 1516, Querini

---

[39] ASMo, Archivio Segreto Estense, *Cancelleria Estero*, Serie: Ambasciatori, agenti e corrispondenti all'estero, Germania, busta 1, unnumbered letters of 1510.

[40] ASMo, Archivio Segreto Estense, *Cancelleria Estero*, Serie Ambasciatori, agenti e corrispondenti all'estero Italia-Venezia, filza 81, dispatches 7 and 8.

was the father of Stefano, who would be inducted into the Immortali with Alfonso's nephew Federico Gonzaga.

Encouraging the turn to farming being made by many Venetian patricians to compensate for reduced commerce, Ruzante praises the Pavan's production of foodstuffs (par. 6), featuring the same goods with which contemporary peasants paid landlords (*Estimo*, reg. 351 [352] fol. 194^r, reg. 355 [356], fol. 98^{r-v}). He may have been alluding to the well-known fact that peasants achieved a greater yield than Venetian owners, even though the latter felt themselves turning into peasants. Pietro Bembo concerned himself with feed and seed, declaring that he had become a 'villanello' (a literary term for peasant).[41] Francesco Badoer, a wealthy patrician whose numerous holdings included pasturage (*Estimo*, reg. 355 [356], fol. 99^v), would have himself portrayed in shepherd's garb (Rylands, p. 33 n. 50) around the time his brother attended Beolco's 1525 performance (Sanuto, XXXVII, 559).

Beginning with bread, the staff of life that Venice had previously sought overseas, especially in Turkey (Olivieri, 'Capitale'), Ruzante's list includes wine, legumes, grains, vegetables and fruits. Grain was a comestible not only for an urban population but for animals, especially during war when it fuelled the horses on which the cavalry depended and the oxen on which the transport of artillery and other equipment depended. Beolco's adolescent humor comes to the fore in the usefulness of the hawthorn's buttscratcher to the 'boaruolo', explained in the opening scene of his *Piovana* (*The Girl from Piove/The Piove Play*) in which a cowherd entertains himself watching a steer struggle to dislodge the thorn he has put under its tail. Ruzante's 'boaruolo' appears to be an apprentice 'boaro' in the system in which peasant men were charged with taking the animals of the 'contadini originari' (peasants with longterm familial registration in a village) to the common pasturage to which they had exclusive right, rather than the contract farm worker into which the 'boaria' was evolving. Cardinal Marco was probably familiar with their work because of his herd of cows and the 'Pietro boarin' to whom the Corner pasture near Abano was rented (Sanuto, XXXVI, 508-09; *Estimo*, reg. 351 [352], fol. 241^r). Ortolano and Immortale

---

[41] Lazzarini, 'Beni' (p. 278 for yield); Beltrami; Ventura; Stella; Rigobello; Varanini. Bembo, *Lettere*, II, 291 lett. 586, 244 lett. 526, 246 lett. 766.

families rented to 'boari' and used the 'boaria' system in the Pavan (*Estimo*, reg. 351 [352], fols 193^v, 201$^{r\text{-}v}$).

The Pavan supported a wide range of useful trees (pars. 7, 11) cheaply and easily transported to Venice via its waterways.[42] Their woods were turned into tools and objects of rural and urban use. The soft wood of poplars and willows was used for basketry, small implements and parts, paper pulp, and firewood. Willows were so useful that landowners required peasants to plant them along streams, and other trees alongside grapevines as supports (Cattini, p. 36; Grubb, p. 144). Oak, elm, maple, ash, and hornbeam provided hard wood for shipbuilding, furniture, barrels, handles, pegs, dowels, and large implements including mill cogs, ox yokes, and cartwheels (Edlin, pp. 98, 108, 116, 134, 168; Rossi, p. 67 no. 81). Oak was especially valuable because shipbuilding had depleted it in Venetian territory, increasing Venetian commerce's disadvantages relative to Portugal's, supplied by New World hard woods.[43] A patrician was even permitted to pay his taxes in wood to the Arsenal (Sanuto, XL, 558). Wood's use for fuel was critical to the capital city. Antonio Grimani made a signal gesture of generosity celebrating his election as doge in opening his private supply of firewood to the populace (Sanuto, XXXI, 11).

In 1517 the Republic renewed its moratorium on the sale of wooded public land, except the Bosco di Legnago (Legnago Wood, near the border fortress). Among the most interested in purchasing it was Dolfin Dolfin, who owned numerous mills in Mirano (Sanuto, XXVII, 401, XXXIII, 280, XXXV, 319, 335; *Estimo*, reg. 351 [352], fol. 155^r). The exclusive woods of rural communities' common lands (C. Ferrari) attracted attempts by powerful outsiders to exploit them, some of which were fended off by the communities with the support of Venetian governors. Unfortunately, Venetian governors themselves were at times tempted to make decisions benefiting their own pockets, apparently the case with Pietro Bembo's father (Viggiano, pp. 158, 166-67, 175 n. 43, 266 n. 132).

---

[42] Bembo, *Historia*, II, 130^r; *Estimo*, reg. 351 (352), fols 205^v-06^r Zuan Dolfin qu. Nicolo; Boschi; G. Ferrari.

[43] Finlay, 'Crisis', p. 75; Lane, 'Venetian Shipping', p. 21, compare Sanuto, XXXIV, 131-2; Del Torre, pp. 148-49.

INTRODUCTION

Trees and woods carried cultural and political connotations. Peasants gathered under an elm or an oak for dancing and singing (Mantuanus, pp. 69-70, *Ecloga II*, ll. 53-108). Moreover, German artists had been developing the wooded landscape in a theme of nature as characteristically German that has been associated with the Habsburgs' renewed dedication to their empire (Wood, esp. pp. 50-54, 63, 100, 128-38, 152-76; Grafton). That their influence reached northern Italy complicates the interest in nature of painters including Dossi and the pastoralists, as well as Ruzante and other playwrights (Carroll, '"Fools"'). Indicative of Beolco's orientation are his references in two works to the emperor but none to the king of France.[44]

The Pavan's fertility extends to the many animals that prosper there (par. 7), although the cows kept in houses and the billygoats with horns might have had human referents as well (Menegazzo, 'Stato', p. 155 n. 41). Ruzante's praise is supported by the statistic that in 1521 Verona had five times as many sheep as in 1516 (compare *Betia*, V, v. 573, *Teatro*, p. 451; Sanuto, XXXI, 100). Cardinal Marco was also familiar with livestock: during his time in the Veneto he sojourned at his farmhouse and he made bequests of his horses and many cows in his will (*Acta Capitularia*, XIII, unnumbered sheet added between fols 22 and 23; Sanuto, XXXVI, 508-09). Animals also had cultural significance. Beyond the Biblical story, Noah appeared in a humanistic genealogy that had the Borgia descend from Noah through Hercules (Dandelet, pp. 21-24) and a work celebrating the peace of Cambrai uniting emperor and France, both descended from him (Tanner, p. 142). Ruzante underlines instead the ark's renewal of fertility in the Pavan.

Pavan women (par. 8) create society with their fertility and feed it with their strength, while retaining their beauty. With big, tough feet and calves like hay presses they stride unhindered across ploughed fields. Their feeding of the hogs produces firm haunches with which their own thighs compare. The boughs as smooth and beams as sturdy as their thighs belong to the peasants' deep woods,

---

[44] *Betia*, II, v. 390 (*Teatro*, p. 259). In the manuscript versions of the *Lettera all'Alvarotto*, 'Insonio d[e] m[issier] Marcho', VR 36, fol. 67^r; in BMV Ital. IX, 309, fol. 8^v; not in the manuscript versions of VR 1636 *Sopra la caccia*, unnumbered fol. but 6^r, or of BCV, Codice Cicogna 3085/IV (*già* Cicogna 691), *La vita humana de Ruzante*, fol. 15^r; not in the Zorzi edition: *Teatro*, p. 1241.

protected from promiscuous cutting (compare Pellegrini, pp. 274-77). With the same candour, perhaps aware of Cardinal Marco's consorting with prostitutes (Cruciani, p. 363), Ruzante audaciously describes the child's oral-genital contact with the mother during birth and the involuntary nature of the male erotic response to females in both humans (even cardinals) and horses. There is a serious underlying theological issue: by demonstrating how to subdue that response, Beolco implicitly refutes Augustine's utilization of it to justify hierarchical social authority, including that of bishop, justified by the assumption that nature's fundamental evilness prevents humans from exercising free will and subjects them to predestination (Pagels, esp. pp. 129-30). Beolco aligns himself with Church Fathers such as Origen and John Chrysostom (whose works were abundantly available then) who continued a pre-Augustinian tradition characterizing nature as good and humans as capable of exerting free will.[45] Moreover, Beolco's position affirms human equality and refutes Luther's revival of the Augustinian position, providing a powerful signal of his loyalty to Catholicism at the moment that Cardinal Tommaso de Vio (Cajetan) was in Germany to subdue Luther. That loyalty, however, as his final veiled threat hints, was contingent upon Cornaro's fulfillment of his request.

Peasant women's eyes pierce Padua's fortress-like walls, which were never breached during the long war and were being rebuilt under the direction of Cardinal Marco's father, a former 'podestà' of Padua (Carroll, 'Dating', p. 917). The inclusion of anvils among pierced objects points to a performance in a mainland city, as, Venice's canals and bridges being inhospitable to horses, anvils were much less common there. Ruzante's invocation in this context of 'Cristo da Loreto', when the Holy House at Loreto was associated with the Madonna, seems to spring from the obverse of his praise for women, a drive to dominate them.[46]

Characterization of the Pavan as the earthly Paradise (par. 9) again denotes it as a locus of free will and human equality (compare Pagels), setting Beolco's social programme on the path

---

[45] It is a position developed in the prologue of the *Betia*, which opens with the declaration that 'El naturale infra gi umeni e le femene è la pì bela cossa che sipia' (The natural between men and women is the most beautiful thing that there is).

[46] This was not the Loreto (Loreo) south of Venice, but the town in the Marches.

away from a theocentric base and toward a purely human one (Carroll, 'Nontheistic'). It also links the oration to More's *Utopia*, of which Beolco could have heard from Ortolano Marin Giustinian. Giustinian, having just returned from London, received a letter praising More in the summer of 1518 from his father Sebastian. The elder Giustinian was completing his service as Venetian ambassador to Henry VIII, an important accomplishment of which had been the resumption of commerce between the two states via Venice's Flanders galleys. A member of More's circle, he had contributed to the text in their discussions. Both Giustinian had ties to Padua and the Pavan: Sebastian owned property in Piove and Marin participated in the defence of Padua.[47]

Scoffing at literary language (par. 10), Ruzante nonetheless flaunts his (flawed) ability to use it, addressing Cardinal Marco with titles punning on insults while declaring that he will only speak at Cornaro's pleasure. Ruzante parses the learned speakers' attribution of the Cornaro origin to the Romagna (the core province of the Papal States, converted by deformation from Rome, to which humanistic genealogies usually linked noble families) as the opposite of praise because of the region's blameworthy race lacking in faith and law. Well known to any local audience were the risks that Romagnol attitudes posed to Venice when combined with the region's military role. The Romagnol town of Brisighella produced the Naldo family of 'condottieri' (hired military captains), who recruited local soldiers to their companies and were often in Venetian employ. Their perceived lack of loyalty derived from the power of their temporal ruler the pope to forbid them from fighting for Venice when it conflicted with his interests (Sanuto, XVII, 429-30, XX, 329). Moreover, as Ruzante bitterly notes, they fled in difficult situations (Sanuto, IX, 337; Buzzacarini, fol. 229^{r-v}). Animosity toward them in Padua and the Pavan stemmed from their depredations during the war despite being Venice's own troops, including ransacking bakeries to compensate for lack of pay (da Corte, fols 47^v, 49^r, 92^v-93^r). Cornaro could be assumed to side with Leo not only because he was a papal favourite but because his archrival Cardinal Domenico

---

[47] Sanuto, XVII, 250, 279, 287, 335, XXV, 233, 560-63 (this last is missing from index); *Estimo*, reg. 351 (352), fol. 88^r; Carroll, 'Ruzante's Early Adaptations'; Carroll, *Angelo Beolco*, Chapter Three provides evidence for *Utopia*'s influence also on the *Betia*.

Grimani sided with della Rovere. A perhaps darker reference was della Rovere's defence of a kinsman cardinal whom Leo accused of trying to assassinate him in a plot in which Leo also implicated Cardinal Castellesi, then hiding in Venice with Bishop Jacopo Pesaro (Sanuto, XXIV, 456, 585-87; Setton, III, 167-69).

Extolling instead the Cornaro family's Venetianness (par. 11), Ruzante proclaims that they are the greatest family in the world and are everywhere. This was not hyperbole when the Cardinal's brother Francesco was ambassador to Spain, his brother Giacomo governor of the border province of Friuli, and their father a leading contender to succeed the elderly doge. Inventing a rustic etymology using the unattested 'cornaro' (cornel or boxwood) rather than the local 'cornolaro', Ruzante likens the family to that wood, which is so strong, firm, and resistant that it would be impossible to make a good dowel, a good knitting hook or cattle prod or paddle or gudgeon, or a good millwheel cog without it. The tools represent the lucrative mainland endeavours attractive to Venetian patricians but in which the Cornaro themselves, despite their Scrovegni ancestor and Zorzi's term as 'podestà', had shown little interest. These included silk knitting, reflecting the locals' contemporary discovery of silk as a cash crop, its importance increased by the loss of the Asian silk emporia of Alexandria and Damascus (Molà, esp. pp. 221-35). Ruzante's suggestions thus unite Cornaro family interests with those of the peasants.

Terming the Cornaro the 'parona' (boss) of the Pavan and from the city that is the boss of both the Pavan and Padua, Ruzante appeals to him to help the peasants. Emphasizing his advice with a punchthrower's question (Does this stink like garlic, now?), he launches into a disingenuous list of states that are not the boss of the Pavan; they were, in fact, the members of the League of Cambrai that almost became its boss, plus Colecut, which had paid for imperial participation with profits taken from Venice. That the pope heads the list alludes to his formation of the league, his initial success with the 1518 truce, and the *papalista* affiliation of Beolco's audience. That in this version Spain precedes France and German land is placed at the end and modified by 'tuta' (whole) indicates that it was written in an environment inclined toward Aragon-Habsburg interests and before the death of the feckless Maximilian (immediately afterward Charles devolved Austria onto his brother Ferdinand). Such was the case of the papal circle and of imperialist mainlanders in late summer 1518 as Francesco Corner reported that Charles of Spain and Maximilian manoeuvred to achieve the unprecedented election of the former as emperor even before the latter's death (Sanuto, XXV, 538-40). A further allusion to imperial affiliation might be concealed in the praise of cornel, acclaimed as the best wood for spears and lances in the *Aeneid* (V. 557; IX. 699-701), a text that Beolco cites in the Paduan prologue of the *Betia*.[48] Given the epic poem's prominence in imperial ideology, contemporary genealogies showing the Habsburgs' descent from Antenor (Tanner), also the putative founder of Padua, and Charles's combining in his person of Spanish (including colonial) and Habsburg treasure and might, Ruzante appears to be recommending the wisdom of agreeing to the truce brokered by Francis. That Venice had lost the Paduan bishopric in 1509 when Maximilian and Julius became 'boss' of the region added to the urgency of the message.

Ruzante's hearty laugh at those proclaiming the cardinal a big man (par. 12) turns to serious advice and a rare (yet backhanded) compliment. Ruzante has heard (not experienced, a goad to future generosity?) that the cardinal has a big heart, which could lead him to stand against a charging boar (an allusion to Cornaro's enjoyment of the the most expensive kind of hunt, the frequent sharing of which with Leo and his circle had cost him considerable sums).[49] As a brother, using the *tu* form and another pre-punch, excrement-based warning, Ruzante warns Cornaro that he could die, which is not worth being pope or lord of the world. Though denigrating the boring speeches, Ruzante covertly boasts that he attended 'with my boss' such prestigious activities. The placing of the detail here in this version points to the importance of the 'boss' and thus a mainland venue, if his 'boss' was Alvise Cornaro, who enjoyed higher status there than in Venice, the Republic having rejected his requests for recognition of patrician status (Menegazzo, 'Alvise').[50] It may also indicate that Alvise was already campaigning to be named administrator of the diocese's many properties (including agricultural ones), efforts that would succeed only with the following bishop. Ruzante, heeded by an

---

[48] Pp. 153-55, pars. 3, 4; Zorzi, 'Note alla *Betia*', p. 1319, nn. 36, 38.

[49] Sanuto, XVII, 217, 490, 512, XVIII, 210, XXIII, 144, XXIV, 51, 94, XXV, 135, 385-86; Setton, III, 194.

[50] 'Stato', pp. 148-49 n. 16; he may also have been someone else, as Menegazzo noted. The present author is conducting research on various possibilities.

early reader who drew a pointing finger in the margin, counsels Cornaro to value life over valour and turn aside.

Clues to the nature of the danger lie behind the form 'reale' and the references to advice that Aristotle and Seneca would not give (par. 13). More than linguistic deformation of 'leale' (loyal, fair), 'reale' meant 'royal' or 'partisan of the king', traditionally the king of France. As Tibor Klaniczay noted (p. 60), the two philosophers were advisors respectively to the first Greek emperor and early Roman emperors, and represented the two branches of philosophy, the logical and earthly (Aristotle) and the emotional and divine (Seneca). The importance of ancient philosophy to Beolco's works is only beginning to be recognized.[51] But while the Stoics are present in Beolco's works, here he counsels Cornaro to reject their views (and the Peripatetics'). The associations of 'natural' here do not derive from Stoic passive acceptance but from the views of free-will theological writers such as Pelagius, Origen, and Thomas Aquinas, more appropriate to Cornaro. While, unlike Domenico Grimani, he was not an intellectual, Cardinal Marco, by virtue of his position at the papal court, was very aware of the rapid strides that the Lutheran movement was making and that were being addressed by Cardinal de Vio, whose commentary to Aquinas's *Summa* was published in Venice in 1518. He would thus have appreciated the opposition to Lutheranism embodied in the free-will position, soon to be championed by Erasmus (Carroll, 'Nontheistic'). Ruzante, then, warns Cardinal Marco of the dangers of (traditional Cornaro) French partisanship and of the growing danger of any association with political power posed by the mounting conflict between Francis and Charles. He counsels him, instead, to concentrate on benefices and becoming pope. The hunting metaphor is continued in the striking image of Cornaro's supporters, presumably Ruzante and the peasants he represents, going to Rome to honour him as pope on all fours wearing dog collars. It reinforces the impression that the character Ruzante was cast as a kind of attack dog protecting Cornaro and acting at his behest.

In the Pavan, Ruzante asserts (par. 13), cardinal is defined not as a 'cardine' (hinge, a common topos) but as a rich man who lives the (sinful) good life yet manages to get into heaven by

---

[51] Carroll, *Angelo*, pp. 30, 69, 82, 97; Carroll, 'Ruzante's Early Adaptations'; Carroll, 'Nontheistic'; Ferguson, pp. 218-24.

unhinging its door. The cardinal who hoards medals was immediately recognizable as Cornaro's rival Domenico Grimani. The detail 'here on the Pavan' seems to indicate that Beolco composed the oration for local delivery when it was learned that Cornaro was coming to the Venetian dominion, as perhaps does Sanudo's explanation that Cornaro avoided Padua to spare himself entrance ceremonies.[52]

Ruzante's avowal that he would not want to exist only as an imprint even if he had been Roland combines a reminder of the useless sacrifice of the French paladin to Moslem treachery and imperial gullibility with a parallel to Beolco's eschewal of (im)printed versions of his works. The living performances and kaleidoscopic adaptations that he prefers multiply the acclaim that he garners in his preferred role of hunter (par. 14). His calling his hound a traitor to goad him into outwitting the wily prey and his bloodthirsty joy at its kill foreshadows Bilora's murder of Andronico in *Bilora* (*Weasel*).

Whether sincerely or disingenuously, Ruzante praises Cornaro's difference from those with ambiguous desires who want to be on top (an allusion to the new vogue for homosexuality as an exclusive activity of the superior classes),[53] urging him to take care of his peasant flock (par. 15). As the elected delegate of his 'visinanza', Ruzante welcomes Cornaro by giving him his hand, a ritualized gesture used to congratulate, to give a promise or seal an

---

[52] The frequency with which Beolco repeats 'chi/ve in sul pavan' (here on the Pavan) may indicate that he drew upon riffs that he performed for Venetian patricians visiting their country properties.

[53] For which see Lawner, pp. 43-45; Ruggiero (pp. 109-45) observed a significant quantitative and qualitative growth in male homosexuality over the fifteenth century, including the development of a 'homosexual subculture' (p. 145), which in turn triggered a harshening of repressive measures. In Tuscany, the presence and even cultivation of male homosexuality was associated with the Platonizing humanistic circle around the Medici, which moved with them to Rome and figured prominently in the two Medici papal courts (compare Cummings, *Maecenas*, pp. 98-101). Curiously, a poem on one of the final folios of XI 66 castigates the Cornaro abbots, Cardinal Marco's nephews, for passive homosexuality (see Cristofari, p. 73, n. 652 and below Section 10). It precedes a poem attributed to Aretino (but see also Romei, p. 21) who, with Berni, was a protagonist in the trend of flaunting male homosexuality (see, for example, p. 58 below).

agreement including a marriage pact, or to make peace.[54] The gesture gives a further indication that the delivery of the oration was planned for the Pavan, as he would not be entitled to welcome Cornaro to a territory not his own. That the new law and statutes are to be reasonable and in good faith shows familiarity with legal norms, as these were prerequisites for valid laws (Menegazzo, 'Stato'). Ruzante's ingenuousness in attributing to him papal powers and the keys to heaven is only apparent, however; a theory of autonomous ecclesiastical entities had long been favoured in the region and was strengthened by the fifteenth-century Conciliar movement (a leader of which was the Paduan Cardinal Francesco Zabarella cited in the *Betia*'s Paduan prologue) among others (Tierney, *Religion*; *Foundations*; see also Seidel Menchi; Logan).

As Emilio Menegazzo pointed out, Ruzante was required to request specific laws because all matters not stipulated were regulated by the existing Paduan statutes (Menegazzo, 'Stato', p. 148 n. 16). Beolco's familiarity with church laws informs the seven that he requests of Cornaro (pars. 16-22), which, like other peasant legal petitions of the time, mix ecclesiastical with civil matters (Carroll, 'Nontheistic'; 'Dating'; '*Charles*'). They are within contemporary trends of peasant claims of equality with traditional authority figures and of abolishing distinctions between the sacred and the secular, as well as those of humanist anticlericalism (Dykema and Oberman; D'Elia, pp. 121-23). At the same time, they recognize the authority of Cornaro, not the peasants, to enact them and appeal to the papal circle's inclination toward pleasurable pasttimes and relaxed spirituality while solving one of their chief worries by parrying Luther's predestinarianism.

In essence, the laws propose means to satisfy humanity's physical nature without interfering excessively with humanity's spiritual nature. Ruzante promises increased peasant devotion if they are enacted but sacrilege and loss of faith if they are not. Choosing a pleasurable hunt over Sunday Mass will not be a sin, nor will fasting be required (did Cornaro understand the reference to famine?), or harvesting a crop on a holy day, or eating for enjoyment. Combining two themes of Beolco's work, the righting

---

[54] See *Anconitana* II, 2 (*Teatro*, p. 807); *Betia* V (*Teatro*, p. 507); *Betia* IV (*Teatro*, p. 387); *Dialogo facetissimo*, Scene 8 (*Teatro*, p. 719), *Betia* V (*Teatro*, p. 423); compare Sanuto, XV, 575, XVI, 28, XXV, 378, XXIV, 269; Bembo, *Lettere* II, 135 lett. 392.

of inequities suffered by peasants and the exchange of sexual favours among multiple partners to manage abundant desire, the final two laws propose novel forms of marriage which actually break laws on monogamy and priestly celibacy. One will require priests either to be castrated or to reciprocate in their exclusive privilege of sharing others' wives. The other, by giving peasants four spouses, will attract city people to the country and reverse the flow of population and privileges to the city (compare Favaretto, *L'istituzione*). It will also solve the problem of city men's seduction and abandonment of country girls (compare Kaplan). Other problems solved are sterility, armed conflict over women, and forced monacation (the relegation to convents of girls whose families are unable to provide a dowry, though peasant girls were too poor to afford even the convent's smaller dowry), and the greatest sin of all, idleness ('nausitè'; VR 1636 'ociositè'; XI 66 'uciositè'). This last detail, curiously, repeats the reason that diarist da Corte gave for Cardinal Marco's taking his dogs and hunters out for a hunt in the Ferrarese, to keep them from being idle ('no vole che stagano ociosi'; da Corte, fol. 149^r). Those familiar with Platonism and Beolco's opposition to it might also have seen a critique of its idealization of immobility (Marsilio Ficino, *Platonic Theology*, Book One, Chapters 4 and 5).

The resulting population increase, in fulfilling the Old Testament injunction, will banish fear of a Turkish invasion and provide a larger force to resist the Spanish and Germans (an appeal to the pro-French Venetian patriciate). Unique to this manuscript, and consistent with an immediate postwar date, is the added benefit that if those invading forces return the peasants will no longer have to flee. That the conclusion of the injunction, to dominate the beasts of the earth, was read by supporters of peasants as opposing servitude because it gave all men dominion over animals and no men dominion over other men (Freedman, p. 250) is consistent with Beolco's philosophy. The espousal of the contrasting interpretation of peasants as animals and not men by those justifying aristocratic rule provided cover from its partisans in his audience.

Appealing to Cornaro's *libido dominandi*, Ruzante declares that the resulting law will be more beautiful than all others, whether civil, canon, or theological. Yet in the next sentence he portrays himself as giving Cornaro advice for his own good. The remainder of the oration oscillates between the two poles with reminders that the cardinal's worth derives from the peasants' support and an affirmation of his power to do exactly as he wishes. In a conclusion blending a father's primary instruments of persuasion, the threat of disownment if the desired action is not undertaken and the promise of familial love if it is, Ruzante requests Cornaro's promise of compliance, closing on the sinister allusion to an epitaph and 'God help you'.

7. A Venetian Audience, and Roman Guests (1518, 1521): VR 1636

The oration's title in VR 1636, 'S Prolico de Ruzante fatto al Cardinale Cornaro nella Inclyta Città di Vinegia', has two unique features: the association with a Venetian performance and the term 'sprolico' (a play on 'prologue' and 'rambling speech', with the accrescitive prefix possibly added later) rather than 'oration'.[55] Both the venue and the rambling character are confirmed by a comparison with VR 36. Evidence points to a performance in September 1518 as part of the 'feste' (parties) and 'piaceri' (pleasures) for the visiting cardinals. The most notable, given in the luxurious Cornaro home, was attended by beautiful patrician women and their husbands, as well as high-ranking Venetian prelates and maskers wearing 'saioni' (an ample garment worn by high-ranking soldiers, typically northern European and imperial) (Sanuto, XXVI, 53-54; Burgkmair).

In this period the rectors of the University of Padua were in Venice to present grievances against the city's Venetian governors and to petition the Signoria to reopen their institution. That presence may be reflected in VR 1636's division of favour-seekers and throneholders (chairholders) into two different groups and the designation of the latter as 'from/of' Padua (par. 1). This would have differentiated them from a Venetian holder, Marino Becichemo, one of the first professors to be engaged and later an orator at Cornaro's installation (Sanuto, XXVI, 14, XXV, 578, 579, 584, 589-90; Oliveira Barata).

Other indications of a Venetian venue appear throughout the text. The simple 'i citadini ne trogna e ne deleza' (city people mock us and make fun of us) becomes 'i cittaini de truogna ne

---

[55] The initial 'S' of the title is detached from the rest of the word and formed somewhat differently. The title is written in Tuscan. On Ruzante's prologues, see in general De Ventura (but on the dating of the 1636 version of the prologue of the *Moscheta*, see Section 10 below).

deleza' (citizens of Truogna make fun of us). The description plays on Padua's founding by Antenor of Troy, vaunted by Ruzante in the Prologue of the *Betia* but here overshadowed by Venetian antipathy for the university city's independent-mindedness. Ruzante has come 'to this place' (not 'villa/ge'). The additions of 'de Talia' and Ruzante's insistence (par. 2) that he does not want to speak Florentine seem aimed respectively at an audience associated with the Medici plan to rule the peninsula and with local resistance to it. In par. 3, a sentence is added defining 'our' language as Pavan and the message as being given to 'Your to you Magnificence', emphasizing the illustrious setting. The Venetian word for swallows ('cesille', par. 4) is used, rather than the Paduan 'cesiole', and their starting point is Colecut and the sun's den, not 'beyond' them. A trace of the Spanish king is thus removed and with it a point of contention between Venetians and Romans, patriots and 'papalisti': Portuguese competition was diminishing, while the renewal of the Flanders galleys made Venice's fortunes subject to Charles's whims.

Noah's vessel (par. 7) is a 'barca' (boat; not 'arca'), and anvils are missing from the objects pierced by peasant women's eyes (par. 8). Emphasizing Venetian dominance, Padua is added to the Pavan that the Cornaro are the 'boss' of, and the assertion of rural primacy in 'Padua of the Pavan' is inverted to the urban primacy of 'Padua and the Pavan' (par. 11). The description of the firmness and endurance of the Cornaro is curtailed (par. 11), as would be consistent with an audience including numerous powerful patricians. Ruzante's 'paron' (par. 12) is mentioned at the end of the phrase, indicating someone less powerful in Venice than on the mainland. To 'mati' (crazies, par. 13) is added 'sperteghé' (without measure); the 29 June authorization of the Estimo instructed Venetian officials to measure ('pertigar') holdings before peasant witnesses (Sanuto, XXV, 507-09). The change from 'We want you to make us' new laws to 'I want you to make me' new laws (par. 15) may reflect a change from a collaborative performance or inclusion of peasants in the audience at Asolo to a single performer.[56] It and the added reciprocity of 'and I yours' to 'you will be my pal' (par. 13) indicate the author's growing status.

---

[56] Calendoli, pp. 69-71, hypothesized that peasants attended the performance in Asolo; the orator's insistent use of 'we' with reference to the peasants correlates with this.

Peasants are 'outside' rather than 'on top' (that the latter was the original is supported by the later reference to their being 'dal lò dessoto' [on the underside]), presenting less of a challenge to the social hierarchy. A similar effect is achieved by 'you know well what I tell you' relative to 'do well what I tell you', 'do it for yourself' versus 'I do it for you' and the added, self-protective 'what does it matter to me' (all par. 22). Gone is 'we would never again flee from this land' (par. 22): Venice never having been invaded, its inhabitants never fled.

Certain variations correspond to differences in political attitudes between the mainland and Venice. States that are not the boss of Venice change from Rome, Spain, and France to Rome, France and Spain, reflecting Venice's preference for France versus the mainland's more extensive imperial partisanship. Congruently, 'bonsegnore Tenore' (par. 3 Goodsir/Prelate Antenor) becomes 'mosignore Tenore' (Monsieur/Sir Tenore), the change to the title of the noble French army officer corps warning of French ambitions in Italy (see Knecht, pp. 62-87). The 'tuta' (all) is dropped from German lands (par. 11), consistent with Charles's and Maximilian's intent to devolve Austria onto Ferdinand, news of which reached Venice by 1518 (Sanuto, XXV, 176, 323, 497, 559, XXVI, 134). That it remains at the end of the list in this and the XI 66 version may correlate with the general view that the older, courtly German imperials posed less of a threat than the ferocious Spanish. The birds' coming from German lands, rather than from beyond them, is consistent with two different stages of support for Leo's truce: the English, Danish, and Portuguese joined early and Maximilian joined at the end. That the truce was seen as a prelude to war may have stimulated a new allusion to the possible loss of the Pavan and its life-giving bread (par. 9). Imminent conflict is similarly implied in the additional properties of wine and alliaceous vegetables (par. 6): the former does not harm the wounded and the latter raise the dead.

To the list of birds (par. 4) are added 'spinchi' (chaffinches). The name of the bird, which is uncommon in the Mediterranean, is extremely rare in Veneto dialects[57] but occurs in central Italian ones as a metaphor for courting men or the male

---

[57] The only attestation that the current author has found is in the present text; the distinctness of 'spinco' from the Tuscan 'pincione' indicates its authentic local origin.

member, as in a poem by Lorenzo de' Medici (*GDLI*, *s.v.* 'pincione', n. 2). Beolco's addition of it is consistent with other efforts to show that illustrious Tuscan with its spiritualizing literature was actually cruder than Veneto (see Carroll, *Angelo Beolco*, Chapter 7). The discussion of the Abano baths (par. 5) occurs before the reference to the 'pavana' dance, perhaps because of the cardinals' visit to the duke, Leo's efforts to extend the papal state in northern Italy, and Cibo's likely role in them. Appropriate to Medici accusations against della Rovere, Romagnoli here lack 'lianza' (par. 10; loyalty or alliance) rather than law.

Adolescent humour colluding with the virility and pulchritude of the cardinals (Aretino said that he committed the sin of lust in gazing upon them) seems behind the added emphasis on the beauty of the bulls (par. 7).[58] The owning of beautiful cows may refer to the beautiful women, their husbands, and the three cardinals dancing the hat dance, also called the 'pavana' and thus the dance praised in the *Oration*. Several passages in Sanudo's Diaries indicate that the dance was frequently held to honour an elite visitor, who was presented with the most beautiful wives of high-ranking Venetians and allowed to choose among them. One such party had been organized by the cardinal's brother Jacomo for the French high command after their 1515 victory at Marignano and attended by the son and daughter-in-law of Polo Capello; the wife chosen was that of Piero Pesaro, then one of the Heads of the Council of Ten (XIV, 30, XXI, 411, XXIX, 546-47). It is unclear whether this was a symbolic or a material relative of an Asian custom of erotic hospitality described by Marco Polo (*Travels*, Book I, Chapter 38).

The list of animals (par. 7) contains various details not occurring in VR 36. Among the most interesting is that the 'bichi' (rams, cuckolds) are the best race and the greatest in the world, a preview of the praise given the house of Cornaro and thus an example of 'blame-by-praise irony' (Di Maria). The cuckolding of patricians, coded in the superlative status of the animals, therefore precedes the cuckolding of peasants in Ruzante's plays.

Some arcane rural dialect features are deleted in the VR 1636 text, consistent with its reworking for outsiders. The Veneto

---

[58] Beolco's adolescent humour is particularly emphasized by Ferguson; see, *inter alia*, p. 44. On Cibo: Cruciani, p. 353; Del Vita, p. 66 (quoting Aretino); F. Petrucci, 'Cibo, Innocenzo', *DBI*.

'in sul pavan' (lit. in on the Pavan) is simplified to 'sul pavan'. In par. 8, the local 'vizia', apparently relating to comunal woods with their dense growth (see Pellegrini, pp. 274-78) does not occur (because of its similarity to Tuscan 'vizzo' outworn?) and the entire passage is simplified. In this version alone Ruzante labels a popular saying as a proverb (par. 3). Numerous Veneto forms are substituted with Tuscanizing ones, e.g. 'chiama' with 'domanda' (par. 2; a Tuscanism then becoming popular: *GDLI*, *s.v.*, no. 7; Colussi, *s.v.*); 'puo' with 'pocho' (par. 3); 'parlare' is added to 'favellare' (par. 3); 'boaruoli' is replaced with 'boari' (par. 6); 'vardè' with 'guardè' (par. 10), 'zugia' and 'caegia' with 'gugia' and 'chaechia', 'foesse' with 'fosse', 'negun' with 'un' (par. 11), 'arbore' with 'albaro' and 'perdomo' with 'prodohomo' (par. 12), 'purpio' with 'propio' (par. 13), 'se lomé' with 'solamen', 'nogioso' with 'otioso' (par. 17), 'fiorin' with 'fiorini' (pars. 10, 22) and, in multiple locations, 'dige', the Pavan form prevalent in the other two manuscripts, is replaced with 'digo' or 'diga', and other -*e* first person singular verb forms with -*o*.[59] The double consonant characteristic of Tuscan and Roman occurs with much greater frequency than in VR 36 (e.g. *tt*). Curious, if it is not a scribal error, is the form 'Petraca' (par. 3), closer to the original form of the poet's Tuscan patronym (Petracco, Petracchi). The sequence of Petrarch's actions is maliciously corrected from 'he came to live (stay) there and died there' to 'he came there to die and stayed there'. Together such details point to Beolco's capitalizing on a hostile attitude toward the esoteric fourteenth-century poet on the part of the worldly cardinals to support his own view.

Some changes, however, correlate with the presence of dignified prelates in the audience, including Bishop Pesaro: the slap on the woman's behind is not given with love, and, unlike in VR 36 where the never-ordained Marco (Sanuto, XXVI, 250) is referred to as a priest, he is 'sì cum preve' (like a priest, par. 8). The intimate 'don't you well know' becomes 'Se l'è ben' (It is indeed, par. 8). 'Che papa la merda' (What pope, shit) (par. 12) is softened to 'Che Pappa, Pappa, la merda' (What pap, what pap, shit) and 'vesco e papa' (bishop and pope) to 'veschoo e Pappa' (bishop and pap), the latter perhaps because of the offense to the

---

[59] This manuscript has several characteristically Veronese forms, such as 'gnu' (we, vs. Pavan 'nu'), probably attributable to the copyist.

papal circle to call a local bishop 'pope'. The honorific 'missier' is added to the name of Jesus (pars. 2, 19, 22) and the honorific 'bonsegnore' in direct address to the cardinal (par. 15), while the semiblasphemous 'dabiu', a distortion of 'corpo di Dio' (body of God; par. 22), disappears. That the same audience contained beautiful women (and their husbands) brought to dance with the cardinals seems to motivate other changes: the addition of 'perqué el ge sa bon' (because they like the taste of it) to city women's desire for four husbands (par. 22), 'che no doerae esser peccò' (that should not be a sin) to coveting another's wife (par. 22), and 'ficchare' (par. 22 'to stuff' with the double entendre 'to screw') for undowered Paduan girls entering monasteries. The proposal to castrate priests adds the phrases ''l n'è zà ben fatto' (that is not well done) and 'E se i serà castrè a no haron sta briga alle spalle' (and if they will be castrated, we won't have to shoulder these problems).

Several modifications belie a preoccupation with old age and death: the addition of 'chiamentre mé ch'a serom vivi' (as long as we are alive; par. 2), vegetables making the half-dead eat (par. 6), and old people, not doctors, propounding the benefits of eating for enjoyment.

Curiously, in this manuscript alone 'chi in sul Pavan' becomes 'chive a Pava' (here in Padua; par. 13). While the detail may indicate that a performance was planned or took place in Padua for Cibo in 1518, its greater importance lies in its correlation with other evidence of a performance in Padua for Cornaro's Venetian patrician and ecclesiastical guests during the 1521 entrance (see below). A Paduan venue, therefore, but a Venetian or Venetian-Roman audience with ecclesiastical affiliations.

8. *Practice Makes Perfect: BMV Ital. XI 66*

The third manuscript version of the *Prima oration* is found in BMV Ital. XI 66. Its title, using the definite article and no forename (*La oration de Ruzante al Cardinal Cornaro*), indicates that it was copied before the second Cornaro brother, Francesco, became a cardinal and received an oration from Ruzante, a partial and untitled version of which was copied onto a later folio. Of the three titles, it is the only one lacking reference to a performance.

A comparison of the text with the others leads to the hypothesis that Beolco approached it as a literary and linguistic laboratory, experimenting with the forms of the original text, variants introduced in 1636 (see p. 62, below), and additional variants (compare Looney, p. 1314).[60] A sensitive consideration of the effects of rhythm, semantics, and sequencing on audience response is manifest in Beolco's modifications. A typical example is his experimentation with 'po' and 'mo' as interjections. Comparison with the other manuscripts shows that even some minute linguistic modifications represent purposeful authorial changes rather than correction of error. An example is 'puorpio' (really; par. 2), where the first *o* is inserted above the line in an amalgamation of 'prupio' of VR 36 and 'pruopiamen' of VR 1636. Another is the experimentation with 'straza' (par. 18; VR 36), 'fraza' (hail, VR 1636), 'sfraza' (XI 66, an apparent neologism).

The XI 66 version is the work of an orator aiming to convince an audience of the rightness of his moral programme. The identity of that audience is therefore crucial: the points on which XI 66 conforms to VR 36 indicate that the audience is again a mainland one. The speech is given in a 'villa' (villa/ge) not a 'luogo' (place); the praise of the 'pavana' is back before the baths; the full meaning of Pavan returns (par. 9); distinctive local verb forms such as 'dige' (I say) and 'foesse' (were) and syntactical structures such as 'in sul pavan' (in the Pavan) and 'se lo mé' (at least) return. The form 'boaruoli' returns, as do 'arca', 'vitia', 'gualiva', 'cesiole', 'gesiò' (church, vs. 'giesia'); in some cases even more distinctive forms are used, such as 'erbore' (tree; par. 12). Peasant women's eyes again pierce anvils, the slap is given with love, the Cornaro hold firm and they are 'parona' only of the Pavan (par. 11), Rome is followed by Spain then France, 'with my boss' is placed early, the definition of cardinal (par. 13) is 'in our Pavan way' and the explanation is long and complex, 'we' rather than 'I' want the laws, the peasants would be on top (par. 22), and the health advice is given by doctors, although the logical progession is spelled out. 'Che papa la merda' returns, while 'bishop and pope' takes on the deformation 'visio' (possibly 'visco' [bishop], an attested dialect form) de papa'.

---

[60] That Beolco was also responsive to changing historical circumstances is confirmed by the additions in the margin to the XI 66 fragment of the *Moscheta*, which indicate that the copyist took account of updates being made by the author, including details showing that war had begun. These *marginalia* having also generally been ignored by scholars, there is no systematic study of them, a project which the present author is currently undertaking.

Of the features introduced in VR 1636, the most important retained in XI 66 are the designation of literary men as from Padua (par. 10); details in par. 13 including 'without measure', the change of 'spendesson' (we would spend) to 'decipesson' (we would squander) and the added 'and I yours' (a sign that he had succeeded in becoming established in those circles?); the honorific 'bonsegnore' (par. 15); the addition of 'missier' (and phonetic variants) to the name of Jesus except in paragraph 15; the change from having the heart 'in heaven with God' to 'ivelo a massier Jesum Dio' (there with Sir Jesus God, par. 19) indicative of the growing emphasis on Christ as personal saviour; all of the details about priestly marriage and castration except that the current situation 'is not well done' (par. 21; also a marginal addition to the *Moscheta* fragment); all of the details about multiple marriage partners (par. 22).

Important changes introduced in this version include the very few examples of buildup, their rarity underlining their importance, as in 'un bel piasere vivo e snaturale' (a lovely live and snatural pleasure; par. 14) compared with the earlier 'un piaser vivo e naturale' (a live and natural pleasure), 'un piasere vivo e snaturale'. In paragraph 4, 'segnor Tenore' eschews both 'bon' and 'mon'; in paragraph 14, where most of the new details occur, 'farte correre' (make you run) becomes 'ti forte corere' (you run hard), 'el can' (the dog) becomes 'el to can' (your dog), and 'un a dire' (one saying) becomes 'vu a dire' (you saying). In paragraph 18 'vostra cara fe' (your dear faith) becomes 'nostra cara fe' (our dear faith); in paragraph 22, 'senza nu che valeseu vu' (without us who would you be) is replaced by 'senza mi che valessevu' (without me who would you be) and 'a ve tegneron' (we will hold you) becomes 've tegneson' (we would hold you). Taken together the details give an impression of Beolco's greater personalization of the situation, accompanied by a loss of illusion regarding achieving his goal and an increased turning to hunting and other pleasurable distractions.

9. Conclusion

Comparison of the texts and contexts of the three versions permits several tentative observations. The first is that the long-held assumption that Beolco's invitations to perform in Venice came through Alvise Cornaro bears re-examining in light of the ownership of agricultural property in the same areas as the

Beolco family or near the Ferrarese state by many patricians associated with the invitations, especially Immortale and Ortolano families. One can imagine that a youthful Beolco's recitation of riffs on the abundance of the Paduan countryside during the pre-war vogue for Giorgionesque pastoralism (Carroll, '"Fools"', 61-63) inspired later invitations to town by property owners, then motivated by an interest in defence and international relations. The extensive imperial connections of Beolco's hosts, whose largely financial motivations are now explicated and documented (Carroll, 'Venetian Attitudes'; '"I have"'), support Lovarini's thesis that Beolco's associates had imperial leanings (Carroll, 'Peasant', pp. 199-200) and open the further question of whether Beolco functioned as a conduit between Venetians and imperials.

The date of the oration's first draft is another point that should be revisited. The VR 36 version exudes the animated confidence of Paduan peasants immediately after the war, when numerous factors supported their aspirations for participation in the direction of their society. Its spirit also conveys the exuberance of a performer at one of his first big gigs. On the other hand, VR 36 expresses great fear of the Turks, understandable in the context of Selim the Grim's recent conquests. By 1521, the Habsburg–Valois war and emphasis on social hierarchy had returned, the Catholic Evangelical spirit had encountered the rapid spread of anti-papal Evangelical movements, Beolco's performances had achieved the approval of a segment of the highest echelon of the Venetian patriciate, and Selim had been replaced by the peaceful Suleiman.

The orator's statement that he is speaking at Cornaro's pleasure, underlining the patrician sponsorship required for his performances, should catalyse a fresh examination of the relationship between Beolco and his patrician associates. While offering himself as an attack dog against Cornaro's enemies, Ruzante also attacks his friends, even the Cornaro, when need be. With a Ciceronian capacity to argue both sides of the question and a matchless ability to say what everyone knows needs to be said, he threatens to function as the boar if the cardinal does not help the peasants. The attack on speakers of Florentine and priests includes Leo's circle, which was taking Cornaro away from caring for his (peasant) flock; by listing the states that are (not) the 'boss' of the Pavan, Ruzante warns that friends may be more dangerous than enemies, reinforcing the message to concentrate on the home territory.

Praise for the Pavan's abundant vitality is also a plea to protect it from the devastation of war by preserving peace, explicated in the theme of the 1525 festivity, 'Concordiae dedicatum' (Dedicated to Peace). Relatively unrecognized by Ruzante studies is that a concern with war is the hallmark of all his plays, not solely those addressing it overtly such as *Reduce* (*The Veteran*). In the *Betia*, for example, the prologue's cows in the city and birds in cages referred to war: cows were brought into the city for safekeeping at the outbreak of war and Venice imprisoned followers of the imperial eagle in cages. The organization of fighting forces (IV), while directed at local conflicts, demonstrates to a patrician audience Beolco's talent at commanding a peasant 'cernida' (fighting unit) in case war again threatened the mainland and their properties.

A master of psychology and possessed of and by an indomitable will to succeed, Beolco employed means to achieve professional success and the implementation of his programme that lie both above and below the threshold of Aristotelian rhetorical dignity. While chiefly using the formal second person plural of the inferior, Beolco at crucial points slips into the familiar *tu* of both the accomplice and the superior (Carroll, 'Linguistic Correlates'). Complicity is reinforced through shared adolescent humour, superiority through bullying. While placing Cornaro at the pinnacle of institutional power in his episcopal role of sole decider, Beolco reminds him that he would be nothing without his peasant flock and will check that the bishop has done the peasants' bidding.

Beolco's role of thinker and reformer intent on ensuring the participation of all social groups in the governance of their society is an extraordinary anticipation of notions that will become the norm only in the eighteenth century and a sign of his importance to the history of democracy.

10. Note on the Texts

The *Prima oration* exists in the three manuscript versions published here, and in a fourth that was extensively rewritten, probably by someone other than Beolco. The Biblioteca Civica of Verona houses two, 36 and 1636, both discovered by Emilio Lovarini and described briefly by Giuseppe Biadego (*Catalogo*, pp. 138-39 [VR 1635-36], 174 [VR 36]). Lovarini says little about VR 36, identifying watermarks spanning Venice to Milan and 1526 to 1566, including one found in Padua in 1536 ('Per l'edizione', pp. 140-45, 147-49, 151-52). He notes (p. 144) that in VR 1636 the titles of two works, *Historia di Phileto Veronese* by Ludovico Corfino and *Sopra la caccia* by Beolco, were added 'di mano moderna' (by a modern hand; it appears to date to the eighteenth century). Richard Wendriner ('Codice') hypothesizes that VR 36 was originally constituted by the first two fascicles, which contain Ruzante's *Anconitana* and other works, to which were added the remaining two containing the *Oratione* and other works (all apparently in the same hand). He gives a partial transcription of remarks scribbled by an early reader lauding its entertainment value. The third manuscript and the reworked version are located in Venice's Biblioteca Nazionale Marciana, respectively in Ital. XI 66 and Ital. XI 90. Lovarini hypothesized that the latter (XI 90) was produced by Alvise Cornaro and Giacomo Morello. Ludovico Zorzi published an overview of the manuscripts in his 'Nota al testo' (pp. 1604-36, 1624-26, 1635). Giorgio Padoan provided a description of the manuscripts in his 'Nota ai testi' (pp. 48-55).

Ital. XI 66, a bulky miscellany containing the largest number of Ruzante's works, was probably compiled by one or more persons associated with the ducal chancellery over many years, with 1530 the last date appearing in it and some works likely added slightly after that date (Cristofari, p. 35 for the oration, mistranscribing 'Ruxante'). While, as suggested by Cristofari, the principal may have been Gaspare dalla Vedova, others, possibly including his son, must have been involved after Gaspare's death in 1524, the period in which the Beolco works seem to have been added. While Danilo Romei has made a number of valuable observations about the prevalent hand of XI 66, his hypothesis that the miscellany was compiled probably in Padua at the direction of the Cornaro family and specifically Alvise Cornaro (pp. 17-18) is based on several flawed premises. Alvise was not a member of the patrician family and it is likely that his surname was not Cornaro but the patronym-based Rigo (Menegazzo, 'Alvise Cornaro', pp. 516-19). Romei cites as evidence of a close relationship between Alvise and the patrician Cornaro a poem copied into XI 66 that names the 'abati Cornaro' (Cardinal Marco's nephews) resident in Padua. However, a reading of the text, relegated to a footnote, reveals that it is a degrading attack on them as passive homosexuals. It is unclear what motivation the patrician Cornaro family would have to include a scurrilous and defamatory poem about the sons and grandsons of some of its most illustrious members in a miscellany of their compilation.⁶¹ Other evidence that Alvise did not enjoy a strong relationship with the patrician Cornaro, pointed out by others, is that he was not named episcopal administrator by Marco Cornaro but by his successor Francesco Pisani, brother of the Zuan who led the 1519 hunt probably attended by Alvise.⁶² While works associated with Padua enjoy a prominent role in the miscellany, it includes others that touch a broad swath of mainland and maritime interests. Having read each folio of the manuscript directly, the present author views the miscellany to have been compiled in Venice probably by individuals with special interests in the mainland and associated with the chancellery (very possibly the two dalla Vedova), probably in connection with a group of Venetian patricians and perhaps under their direction. That the Cornaro figured in such a group is certainly possible but, at the current state of evidence, it is unlikely that they directed it, at least in its entirety.

Neither Lovarini nor Wendriner expressed an opinion on the chronology of the three versions. Zorzi viewed XI 66 as probably the oldest or at least the one with the fewest intervening copies. Observing that it is close in form and in time to the first printed version (1551, by Venetian printer Stefano Alessi), he hypothesized that it was derived from one owned by Alvise Cornaro and accepted Lovarini's Cornaro-Morello hypothesis. Padoan hypothesized that VR 36 and the earliest printed version were based on the same manuscript source because they share certain omissions. He saw shared incorrect readings of VR 1636 and XI 66 as indicating that they belong to a second family.

A closer examination of the variants provides additional insights. An erroneous abbreviation in the VR 36 version (par. 22) 'ben el sarà p[er]e vu' (it will be good for you) may be related to its

---

[61] The poem may well have come instead from the circle of Aretino, who in those years was supporting Pietro Bembo in a conflict with the Corner over whose client would be named to an office (the Corner prevailed) and over a delay in paying Bembo the pension owed him from a benefice occupied by one of the 'abati Cornaro', Cardinal Marco's nephews (for which see Virgili, 244-46).

[62] Alvise did cultivate a relationship in late second and early third decades of the century with the patrician group around the Immortali, in which the Corner figured prominently, a development in which it is beginning to appear that Federico Gonzaga played an important role (Carroll, 'Venetian Attitudes', esp. pp. 18, 24-25; Carroll, 'Shepherd'; compare Carroll, '"Fools"').

inaccurate XI 66 counterpart '"l serà ben pre vu' (1636 abbreviates correctly: "'l serà ben p[er] vu'). The *Anconitana* manifests a similar problem. In VR 36 (fol. 5^v), 'un putato boaruoLo' (an adolescent cowherd) shows the clever correction with a capital 'L' of an underlying 'v', demonstrating the copyist's familiarity with the rural word and his willingness to intervene. XI 66 (fol. 127^r) has 'un putto boaruovo' (a child oxegg), where the unfamiliar rural 'putato' (adolescent) is substituted by 'putto' (child), familiar to a Venetian or Tuscan but showing ignorance that a child would not be entrusted with cattle, while 'boaruovo' is not recognized as a nonsense term resulting from a misspelling. These details suggest that VR 36 and XI 66 shared a matrix.

The variations among the three manuscripts sometimes give the impression that the work did not involve transcribing a clean copy but untangling a cat's cradle of scribbled corrections and collated bits. Here Lovarini's sound intuition of Beolco's closeness to the three manuscripts in time, geography, and influence is relevant. Finally, the chronological order of the manuscripts is unlikely to reflect the chronological order of the performances, as they apparently were copied for different reasons for different audiences.

The *Oration* of VR 36 (fols 48^v-49^v) is followed by a bizarre work entitled *Querella contra Madonna Trucignicignacola* (The Case against Lady Trucignicignacola), set in Venice in 1514. Lovarini's speculation that it was by Andrea Calmo ('Per l'edizione', p. 148) is unlikely for chronological reasons. Its resemblance to the heavily reworked *Oratione* and its setting in the time and place of Alvise Cornaro's case for patrician status support the hypothesis that Cornaro was its author.

Beolco's works in VR 1636 occur in the following order: *Sopra la caccia* (*On Hunting*), *Intermedio d'una comedia de Ruzante alla Pavana* (*Intermezzo of a Pavan Comedy by Ruzante*), *S Prolico de Ruzante fatto al Cardinale Cornaro nella Inclyta Citta di vinegia* (*SPrologue/Rambling Speech Made by Ruzante to Cardinal Cornaro in the Illustrious City of Venice*). *Sopra la Caccia* (the title added in a later hand), a version of the *Lettera all'Alvarotto*, has its own folio numeration (although only the first three folios have the numbers written on them). The *Intermedio* and the *Oration* and several non-Beolco works that follow (see below) share a separate numeration. The *Intermedio*'s title provides the valuable information that it was then a between-act sketch; it later reappeared as the prologue of the *Moscheta*, to which it apparently gave rise. The manuscript concludes with an unusual assortment of works by other authors including a sonnet citing Priapus, a Latin translation of a poem of Hesiod's, and distichs addressed to the pope (Biadego, *Catalogo*, p. 208).

VR 1636 is bound with VR 1635, the romance *Historia di Phileto veronese* (*The Story of Phileto from Verona*) by the Veronese Ludovico Corfino. It recounts the adventures of the exiled imperialist Phileto between about 1515 and 1518, referring to a fictionalized version of Ludovico's brother Girolamo as a personal attendant of Cardinal Cibo in Rome.[63] A connection between the Roman cardinals' 1518 visit and VR 1636 could explain some of the idiosyncracies of the *Intermedio*. Unlike the other manuscript version (XI 66) and the printed version, it lacks the statement 'E questa che è chialò no è Cremona, né Ferara; mo l'è Pava' (This that's over here is not Cremona nor Ferrara but Padua). Cremona being the city in which Ariosto's *Negromante* is set, the *Intermedio* dates to before 1520, the year in which Ariosto, at the request of Pope Leo, wrote the play for the Roman Carnival season. The pope had come to know the playwright's work through Cibo, who so enjoyed Ariosto's *Suppositi* in Ferrara that he staged it in Rome in 1519.[64]

The *Intermedio* does refer to a writer present who could write in his own language but who writes in Florentine. It also castigates male fashions of the late second decade of the sixteenth century, Spanish influence on language, and the wearing of earrings (a fashion arriving in Italy from Spain and Africa in that period) by members of the audience.[65] The writer is clearly Ariosto and the other details point to Ferrara. In the preceding forty years, Eleanora d'Aragona of Naples and Lucrezia Borgia as duchesses of

---

[63] Biadego, 'Introduzione', p. xxv. Biadego's research showed that the character died earlier than the historical brother but did not produce evidence that he had served Cardinal Cibo.

[64] Casella, Ronchi, and Varasi, pp. ix-xlix, xxvi-xxxii; Cummings, 'Music'.

[65] For earrings' origins, Hughes; for images of them in use in northern Italy, including Ferrara, much earlier than in Venice, see Lorenzo Lotto, *Mystic Marriage of St Catherine [of Alexandria]* (ca. 1505-06) in Humphrey, figs. 28 (p. 23) and 29, detail of 28 (p. 24); *Judith with the Head of Holofernes* (1512), fig. 44 (p. 40); Dosso Dossi, *Soldier and Girl with Flute* in Gibbons, cat. no. 76 and plate 26; *Poet and Muse*, cat. no. 33 and fig. 56; compare Ariosto, *Orlando furioso*, VII.54.

Ferrara had brought significant Spanish influence to it, and the Este had employed numerous Spanish troops in their wars (Rigobello, *Lendinara*, pp. 99-120). Dosso Dossi, the court's painter, includes earrings on women figures in this period when they were still unknown in the Venetian dominion. The cardinals' enjoyment of the *Intermedio* in Ferrara perhaps led to the performance of the oration in Venice, explaining the texts' sequence in the manuscript.[66]

VR 1636, whose watermark was found by Lovarini in Vicenza in 1536, seems to have been assembled for Cardinal Cibo from texts performed for him and others added out of interest. Cibo is also mentioned in a BCV miscellany shortly after a version of Ruzante's *Lettera all'Alvarotto* in a group of letters arranged chronologically for the first months of 1537 (Codice Cicogna 3085/IV [*già* Cicogna 691], fols 26^v-27^r). The extract from the letter containing his name alludes to the assassination of Alessandro de' Medici, which could have put Cibo, the tutor of Alessandro's infant son, functionally in charge of the Medici state.[67]

As to the identity of the compiler of VR 1636 or its archetype, there are several possibilities. Marco Cornaro had been bishop of Verona long before becoming bishop of Padua. Francesco Berni, a devoted admirer of Ruzante, spent some years in Venice, Padua and Verona after the 1527 Sack of Rome and participated in a poetic exchange with Ludovico Corfino.[68] Dolfin Dolfin was interested in property near Verona and his poetry was included in an anthology of works by friends of the Veronese dialect writer Girolamo Verità and possibly also Corfino. However, the most persuasive evidence is the Estimo declaration of Paolo Alvarotto (*Estimo*, reg. 5 [6], fols 134^r-37^v, dated 1562), whose father Giacomo had joined the diplomatic staff of the duke of

---

[66] Lovarini's original analysis of some versions of the *Lettera all'Alvarotto* as early appears correct.

[67] In 1535 Cibo had been accused of poisoning Francesco Berni when Berni refused his directive to poison Cardinal Salviati for opposing Alessandro. Although knowing of the accusation, Charles V met Cibo in May 1536 and was with Alessandro when his bride, Charles's illegitimate daughter, arrived in Florence (F. Petrucci, 'Cibo, Innocenzo', *DBI*).

[68] Reynolds, pp. 47-51; Virgili, pp. 200-62, 411-20; Biadego, 'Notizie', pp. xviii-xx; Lovarini, 'Per l'edizione', pp. 139-49.

Ferrara. Its hand is almost identical to that of VR 1636. That branch of the Alvarotto, which had strong connections to Rome and a history of acquiring benefices, had worked hard in the decades after 1509 to repair the damage caused by their participation in the rebellion against Venice, the extent of their properties indicating their success. VR 1636's apparently Vicentine watermark poses no obstacle, as the towns are close together and there are similar Veronese watermarks of the same period.[69]

The *Prima oration* may have resulted in word of the *Utopia* and *Praise of Folly* being taken to Florence by Cardinal Cibo, where, ironically, it was the members of the anti-Medicean faction who were inspired by them. The Giuntine press published *Praise of Folly* in Florence in December 1518 (it had been printed twice in Venice in 1515) and *Utopia* in 1519 with works by Lucian of Samosata. Carlo Dionisotti saw the latter volume, which appeared shortly after the death of Lorenzo duke of Urbino, as inspiring the anti-Medici plot put into effect after Leo's death in 1521 against his nephew Cardinal Giulio, regent of Florence.[70] A poem by conspirator Jacopo da Diacceto was transcribed into XI 66, with a note that he was executed for his role (Cristofari, p. 25).

Although in the present edition modern punctuation has been introduced, efforts have been made to preserve the appearance of the texts in the manuscripts. While capitalization has been added where it would be found in modern usage, non-standard capital letters present in the manuscript have been retained where they appear to bear meaning. For example, the VR 36 text, unlike the others, consistently capitalizes 'papa', an interesting correlation with the hypothesis that it was destined to a cardinal who was a member of a papal family. Abbreviations have been expanded silently. Original spellings, even where apparently irregular, have been retained because of the valuable clues they may offer, it being rarely clear whether variants are mistakes, deliberate malformations, or unattested dialect variants. In the rare cases where a variant spelling appears to embody genuine error, it has been corrected, with the change recorded in a note. Accepted word

---

[69] Lovarini, 'Per l'edizione', p. 147 n. 3 identifies it as Briquet, I, 3565 (*sic, recte* 3505), whose appearance is quite close to that of 3504, attested in Verona in 1538.

[70] Dionisotti, pp. 210-13; Lowe, pp. 121-31; Cummings, *Maecenas*, pp. 23-24, 169, 185, 190, 208 n. 33.

divisions are followed, although in the manuscripts spaces within words may be as large as those between words. Accents, which are generally (but not entirely) lacking in the manuscripts, have been added sparingly, following modern usage, to assist the reader, although some of them are rendered uncertain by geographical and historical variations in accentuation. The one radical intervention into the text is the introduction of paragraphing. While in some cases a dividing point was relatively self-evident (e.g. 'Pavan, an?' tends to open a new topic), the run-on character of other sections resulted in more arbitrary choices.

The paucity of available authentic texts in the rural Pavan dialect of the sixteenth century, and therefore of complete information about it, leaves many open questions about its use in the three texts, which are increased by the lack of information about intermediary manuscripts and copyists. For example, the same manuscript uses both *-e* and *-o* as the first person singular present verb form. It is well documented that *-e* was a characteristic Pavan form, raising the question of why *-o* is also used in the text. Was it beginning to infiltrate the countryside as a prestige form? Did it co-exist in free variation in some regions, such as those closer to Venice? Did the playwright introduce it to make the text more understandable to a larger audience? Are all the *-o* forms attributable to the playwright or were some introduced by the copyist(s)? By comparison, in the two texts of the *Betia*, 'dige' occurs much more frequently than 'digo', especially in the Marciana version, whose single prologue for performances in Padua apparently indicates it was not to be performed in Venice. Some interesting hints about usage are provided by the third plural masculine subject/object pronouns 'egi' and 'igi' (they/them). VR 36 uses both 'egi' (4 times) and 'igi' (7 times) as the tonic (stressed) pronoun, and *-egi* as the postclitic (two examples). What is most interesting is that in at least two visible instances, 'igi' was corrected to 'egi' ('che 'l cancaro i magne egi', par. 13; 'cossì nu de sora con igi è egi', par. 22) in a tonic form, indicating that some semantic principle was at work. VR 1636 uses 'igi' exclusively as the tonic pronoun, and *-egi* as postclitic (two examples); XI 66 uses 'egi' (3 times) and 'igi' (15 times) as tonic pronoun, and *-egi* as postclitic (few examples).

Some of the linguistic differences may provide information about the performances themselves. In VR 36, the literary men's lack of knowledge is related in a past tense but in the other two manuscripts in a future perfect, used in Italian to express probability or conjecture about the past. The change in tense might indicate that Beolco himself was present during their speeches on the first occasion, the informal 1518 Asolo context, but not on the other two, the formal contexts of a government body (Venice) and the episcopal entrance (Padua). The number of Veronese dialect features, especially the palatalization of *nu* (*gnu*) and the exclusive use of 'intendivu' rather than 'intendiu' (do you understand?; the latter much more frequent in Beolco's plays in general), as well as the increased instance of humorous linguistic deformation ('altro moio') may add to other evidence that Beolco's works were restaged by others interested in them.

Systematic descriptions of what is known of the Pavan dialect of Ruzante's time are available in Wendriner (*Die paduanische Mundart*) and Carroll (*Language*, Chapter Two). The following are some of the basic features that appear in the oration.

Two characteristic phonetic features affecting many words are lenition, which produces a massive loss of intervocalic single consonants, and heavy diphthongization, which occurs even in closed syllables.

Both tonic and clitic subject pronouns are used, the clitic *a* serving as a generic pronoun but most frequently used with the first person and least frequently with the second person singular; postcliticization occurs in the interrogative. The subject pronouns are: *a* (also *e*), *mi*, *io*; *a*, *ti*, *te*; *a*, *el*, *l'*, *elo*; *a*, *la*, *ela*; *a*, *nu*; *a*, *vu*; *a*, *i*, *igi*, *egi*; *a*, *e*, *ele*. The postclitic form for the first person singular is *-io*, often palatalized to *-gio*. Lenition may result in the reduction of the second person plural *-vu* to *-u* in the postcliticized form. Object pronouns also occur in tonic and clitic forms and are similar in most cases to the subject form, with the exception that *a* does not function as an object pronoun. The clitic locative pronoun has the forms *ge* and *gie*, the third person indirect object *ge*, and the partitive pronoun *in*.

For verbs, the first person singular in the present and the future ends in *-e* (reflecting the first person singular of *avere*, *he*), although, as noted elsewhere, the ending *-o* also occurs. The second person singular of *avere* also has the form *he*. The characteristic first person plural is *-om*. The second person plural, used also in formal address to one person as here to Cornaro, is *-é* for the first and second conjugations and *-i* for the third. The third person forms are identical in the singular and plural, and tend to be *-e* even for first conjugation verbs. The transcription here uses the form 'pò' for the third person of *potere* to distinguish it from 'po', the form used here for both the adverb of time (='poi') and the interjection. Forms of the verb *volere* occurring here are 'vuogio' (first person singular), 'vo' (third person singular), 'vogiom' (first person plural). The third person present subjunctive of *essere*, which occurs frequently in the oration, is 'supia' or 'sipia'. The conditional occurs in the first person singular form -*rè* and the third person form -*rae*. The past participle ending of regular first conjugation verbs is -*ò* in the case of no agreement, while -*è* is the reflex of -*ati*. The past participle of the second conjugation is -*ù* and of the third conjugation -*io*. There is a preterite (many of whose forms resemble those of the imperfect subjunctive) as well as a present perfect. A distinctive formation is the use of the preposition 'a' followed by the gerund. The particle 'an' is used for both emphasis and to mark an interrogative.

The almost universal possessive for both third person singular and third person plural is 's(u)o''. The masculine plural definite article is 'gi'.

The form of the cardinal's surname used requires a note. Its Venetian form, as may be observed in Sanuto, is Corner. The Paduan form, used in the oration, was Cornaro, one of Beolco's many means of aggregating the cardinal to his side. For that reason and because all of the titles in the manuscripts use that form, it is used here. It is significant, in light of Beolco's patron's ardent desire to be recognized as a Venetian patrician but his fortune's source in the mainland, that the signature on the petition to Federico Gonzaga used the hybrid form Chornero.

The Cornaro barco at Asolo
Photo credit: Edward Muir

Angelo Beolco (Ruzante): La prima oration

An oration of Ruzante's recited to Cardinal Cornaro at his barn below Asolo in the Trevisan countryside

VR 36

1) Because it's the clap to shove yourself where you're not supposed to and where it isn't proper and now I, who am what I am now and — like the man said — a polite man, I watch what I do, and for that reason, Most Rebellious Sir Scardinal, I did not want to come to Padua to give this peroration to you because — why because those clap-creaking favour-hounds who sit on the sliterary shit-thrones of treason would have taken it the wrong way. Because, as the saying goes, it is not seemly for Jews to mix with Samaritans, which amounts to saying that bachelors should not mix with married men. Now because, now because just as bachelors try to put horns on married men, so city people poke fun at and ride us poor folk from the villages. And for that reason we flee from them more than sparrows flee from hawks. And this now is why I didn't come to Padua.

2) Now I came right here, just here, in this spot, where else, in this villa(ge) so I could easily tell and spell out my counsel in the name of the whole Paduan territory that elected me, a well-spoken man and orator, and don't look, don't even check if we wanted to send a priest or one of those guys with saffron belts who speak in standard sin-tax or in Florentinish lawyerspeak, of those, you know, that are called duotowers, well I there am three of those towers. Now we, don't you know, take pleasure now in holding our natural straight up and straight on through Mother nature, stirring our tongue in our own way and not in the Florentinish way. And I want to say about myself that I from now on would not exchange my tongue with two hundred Florentinish ones, nor would I grab at being born in Egypt of Bethlehem where Jesus God was born, because then I would not be born in the Pavan. Now wouldn't I too know, if I wanted to, how to talk Florentinish? I would talk, I say, so valiantly that you would say that I was a real Politan from Robbing. Now listen, Goodsir: I we is a peasant from the country that we lives and stays on the Pavano and I me bows himself down before your Lordship of you. Does it

Oration de Ruzante recitata al Cardinal Cornaro al barcho soto Asolo in Trivisana

VR 36

1) Perqué l'è el cancaro a cazarse on no se de e don non è honesto, e mo mi che a son mi — mo e, con dise questù, hom compìo — a guardo ben co a fazo. E perzontena, Rebelissimo Missiere lo Sgardenale, a n'he vogiù vegnire a farve sto sproleco a Pava. Perqué? Mo perqué qui cancari de quigi sbaiafaore de quigi chagariegi sletran harà habù per male. Che com dise el provierbio, 'No bene conveniunte zudie con samaritani'. Che ven a dire che no sta ben donziei con mariè. Mo perqué? Mo perqué così con i donziegi cerca de far bichi i mariè, così i citaini ne trogna e ne deleza nu poviriti da le ville. E perzontena a muzon pì da igi che no fa le celege dal falcheto. E questo è mo che a no son vegnù a Pava.

2) Mo a son vegnù chialò chive quencena chialondena in sta villa per poere ben dire e slainare la mia reson per lome de tuto el terramuorio pavan che m'à aslenzù mi si com hom bon parlente e sprolegaore. Nè gnian gnian guardè che haon vogiù mandare un preve nè un de quigi da le centure insofranè che favela per gramego o in avogaro fiorentinescho, de quigi — savì? — che se chiama dottore. A ge son an mi tre de le torre. Mo nu, savìu, haon mo piasere de tegnire el nostro naturale derto in pè e dertamente per la natura, smissianto la lengua a nostro muò e no | [40ʳ] a la fiorentinescha. E a vuo' dir de mi che mi inchindamo a no cambierae la me lengua co dosento fiorentinesche. Nè no torae de essere nassù in l'Agito de Beteleme, donde nassè Iesum Dio, per no essere nassù sul Pavan. Mo no saravigio an mi se ha volesse favellare fiorentinescho? Favellerae a dige sì fieramen che a dissè che a foesse prupio un politan da Rubin. Mo ascoltè Bonsegnore: 'Io me a siamo contadino de la villa che habitamo et stasamo sul Pavano et io me si rebutamo a la vostra de vu Segnoria'. Ve par mo per la vostra cara fe che a parerae mé che a foesse nasù in sul Pavan? Po l'è un gran cagare. [Ve par mo che

appear to you, on your dear faith, that it would appear at all that I was born in the Pavan? Boy, that's a load of shit. [Does it seem to you that I could be there too, if I wanted to?] I don't want to now; I want to go with my natural standing right up and in a straight line, like I say.

3) Now tell me this, Mister Francis Petrarch, wasn't he born in Florentinery? Yes, by the pox, that's it, and because he was unhappy at having been born there, because he wished he'd been born in the Pavan, he came to live there and died there and wanted to be buried there. How's that? And this was no joke or trick, and yes he did not hesitate to leave the place where he was born and leave behind relatives and friends, and even though they say, you know, 'Tie my hands and feet and put me with my pals'. He left there and came to the Pavan and left everybody behind, even though he knew everything that can be known. And now why did he do that? So that he could be one of us after he was dead since he wasn't able to be born here, because he knew that ours was the most beautiful language in the world and the most beautiful country. Now then, goodsir Tenor came from across the sea, from Turkeyland, to found Padua on the Pavan, because the Pavan came before Padua. And our old ancestors wanted him to put a woman's name on Padua so that she would always stay underneath the Pavan and the Pavan would keep Padua sodomitted and now it's going a different way. Now because you have the power to do so, you will fix this, because it is a sin against this poor Pavan.

4) Pavan, huh? Now, don't the swallows who leave from beyond Colecut, and even from beyond the sun's den come here to the Pavan and come to have their young with us in our houses without fear as if they didn't notice a thing and sing the whole morning long to please us? And they pay no attention that, in order to come here to the Pavan, they have to cross so many seas and so many desolate places. And what about the quail that come too from there, to fatten themselves here, to give us in the Pavan good eating. Pavan, huh? And the robins, titmice, redstarts, nightingales, thrushes, and so many other kinds of birds who come from beyond the German land and cross so many mountains and so many snows, Oh and where are they coming? To the Pavan, now. To do what? To get fat now.

sarae an mi esserge s'a volesse?] Mo a no vuogio — a vuogio andare co el me naturale in pè derto e dertamente con a dige.

3) Mo dime un puo': Missiere Francesco Petrarcha no nassilo in Fiorentinaria? Mo cancar'è e perqué el fo mal contento a esserge nasù, che 'l vorae essere nasù in sul Pavan, el ge vene a stare e ge morì e ge vosse essere soterò. An? Questa no fo buffa ne capelleta. E sì no guardè a partirse don l'iera nasù e lassare parentò e amisté, che saì pure che se dise, 'Ligame le man e i piè e metime de brigà d'i mie'.' El se ge partì e vene in sul Pavan e lagè tuto hom e sì saea pur quello che se pò saere. E perché el felo mo? Mo per essere da po morto pavan e dasché el no g'havea possù nasire, che el cognosea che 'l | [40ᵛ] nostro giera pì bel favelare del mondo e pì bel paese. Po bonsegnore Tenore che vene d'oltra el mare de Turcaria per fare Pava in sul Pavan, che prima fo el Pavan de Pava? E i nostri antessore vegi vosse ch'el metesse lome a Pava de femena perqué la staesse sempre soto el Pavan e ch'el Pavan tegnisse sotomitò Pava e la va mo a un altro muò. Mo a dasché a 'l poì fare, ala conzarì, che l'è pechò de sto povero Pavan.

4) Pavan an? Mo no ge ven le cesiole che se parte de là da Colecuta e chiamentre de là dal coato del sole per vignire chi in sul Pavan e per vignire a fare i suo' furti con nu in le nostre ca senza paura con se le foesse desmentegè e canta tuta la doman per farge apiasere. E sì no guarda che a vignire chi in sul Pavan le habbi da passare tanti mare e tante salbergure. Mo le quagie? Che ven an elle de ivelo e ven a ingrassarse chi per darge ben da magnare a nu pavani. Pavan an? Mo i betuzi, paruzole, coarussi, rossignati, turdi, e tanta altra fata de osiegi che ven de là oltra la terra toescha e passa tante montagne e tante nieve, o per vignir mo onve? Mo sul Pavan, a far mo che? Mo a ingrassarse.

5) Pavan, huh? Now you can't even go to Rome, if you take the Treviso road, without passing over the Pavan. Pavan, huh? Now tell me if somebody knows how to do a nice dance who does not do the pavan. Now if there were nothing else in the Pavan except the Abano hotspring baths, and there are so many others that are better, where all day long foreign men who are sick to death come with their coffins hanging off their butts and leave the Pavan healed. Pavan, huh? Now, what air there is there and Christ of Loreto, when someone is sick and especially those guys from Venice when they are pretty messed up and sick and they have themselves brought there and, I say, without either baths or medicine they are immediately restored to health right here in this Pavan.

6) Pavan, huh? And what about that bread that is born there, isn't it good? They make friar's bread, that puffy kind, and bread that is so crusty that when you eat it bits of crust shoot right up into the sky, so that a stonecrusher would pale in comparison. And it's better than frosted cakes or doughnuts. Now that rough wine, isn't it good? And it says 'Drink me' and jumps in the cup, a wine that could really raise the dead and digest stone. Pavan wine, huh? Now isn't that the place where all the kinds of legumes of the world are born? Let's not talk about broad beans, because whoever starts eating them can't help eating four bowlsful. And chickpeas, now beans that call for smothered cabbage a thousand miles away. Now then there's chicklings, and lentils, peas now and panic grass and fodder grains, with millet, sorghum, spelt, rye, barley, orzola, oats, and vetch. And greens now? Now savoy cabbage, tall savoy cabbage, head cabbage, herbs, lettuces, parsleys, and chicory, now onions and scallions, garlic, leeks, cucumbers, squash, melon, turnips, radishes, parsnips, and carrots. And now fruit — don't talk about fruit now: pretty apples, russets, dark red apples, spicy apples, blood-red apples, ugly-but-good apples, mottled apples, that alternate red and white like a silk velvet, now. What about pears: orange pears, muscatel pears, zucchine pears, St. Peter's pears, painted pears, priest-choker pears. Now walnuts and hazelnuts, what should I say? Even the hedgerows and thorn bushes in this land bear fruit. Now don't the brambles bear blackberries? And don't the blackthorns make plums, and don't the hawthorns make butt-scratchers, and aren't they fruits and good for cowherds? And what is in the ditches? Isn't there some usefulness

5) Pavan an? Mo a no se pò gnian andare a Roma chi vien da la volta de Treviso ch'i no passa sul Pavan. Pavan an? Mo di' che se sapi fare un bel ballo chi no fa | [41ʳ] la pavana. Mo se no foesse se lomé i bagni da Abano sul Pavan che ge n'è tanti altri meiore che ge ven tuto 'l dì gi huomeni folestieri morti amalè con le casse al culo e torna via arsanè dal Pavan. Pavan an? Mo che aire ge è Cristo da Loreto! Con uno è amalò e tramente de quigi da le Veniesie con giè ben impocolè e amalè e che i se ge fa portar, e dige, senza bagni nè mesina de fato i varisse chi in su sto Pavan.

6) Pavan an? Mo quel pan che ge nasse, an, bon? Che se fa pan da frare de quel boffeto e pan scafeto che con te 'l magni le croste borre inchiamentre mé in cielo — a ge perderae un speza pria — miegio che nibie o braciegi. Mo quel vin garbozo an bon? Che dise, 'Bivime', che salta in tol migiolo, vin purpio da resusitare muorti e da far paire pri. Vin pavan an? Mo no ge nase de tuta fata legume del mondo? De fava no favellare, che no se pò fare che no se g'in magne quatro scuelle chi scomenza. Pizuoli, mo fasuoli che chiama verze inbragè de milli mi. Mo cesere, mo lente, mo bisi, mo panizo. Mo biave po, con megio, sorgo, spelta, segalla, orzo, scandela, vena, e veza. Mo herbame mo? Verze, verzuoti, capuci, herbete, latuge, persemoli, e radichio. Mo ceole, scalogne, agio, puori, cogombari, zuche, molon, ravi, ravaniegi, pestenagie, e carote. Mo furti po, mo de furti no favellare. Pumi musiti, pumi ruzene, pumi piola, pumi calaman, pumi dolzani, pumi burti e boni, pumi cielà che è russi e bianchi con è un velù de sea. Mo piri, po, piri ranzi, | [41ᵛ] piri moscatiegi, piri zuchuoli, piri da San Piero, piri invernici, piri strangola preve. Mo nose e noselle, mo che bisogna dire? Inchiamentre mé le ciese e spini in sto paese fa furto, mo no fa le rove more? E i spini nigri brombiuoli e i bianchi sbroiacoli che è pur an egi furti e boni per i boaruoli? Mo sì che in ti fossè? No ge ven utilitè? No gh'i a mosche, i vo essere per gnente igi? Sì, i no sa fare de le scardoe che soto le bronze roste g'in magnerae i muorti. E i no sa fare an de le rane? Che in gresta se g'in porae dar a un papa. Che a pensanto co le è bone, a se me desconisse el cuore che a no me posse tegnire che a no spue. E on è sti fossè? e ste rane? Mo in sul Pavan.

that comes from them? Don't they have flies? And wouldn't they be there for nothing if they did not know how to make rudd, that when they are roasted under the coals even the dead would eat them. And don't they know how to make frogs as well, that when they are pickled could even be given to a pope and just thinking about how good they are makes my heart melt, so that I can't keep myself from spitting. And where are these ditches? And these frogs? In the Pavan, now.

7) Pavan, huh? Now then, then, don't talk about trees. Were there ever seen more beautiful poplars, more beautiful willows, more beautiful oaks, elms, maples, ash, hornbeams? Now what about livestock? How beautiful the oxen are! And beautiful cows! Who, by the pox now, is such a poor man that he doesn't have a lovely cow in his house? Now aren't there sheep and wethers? Now horses and mares, now hogs and sows, now nannygoats and billygoats with horns. By the pox, there are some big ones of those, the most beautiful in the world, I say. Now jenny asses and big male asses. Well, now, what would I get from keeping on grifting? In colusion, I truly believe that the Lord God made the sflood and that he gathered into Noah's ark some of all the beasts of the unirevolved world, and that he dug out and unloaded the ark's livestock here on the Pavan.

8) Pavan, huh? Now let's talk about women, better than animals. For sure there are beautiful women, starting from the bottom and moving up. And from the feet, cunt, what beautiful big ones they are, broad and firm. Look, do the clods or the cane stubble hurt them, going barefoot as they do? Yes, up your rear. You wish there was stubble that did not bend or a clod that did not crumble. And then those beautiful big legs, with that well-fed calf that would put a haypress, and I mean one of the big ones, to shame. And those big old thighs! Your Scilentiousness, have you ever seen one of those beautiful logs or shafts of walnut, of the kind that have smooth, even bark from growing in a deep wood, with little bumps that give you a lascivious thrill, and as big as a beam and that tends so toward white. Well, that's what their big old thighs are like, and just that hard when you pinch them. Then go up higher — their beautiful buttocks, white and round sprecisely like a nice fat hog when it has been freshly skinned. So that when you see them, you can't keep yourself from giving them — like this — a little slap with your open hand, out

7) Pavan an? Mo de erbore po? Po no favellare. Fo vezù mé i pì biegi polari? I pì biegi salgari? I pì bie' rovre, ulmi, upii, frassini, carpene? Mo de bestiame po? Con è biegi i buò! Belle vache, mo chi cancaro è mo quel sì poverom che n'habij una bella vacha in ca, mo piegore o castron ge n'he mo? Mo cavagi e cavale, mo puorci e scrove, mo cavere e bichi. Cancaro el ge n'è de grande, a digo, sì biegi con sipia al mondo. Mo asene e asenon grande? Poo mo che vuogio pì stare a frapare. In colusion a cherzo verasiamen che Domenedio fè el sdeluvio e che l'arsunè in l'archa de Loe de tute le biestie del roverso mondo, che el cavè fuora e descargè l'archa de bestiame chi in sul Pavan.

8) Pavan an? Mo favelon mo de femene ch'è miegio | [42ʳ] cha biestie per certo. El g'è pur le belle femene, e comenzanto de soto in su e da i piè. Pota che biegi piazon largi e firmi! Guarda che le zope o scataron andando con le va descolce ge face male. Sì in lo culo! El vo esser ben scataron che non se intorza o zoppa che no se sfregole. E po quelle belle gambe grosse con quel lacheto passù che persenari — e dige dal grosso — ge perderae. E quelle cossonace! Haìvu mé vezù, la vostra Scislencia, de qui biegi cieffi o ramonaci de nogara, de quigi ch'à quella scorza vizia gualiva frisia da morbezo, che è gruossi con è un atraverso, che tra cossì al biancho? Mo ben cossì è le sue cossonace e cossì dure in tel picegare. Va' po pì in su — quelle sue belle nege bianche e reonde sprecisamen con è un porco ben grasso quando l'è pellò da frescho. Che con te le vi, te non te può tegnire de no ge dare, d'amore, a man averta — cossì — una schiapeza. Mo quello che è po da l'altro lò dananzo, in fra le gambe, un somesso alto, che pensanto se me desconisse el cuore, e per rebelentia de la vostra Spetabilitè, che pur si un preve, a no 'l vuogio

of love. Now, the thing that is on the other side, on the front side, between their legs, a little higher, that thinking about it my heart melts and for rebellence of your Spectability, because after all you are a priest, I don't want to name but I am saying what my heart tugs me to say, don't you well know? That thing that even you kissed, when you came into the world — let's leave it alone, because it isn't very safe to talk about it, because even men can go all ropey, like horses do. And then that tummy round enough to carry three babies in a litter, with those big old tits where you can hide your head right in the middle. Tits, now? In truth, they are like milk buckets, with those big shoulders that could carry any big load, and that say, 'Load me up if you know how, because I will carry it over my shoulder like a sack or use a yoke'. With those arms and those hands, crossarms made for work, and hands made for a shovel that would not tire if they loaded a hundred barrows a day. With that big old round, well-fed face, against whose white and red a slice of marbled ham would lose, as would turnips, those there white-and-red ones, when they are well washed. And then with those eyes like shining suns, whose piercing gaze penetrates the walls of Padua and anvils. Christ from Loreto, now they are beautiful. And in fact all of our women are beautiful. And where are they born, these beautiful women? On the Pavan, now.

9) Pavan, huh? Aren't we talking about the Pavan then? In colusion I truly believe that it is the earthly paradise, and even more beautiful and better because up there you don't eat but down here you do. Spectable mister scardinal, do you know what 'Pavan' turns out to mean? 'Pavan' adds up to meaning 'go to bread' and without bread we can't live, and those who want to live should go to bread and those who want bread should go to the Pavan. Pavan, huh? And these cucumbers of these sliterati want to talk in sin-tax or in Florentinish and go around looking for bread that is better than the kind made from wheat. And for that reason I will let them bay, and, yes, I will talk in our styles, which are the most beautiful in the world, as a good Pavan.

10) And it pleasing you, Your Silence, Paternity, Magnificence and Illustrious Serenity too now will listen to me now, and me I will speak, it pleasing you, as I speak. And pay no attention when I want to continue grifting and talking and baying about your family

dire — a dige mo quello che me tira el cuore de dire, saì ben? Quello don fin vu vegnanto al mondo el basassi. Lagonlo pur stare, che la n'è troppo segura a favelarge, che an l'homo se porae incordare con fa i cavagi. E po quella panza reonda purpio da portare tri puti in t'un portò, con quelle tetonaze che se ge po | [42^v] ascondere el cao in migola mezo. Mo tete? Veramen da vregola da late, con quelle spalace da portare ogni gran carga, che dise, 'Cargame se me sai cargare, che a porterè o in spala da sacho o a bigolon'. Con quelle brace e quelle man, purpio braci da faiga e man da baìle che no se stancarae a cargare cento barelle al dì. Con quel voltonazo reondo norìo, biancho e rosso, che ge perderae fete de persuto verzelò e ravi de quigi bianchi e russi quando igi e ben lavè. E po con quigi giuochi de sol in razè che tra de ponta che passerae le muragie de Pava e gi ancuzene. Cristo da Loreto, mo i giè pur biegi. L'è pur a bel fato tute belle le nuostre femene. E on? nasele ste belle femene? Mo in sul Pavan.

9) Pavan an? Po no favellemo del Pavan? In colusion a cherzo verasiamen che il sipia el paraiso terrestre e tanto pì bello e megiore con che là su non se ge magna e chialò sì. Spetabel missiere lo sgardenale, saìu zo che ven a dire pavan? Tanto vol dir pavan co, 'Va al pan', e senza pan no se po vivere e chi vo vivere vage al pan e chi vol pan vage in sul Pavan. Pavan an? E sti cogombari de sti sletran vo favellare per gramego o in fiorentinescho e va cercanto megior pan cha de formento. E perzontena a i lagerè baiare e sì | [43^r] favellarè a le nostre divise, che è le pì belle del mondo da bon Pavan.

10) La vostra silentia, paternitè, Magnificentia, e Serenitè Lostrissima, piasantove mo, an vu me ascolterà mo mi e mi a dirè piasantove, con a dige. Nè gnan vardè con a vuogie star a frapare nè a dire nè a sbaiafare de la vostra schiata, zenia e naration che à

stock, breed and narration like those Paduan sliterati did in their speeches. And they made so many of them to you that, God help me, you must be good and fed up. And, like the guy said, they must have dropped out of your rear because, as you know, thinking that they were praising you, they talked against you because they said that you are from a stock that came from Romagnolery from Rome. On my faith, they gave you a nice bit of praise. Now, there is no worse breed than the Romagnolers. Now aren't they Eezy-beezies or Politans from Robbing? There is very little difference between them and the Spanish. Now haven't they proved that in these wars and shitermishes and routs? There never was a Romagnoler who had either faith or law. Now aren't they all blasphemers when you get down to it? Do they treat the Lord and the saints as if they had carved them with a bowie knife? Do they stab them, the pox on it, as if they were stabbing a willow? Cups and florins! Does it seem to you now that they have given you a nice bit of praise? I tell you now, I who am no sliterato like they are, that you are from the Venetian isles, a Venetian of the good kind and of the most important.

11) Now who the pox does not know that the House of Cornaro is the greatest house in the world? Now don't they have members everywhere? On my faith, and this is no joke, likewise there is no better wood in the world than cornel, I say. It is the most lasting, the firmest and the hardest and in the same way the House of Cornaro is the firmest and will maintain itself more than all the others. Believe it that one can truly say that the House of Cornaro is made firm by cornel wood. Now what do you make a good peg with if it is not with cornel, or a good knitting hook or pivot, or mill wheel cogs now? Yes, would we mill tomorrow if millwheel cogs were not made of cornel? Now if there were no House of Cornaro that is at present the boss of the Pavan, what state would we be in? Because we have hope that you will help us. It is enough for this that you are from the House of Cornaro and from the city that is the boss of the Pavan and of Padua. Now isn't that a lot? Does this stink like garlic, now? There is no other city in the world that be the boss of the Pavan — Rome of Romagnolery not at all, Spain of Spainery not at all, France of Frenchery not at all, Robbing not at all, Colecut not at all, the whole Germanland not at all, so that, goodsir mister scardinal, you are one from the city that is the Venetian isles, boss of Padua of the Pavan, because there is no other at all like it among

fato quelli sletran de Pava in le so rengaure, che tante i ve ne ha fate che, se die m'ai', a doì esser bell'e stufò, e con dise questù, le ve d'essere cazù dal culo perqué, con a saì, credanto laldarve, i ve disea contra, per che i dise che a si de schiata vegnua de Romagnolaria da Roma. A la fe i v'a do un bel laldo. Mo no g'è la pezor zenia de romagnaruoli. Mo no ègi sbissigiegi o politani da Robin? Da igi a spagnaruoli e g'è puocha differentia. Mo no ghi haonte provè in ste guerre e scagaruole e muzaruole? No fo mé romagnaruolo che havesse fe nè leza. Mo n'ègi tuti a bel fato biastemaore? A fagi de domene e de santi con se i ghi avesse fatti col cortellazo. A ge tragi el cancaro co si el traesse in un salgaro. Coppe fiorin! Te par mo che i v'habbi dò un bel laldo? A dige mo mi, ch'a no son sletran con giè igi, che a si da le Veniesie, venitian d'i buoni e d'i maore.

11) Mo chi cancaro no sa che ca Cornaro è la maor ca del mondo? Mo no ge n'è da per tuto? A la fe, no trogniando, così co no g'è megior leg | [43ᵛ] no al mondo del cornaro, a dige, pì tegnente, pì fremo e che dure pì. Cossì è ca cornaro la pì frema e che se mantegnerà pì cha tute le altre. Cherzi che se po ben dire che ca cornaro sipia da cornaro frema. Mo di che se faza una bona caegia se la n'è de cornaro? Nè una bona zugia? Mo dente da molin? Sì, se masenerae doman se i dente da molin no foesse de cornaro. Mo se no foesse ca Cornaro che è adesso parona del Pavan, co stason nu? Che haon speranza che n'aigià. Ge basta cha si da ca Cornaro e de la terra che è parona del Pavan e de Pava: n'è el mo assé? Puzela mo da agio questa? El no g'è zà altra terra al mondo che sipia parona del Pavan: Roma de Romagnolaria no zà, Spagna de Spagnaria no zà, Franza de Franzosaria no zà, Robin no zà, Collecuta no zà, terra toescha tuta no zà. Siché, bonsegnore missier lo sgardenale, a si un de la terra che è le Veniesie, parona de Pava del Pavan, che no ge n'è zà de tante negunaltra. E egi dise cha si da Roma Romagnaruolo. Cancaro i magne!

so many. And they say that you are a Romagnoler from Rome. The pox eat them!

12) Now they almost make me shit from laughing when they say that you are a great man. Now, can't they see, the plague eat them? You actually are a little man. Now don't they know how to say that you are a great little man and not a great man? You do truly have one great thing, as little as you are, that they don't know how to say. Now I will be the one to say it: you certainly have a great heart, that is what I have heard. Now tell me something for your dear faith and as a brother, since I hold you, God help me, in no way different. Who, the pox, would be the pox of that guy who was on horseback and who when he saw a wild boar heading toward him who was foaming at the mouth, would fail to get out of the way and flee? I, let me tell you, would get myself out of there and if I were on foot such that I could not flee, I would shinny up a tree. And you, mister goodsir, dismounted down from your horse and you went — more than once, too — to face it, I say, like a man of valour. And yes, you jousted with it. Does it seem to you now that this sticks to the shovel? Don't do it, on my faith, because it isn't too safe, it could even turn out badly and once you were dead, you would be deprived of this world. And even if you had scooped up that plum, whatever would you do with wild boars or with bishoprics? Now as poor a man as I am, I would not agree to be dead and to be pope — what pap-all shit — pardon me. Moreover, I say that I would not agree to be lord of the unirevolved world. I want to give to you, your rebellence, some advice that those sliterati from Padua did not know how to give you. Yeah, did I heard them too, with my boss, a lot of their speeches that they made you? Now tie this around your finger, because it is important: that it is better to live a coward than to die a hero. So don't pay any attention to your big heart and when a wild boar is coming at you, pull off to the side.

13) Be a royal companion and tell me: have you learned as much in their speeches? No, God help me, may I believe it, so then I would teach them the kind of point that not Aristotle and not even Seneca ever thought up. They only know enough to say that you are a scardinal and that saying scardinal amounts to saying those things that hold up the doors of Paradise, [Oh, if they have ever seen Paradise] or the doors or those things that hold them up that they

12) Mo a me fagi ben po squase cagar da riso quando che i dise che a si grandhomo. Mo no vegi, morbo i magne? A sìu ben pizolo homo, mo i no 'l sa dire. A si un gran pizolo e no grande homo. Haì ben una gran cossa per pizolo che a si, che i no 'l sa dire. Mo a 'l dirè ben mi. Haì per certo un gran cuore, per quello che ha e intendù. Mo disime un puo' per la vostra cara fe, e da frello, che a no ve teg | [44ʳ] no — se die m'ai' — gnan altramen. Chi cancaro sarae quel cancaro de quelù che foesse a cavalo e che veesse un cengiaro abavò che ge vegnesse in contra che non tolesse da un lò e muzare? Mi inchindamo a me torae via, e se foesse a pè che a no poesse muzare, a me rovegerae su 'n arbore. E vu, missier bonsegnore, a desmontè zó da cavallo e sì l'andè pur tal bota a frontare, a dige, da perdomo e sì l'armezè. Te par mo che questa se tegne al baìle? No fé, ala fe: che la n'è troppa segura — la ve porae an butar male. E con a foesse morto vu, vu asisse deroinò del mondo. E si hasse scapò su quella bromba, che vosseu mo pì fare de cengiari? Nè de vescovè? Mo cossì poveron co a son, a no torae de essere morto e essere papa. Che papa, la merda — perdoneme. Ampò a dige che a no torae da essere segnore del roverso mondo. A ve vuogio dare a la vostra rebelentia un consio che quigi sletran da Pava no ve l'à sapù dare. Ampò e gi ò sentio an mi con el me paron assé de le suo' rengaure che i v'ha fato? Mo ligevela al deo, che l'è de importantia. Che l'è miegio vivere poltron cha morire valenthomo. Siché no guardè al vostro gran cuore, e co un cengiaro ve ven incontra, andè da un altro lò.

13) Haìu imparò — diséme da compagno reale — in le suo' rengaure anchora mé tanto? Se diem'ai' no, che a cherza, po a ge insegnerae a igi tal ponto, che Stotene, gnié Sinica, no se 'l pense mé, i sa se lomé dire, che a si sgardenale e che a dire sgardenale el ven | [44ᵛ] a dire quigi che ten su le porte del paraiso. [E se gi à mé vezù igi paraiso,] nè le porte, nè quigi che ten su le porte del paraiso, che nu a i chiamon cancari, a vorae che 'l cancaro me magnasse mi, e

say you are that we call poxes [hinges], I would like the pox to eat me, and if they haven't seen them, I would like the pox to eat them instead. Oh, let the pox eat those crazies, because they want you to be the pox. You are a scardinal and not the pox, may they have their eyes gouged out! You would be in real trouble if you were what they say. You are a scardinal like I will tell you and will spell out to you. They really ought to recognize you by your red hat and many incomes. May the Lord be generous with you. May you indeed be pope and we would all come to you, to Rome, to see you on all fours with a dog collar around our necks. Scardinal, huh? Hey, a pox on the sliterati. Do you know what scardinal means in our Pavan way of talking? I'll tell you now, it amounts to saying, scardinal as I will say, a great rich gentleman who gives himself pleasure in this world. And when he dies (because we all die) even though you have not done too much good, you go right along to Paradise and if the door is barred, then you take it off its hinges and you get inside through any path or any hole. And this is what scardinal means, someone who unhinges and not a pox that holds up the door, may the pox eat them and their sliterature, the crazies. Isn't that the way it is? Now, can you see that I understand it better than they do, scardinal, huh? It is truly quite a nice thing to be, God help me, and I would agree in exchange to never more eat wheat bread, and I would be exactly as you are. You would be my pal, and I would not give alms in the walls with coins as a certain scardinal did, who has already been here in the Pavan, because he didn't have the heart to spend them, if there were some, isn't that true? Well, now, how would we spend them? I don't believe that we would ever spend them on stones for cut statues either or on those pennies that have figures on them that they call merd-alls. If only you could spend them like you spend coins. Oh, pox on merd-alls and on garlic and on onions. It seems to me that it's like talking [with the dead to talk] about those whorehouses. I would never agree to be imprinted on one and to have been Roland and to not exist any more except in imprinted form, God help me. Because those who enjoy them don't understand that it means to take pleasure with the dead. Dead with dead and living with living.

14) It is truly a living and natural pleasure to hear a harrier flush and chase the prey out of a big thicket. And you see her and loose your hound after her and and as she flees you have to run where

se i no la vezù che 'l cancaro i magne egi, do' cancaro i magne mati, dasché i vo che vu sie el cancaro, a si sgardenale e no el cancaro. Haessegi cavò i giuochi. A stasse frescho se a stasse co i dise egi. A si sgardenale con a ve dirè mi e, con ha ve slainerè mi, i dorae pure cognoscerve al capelleto rosso e a tante intrè. *Sproficiata vobis domine*: posseu an esser papa e che adesson tuti vignirve a verve a Roma in gatolon con una morisse da can al collo. Sgardenale an? Do', morbo a i sletran. Saviu zo che ven a dire sgardenale al nostro muò pavan? Mo a ve 'l dirè. Tanto ven a dire, sgardenale con a dirè, un gran segnore richo che se dà a sto mondo piasere. E con el muore (perqué tuti a moron) se ben vu a no haì fatto massa ben, andè de lungo al paraiso. E se la porta è apassà, a la sgardenè e intrè entro per ogni via e per ogni buso. E questo ven a dire sgardenale — che sgardena, e no un cancaro che ten l'usso su, che cancaro i magne egi e le suo' sletre, mati. N'èla mo cossì? Mo ben viu mo se la intendo pì de egi, sgardenale an? L'è pur bella cossa a esserge. Inchindamò, se die m'ai', che mi torae a no magnar mé pan de fromento e esserge, e sarae purpio con a si vu, a sesse me compagno. Gnan mi a no farae me mosina de dinari | [45ʳ] in le muragie con ha fato tal sgardenale che à zà stò chi in sul Pavan, che n'havea cuore de spendergi, gin foesse pure, n'è vero? Mo ben co a i spendesson! Nè a no cherzo mé che a i spendesson in prie de statoe intaiè nè in quelle parpaiole che ha quelle figure su, che i le chiama merdolagie. A manco se spendessele con se fa la monea. Do', cancaro a le merdolagie e a l'agio e a le ceole. El m'è mo doviso che sipia un favellare [coi morti a favellar] de quigi bordiegi. A no torae zà de essere stampò su e essere stò Rolando e no ge essere pì se lomé in stampa. Se die m'ai' che chi de elle n'ha piasere no la intende ha havere piasere de muorti. Muorti co muorti e vivi co vivi.

14) L'è pur un piaser vivo e naturale a sentire a borire un braco e cazar fuora una selbegina de un machion, e ti verla e lassarge el to levriero drio e ella muzanto farte corer don la va, e ti criare e

she does and yell and say, 'Ah, sluggard, ah traitor, ah scoundrel, ah dawdler, catch her!' and see that your dog caught her and you reach them and get there to do the killing and kiss the dog and pick it up to put its guts back in place. And then you call your pals and say, 'It's dead, it's dead' in as loud a voice as you can and blow the horn to celebrate (everlasting merd-alls up the rear). And then you catch up to your pals and tell them how it went and one will say that he saw the whole thing and that the harrier flushed it well and that you were right to loose him and that that hound of yours is a good one and that you reached them right away and that you are a good hunter. And you say, 'Whatever beasts they were, even if they were lions'. And you feel, brother, that your shirt doesn't touch your butt because it seems like you have it in a basin of fresh warm milk, and you give a jump and you rub your hands together and look at your dog and you see the others say, 'That was the one'. And then you look at the beast, which is one of the long-lived ones. Now isn't this a pleasure? Look, merd-alls are not, because they can't be spent.

15) Well, now, there are some who understand it and some who do not understand it. I know that you, lord, understand it, your spaternity, and yes I know that you are going along the high road. Believe me, on faith, that you have a great brain and that you are a great little man, a well-intentioned man. And if you were anything else, I myself would tell you because what does it matter to me, do you understand? The only way I know how to tell it is like it is, do you understand? You are also an openhanded good pal, a stand-up guy, and you're not at all one of these depraversed, these wilful obsessives that you never know what impulse they are acting on, do you understand? Of these arrogant ones who always want to be on top of everyone and make everyone submit to them, because, faith, they don't think that there is anyone else in the world. I like you and for this reason I want your wellbeing, so, like a brother, I tell you to continue straight along the high road as you are doing, your rebelliousness and magnificence, and do a good job tending your sheep, that is us of the Pavan, because you are our shepherd and pastor and our bishop and pope who has the power, as Jesus God said, to do and to undo and, in colusion, to turn the cakes in your own way and for that reason we poor people have desired you more than a skinny, bony and skittish mare desires tender new grass. And

dire, 'Ha poltron, ha traitore, ha ribaldo, ha poltron, pigiela!'. E vere che 'l to can la pigie e ti arzonzerge a dosso e rivarla de amazare e basar el can e alzarge per tornarge le buelle al so luogo e po chiamar i compagni e dire, 'L'è morto, l'è morto!' quanto se pò mé de vose. E sonare el corno fazanto alegrezza (merdolagie mé nel cullo). E po arivare a i compagni e dirge con la è andà e un a dire haver vezù el tuto e che el bracho l'a borì ben e che te ge lassasi con reson e che l'è bon levriero quel to e che | [45ᵛ] te fossi presto azonzerge a dosso e che te si bon cazaore. E ti a dire, 'Mo g'in foesse pure de gi animale, se i foesse ben lion!'. Te te sinti frello che la camisa non te tocha el culo, che 'l t'è doviso de haverlo in t'un cadin de late lomé monta. Te tre un salto, te te fregoli le man, te guardi el to can, e te vi che gialtri dise, 'L'è stò quello.' Ti guardi po l'animale che è di vegi. È mo questo un piasere? Vìu, no le merdolagie che n'è bone da spendere.

15) Horbentena chi la intende chi no la intende. A se che vu, segnore, a la intendì, la vostra spaternitè. E sì a se che andè per carezà. Cherzime a mi, a la fe, che haì gran celibrio e che a si un grande pizolo, homo da ben, e se a fosse altramen a ve 'l dirae mi. Perqué? Che me fa a mi? Intendìu? A no se dire se lomé con la è, intendìu? A si an slibrale bon compagno, moregole. A no se gnan de sti provieri, di sti stinè, spisemusi che no se sa me de che vuogia i sipia. Intendìu? De sti altieri che vo star sempre de sora da tuti e sotomitar tuti, che i non cre che ge sipia altri al mondo. A la fe che a me piasí e per questo a ve vuogio de bon ben, a dige sì con da frello. Andè pur drio per sta carezà con a fé, la vostra rebelentia e magnificentia, e governè pur ben le vostre piegore, che a seon nu del Pavan. Perqué a si nostro pegoraro e pastore e nostro vesco e papa, che haì lubertà, con dise Jesum Dio, de fare e desfare e in colusion de volzere le torte a vostro | [46ʳ] muò. E perzontena nu poveriti a ve haon desirò pì cha no fè mé cavala magra, secca, e rostìa l'herba nuova. E avon fato per visinanza che mi a son vegnù per lome de tuti a alegrarme de la vostra vegnua. Tochéme la man, che a sipie el ben vegnù e 'l ben trovò. A vogion che a ne face no so que leza e stratuti nuovi, che è ben de rason. E madequide, in bona fe, sì:

we decided in the local assembly that I would come in the name of all to celebrate your coming. Take my hand, and may you be welcome and well found. We want you to make us some kind of new laws and stratutes that are well thought out and, yes indeed, in good faith.

16) The first: that every hunter or birder who goes hunting or birding for pleasure and not for profit can do so on Sunday without hearing mass and that would not be a sin because, as you know, in that hour is the height of pleasure for many reasons and if you lose that hour, it never comes back again.

17) Number two: that no one from the country be obigated to fast because, as you know, working gives you such an appetite you could digest rocks and once you have an appetite, if you don't eat, your heart melts and you risk dying or spitting out your lungs along with all the saliva that fills your mouth. And then you go to bed but you can't sleep and if you have a wife, to fend off your hunger and fall asleep, you do that thing that you would not do if you were asleep. And if you don't have a wife, it will be a wonder if by morning you don't get one, and to keep from being bored people do even worse things, as you know. Do you get it?

18) Number three: that when it is grain harvest time it not be a sin to work on feast days because from one hour to the next a nasty storm can blow up and ruin us, and then we swear like dogs. And who wouldn't swear? Tell me, on your dear faith. And then we have to steal if we want to live, and right away we commit two sins, and even if it isn't our fault, that is the way it is.

19) Number four: that you can eat in the morning before mass so that you can then give your heart to God, because it is the pox when you are hungry, and if you are in the church-house your heart is forced to be at home, on eating. And if we have eaten, our hearts will be in heaven and on God and not at home on bread.

20) Number five: that eating not be a sin of gluttony when you eat because it tastes good and even though you are not hungry. Because the doctors say that what tastes good is good for you and makes for good health, and staying healthy you live a long time, [living a long time] you become old, becoming old, you do good

16) La prima: che ogno cazaore o oselaore che va per piasere e no per guagno a caza o a osellare posse andare la domenega senza aldir messa e no sipia peccò perqué, con assaì, in quel'hora l'è el bello del piasere per pì reson, e chi perde quel'hora la no torna mé pì in drio.

17) Le do: che neguno de villa sipia ubigò a zunare perqué, con a saì, el faigarse fa pair pri. E con se a paìo, chi no magna se desconisse el cuore o va a risego de morire o de spuare el polmon da salivo che te ven in bocha. Te ve po in leto e te no può dormire. E s'te he mogiere, per pararte la fame e farte vegnir sono, te fé quello che te no faressi, che te dromeresti. E se te n'he mogiere, gran fato che de doman te no ge n'habbi una. E per no star nogioso se fa po piezo, con a saì, intendìu?

18) Le tre: che dal tempo dal taiare i fromenti no sipia peccò a lavorare la festa. Perqué da una hora a l'altra po vegnire una straza de tempesta e deroinarge. A biastemon puo a muò can, e chi no biaste | [46ᵛ] merae? Diséme per la vostra cara fe! E a sconvegnon po an robare se a vogion vivere, e da muò a fazon due pechè e sì no haon la colpa. La è pur cossì.

19) Le quatro: se possa magnare la doman nanzo messa, per poere po pì stare con el cuore a Dio, che l'è el cancaro quando se à fame, e che se è al gesiò, l'è pur forza haver el cuore a ca al magnare. E se haron magnò, haron el cuore in cielo e a Dio e no a ca al pan.

20) Le cinque: che per magnare no sipia peccò de gola quando se magna perqué el sa bon, si ben no se ha fame, perqué i miegi dise che quel che sa bon fa bon pro e 'l fa sanitè. Staganto sani se vive assé, [vivendo assé] se ven viegi, vegnanto viegi se fa del ben, fazanto del ben se va imparaiso. Siché no pò essere male nè

deeds, doing good deeds, you go to paradise. Therefore it cannot be bad or a sin because just as whoever ate poison knowing that it is harmful would commit a sin, so eating something beneficial must be meritorious, and that's what good eating is.

21) Number six: that you make it so that every priest can have a wife or be castrated because the weakness of the flesh is the pox. Sometimes it bothers you so much that you don't know what hole to stick yourself into, and even if they are priests, they are still men like we are and of the kind that are even more male and because they don't have women they go into such heat that the first time they bang into one of our women, they get her pregnant on the spot and we poor guys bear the expenses for their children and that is not right at all, and if they will have wives, they will not be so hot-tempered or always in heat, because the wives will keep them milked. And if they still get our women pregnant, we will get theirs pregnant too, and if we support their children, they will support ours, and we will be even.

22) Number seven: because there is such a pox of enmity and ill will between us peasants from the villages and the citizens of Padua that we could eat our hearts out about it, and all day because of this we are in torment and if we were to be on top as they are now, bow wow bow bow, cups and florins! they would not last an hour in our hands. Let it go, now. They call us peasants 'clods, snakes, lizards' and we call them 'shit-thrones, dogs, usurers, bloodsuckers of the poor folk'. Now we would like, as I said because we are the underdogs, for you to fix this difference and make it so that we might all be one and the same. Therefore we want you to make this law for us that every man from the country can take four wives and every woman from the country can take four husbands because when those shit-thrones from Padua see this, and because they are drawn to our women, all of them will become countrymen to be able to take four wives, since their status lets them make that change. And all the city women, to be able to have four men, will make themselves countrywomen. And we'll scoop up those little plums, and in this way we will all be one and the same thing, nor will there any longer be envy or enmity because we will all be one big family. And all the women will go around with big bellies and the law of Jesus God who said, 'Increase and smultiply' will be fulfilled. See if we will

peccò perqué cossì con se farae peccò chi magnasse tossego sapianto che 'l fa male, cossì magnanto cossa che face pro dee essere mierito co è a magnar de bon.

21) Le sie: che a facè che ogno preve possa haver mogiere o che 'l sipia castrò, perqué l'è 'l cancaro la fragilitè de la carne. La dà qualche botta tanto fastibio che no se sa in che buso cazarse, e se giè ben preve giè huomeni co a seon nu e de quigi an più maschi. E perqué i n'ha femene i va in tanta veregaia che con i s'embate la prima botta in una de le nuostre femene i la ingravia de fatto. | [47ʳ] E nu poveriti fazon le spese a' so figiuoli, che la n'è zà de reson. E si gi'arà mogiere i no sarà sì rabiusi nè sempre in veregaia che elle i tignerà monzù. E se pure i ingravierà le nuostre femene, e ingravieron an nu le suo', e si nu a faron le spese a i suo' puti, i farà a i nuostri. E a saron su e su.

22) Le sete: perqué l'è tanto cancaro de nemistè e malivolentia tra nu containi da le ville e citaini de Pava, che a se magnesson del cuore e tuto el dì per questo a se tragaion. E se a fosson cossì nu de sora con igi è egi, bao ba bao bao coppe fiorin! a no ge dureravegi un'hora in le man. Mo passintia. I ge dise a nu, 'Containi, vilani, marassi, ragani'. E nu a ge digon a egi, 'Cagariegi, Can usulari, magna sangue de' poveriti'. A voson mo, che con a v'e ditto perqué a seon dal lò del soto, che conzasse sta diffirentia e che a fasse che a fosson una cossa miesma. A vogion perzontena che a ne facè sta leza: Che ogni hom da villa possa tuore quatro mogiere e ogni femena da villa possa tuore quatro marì. Perqué con quigi cagariegi da Pava vega cossì, e perqué i tra a le nuostre femene, tuti per poere havere quatro femene se farà de villa, che el sta a egi a farsege, e tute le citaine per poere havere quatro huomeni se farà da villa e nu scaperon su quelle brombete e a sto muò, e a saron una cossa miesma, nè no ge sarà | [47ᵛ] pì invilia nè nemistè perqué a faron tuto un parentò e tute le femene andarà pine e se impirà le leza de Jesun Dio che dise, 'Cressì e smoltiplichè', guardè che haron mé pì paura de Turchi che ne impale — sì — in lo culo. Se verà se no cielo e femene gravie e puti perqué adesso el g'è tal una che con uno homo sola la no pò ingraviare che con la n'haverà quatro, gran fato

ever again be afraid of the Turks who impaled us, yes, in the rear. You won't see anything but sky and pregnant women and children, because now there is a woman or two who with only one man can't get pregnant but when she has four of them, it won't be a big deal if one of them finds the way to knock her up. No one will make anyone else a cuckold and [commit] that sin of approaching other men's women, because everyone will have enough to do at home. Won't this be a fine benefit, huh? How many arguments about this would not take place, how many who are killed would be alive, how many pretty poor girls in Padua who have no way of getting married would marry, who, yes, now become nuns in convents? All women would have lots of children. Aren't there some of them now who are idle who would have something to do, because there is no greater sin than naushirkishness, and perhaps there are some now and some pretty good ones? The pretty ones and the ugly ones, all, all would have a good start: for each relative that you have, you would have four, everyone would have four times more power to kick out Spaniards and Germans. If they ever came back to bother us in this land, we would never again flee from this land. You would not make, God help me, a more beautiful law, because you will make the entire civil law of the world, not the caloric or the beweaveral. Make it, mister scardinal, because, may bod help me, you will give as many blessings as will be given to you. To me — what does it matter to me, do you understand? I'm saying this for your benefit now, do you understand when I say, yes, because why ever, do you understand? I'm doing it for you, do you understand? Go ahead and do it because you will be adored by us as if you were a saint. If I didn't love you I would not give you this advice, but do well what I tell you because the benefit will be to you. You have the power to say 'I want it this way' and it will be that way, and without us, what would you be worth? And yes we all will hold you to be like a father, like a son, like a brother, because we do not hold you otherwise at all. Give me your hand and promise me that another time I will come to pick up the epitation. God help you.

che uno no ge cate la stralecha, a no se farà gnan neguno becho e quel peccò d'andare da le femene d'altri, che tuti hara da fare assé a ca so. Saralo mo questo un bel ben, an? Quante costion che se fa per questo che no se farae? Quanti ven amacè che sarae vivi, quante belle pute poverete in Pava che n'ha muò de poerse mariare se marierae, che sì se va a far monege in ti monestieri? Tute sfigiuolarave. Ge n'è mo che sta indarno che harae da fare? Che maor peccò è de la nausitè? E fuorsi mo che ge ne è de belle? Le belle e burte tute tute harae bon inviamento. Per uno parente che se à, se ne harae quatro, ognuno harae quatro fiè pì potintia da cazare spagnaruoli e toischi se i tornasse pì a darge fastibio in sto paese. A no mucesson mé pì de sto paese. A no fiessi, se die m'ai', mai la pì bella leza, che a farè tuta la leza zoile del mondo, nè la caluorica nè la teluorica. Féla missier lo sgardenale, che, dabiu m'ai', vu dé tante benission | [48ʳ] che ve serae dee. A mi che me fa a mi, intendìu? A dige mo mi per vostro miegio: intendìu con a dige? si perqué me intendìu? A fazo per vu, m'intendìu? Féla pure che a sarì adorò da nu co se a foesse un santto. S'a no ve volesse ben, a no v'in consegierave. Ma fassè ben quel che a dige, che ben el sarà pere vu, a porì dire, 'A vuo' cossì' che cossì sarà, e senza nu che valeseu vu? E sì a ve tegneron tuti da pare, da figiuolo, e da frello, che altramen no ve tignon: Deme la man e promitime che un'altra volta vegnerò a tuore el spatafio. Die v'ai'.

Note on the text

The text above has been transcribed from Biblioteca Civica Verona, MS 36 (Cl. B. Lett Ubic. 82.1); it begins on fol. 39^v and concludes on fol. 48^r. At the bottom of fols 39^v and 40^r, a reader's comment is added in a hand that could be contemporary (compare *Estimo*, reg. 357 [358], unnumbered folio between fols 198 and 199, dated 1519) or slightly later; a hasty scrawl, it is extremely hard to read and is reproduced in part by Wendriner ('Codice'). While the text is written in a well-formed if florid script, numerous words and phrases were left out and added interlinearly or marginally by the copyist, although not all omissions were noted. The copyist also made careful, superimposed corrections in a slightly darker ink. The list of corrections by paragraph follows; it includes erroneous readings (marked with *sic*) and explanatory remarks (in parentheses) to avoid notes that would disturb the alignment of the facing page translation. Visible underlying forms are given between parentheses, interlinear additions between single slashes, marginal additions between double slashes, and omissions between square brackets. Par. 1 *prov/i/erbio*, /le/; par. 2 *son /an/ mi, derto, dertamente, me, na/s/sù, che*; par. 3 *puo', contento*; par. 4 *Colecuta*; par. 5 *Mo a* (*sic*; *recte* Mo); par. 6 *f/r/are*, //*mo lente*//, //*herbete, latuge, persemoli, e radichio. Mo ceole, scalogne*//, *Mo*; par. 7 *b/i/egi i, che el* (illeg.), *bestiame*; par. 8 *comenzanto de soto in su e da i piè. Pota che biegi piazon largi e firmi! Guarda che le zope* (repeated then crossed out), //*belle*//, /*te*/, //*a dige mo quello che me tira el cuore de dire*//, *cavagi* (*cavegi*), *portò, bianchi chi* (*sic*; *recte* bianchi), *quando igi e, g/i/uochi, i giè* (*sic*?; *recte* igi e?); par. 9 *e chi vo vivere vage al pan, e senza pan no se po vivere* (repeated then crossed out); par. 10 *renga/u/re, bell'e e* (*sic*; *recte* bell'e), *de, e g'è* (*sic*; *recte* el g'è); par. 11 *Robin, zà /de/*; par. 13 *egi* (*igi*), *a no* (*sic*; *recte* e), *egi, pure, ver/v/e, vu a no haì fatto massa ben, andè de lungo al paraiso. E se la porta è apassà* (the preceding passage emphasized by a mark in the margin), *egi, egi, sesse, bordiegi*; par. 14 *pig/i/ela, dirle* (*sic*; *recte* dirge); par. 18 *e a* (*sic*; *recte* a); par. 20 *assé, viegi, viegi*; par. 21 /*i va*/, *i s'embate la prima botta in una de le nuostre femene* (*i s'embate in una de le nuostre femene la prima botta*); par. 22 *egi, per*//*qué*//, *egi, a, sarà p[er]e* (apparently corrected from *p[er]*; compare XI 66 'pre vu'), /*nu*/.

S Prolico de Ruzante fatto al Cardinale Cornaro nella Inclyta Città di Vinegia

VR 1636

1) Perqué l'è el cancaro a cazzarse do no se de e do no è honesto, e mi ch'a sum mi — e ch'a sum, cum dis' questù, un huom complo — a guardo ben cum a fago. E perzondena, Rebellissimo Missier lo Sgardinale, a n'hem vuogiù vegnire a farve sto sprolico a Pava. Perqué? Mo perqué qui canchari de quigij sbagiafaori e de quigi cagariegi sletram da Pava harae habù per male. Che cum dise el provierbio, 'No bene conveniente zodie cum samaritè'. Che ven a dire che no sta ben donziegi cum mariè. Perqué mo? Per cossì ch'i donziegi cerca de far bichi i mariè, così i cittaini de truogna ne deleza gnu puoveri containi dalle ville. E perzondena a muzzon pì da igi che no fa le cellege dal falcheto. E questo è mo quello ch'a no son vegnù a Pava.

2) Mo a son vegnù chive chialò quenzena chialondena in sto luogo per poere ben dire e slainare le me rason per nome de tutto el territuorio pavan che m'ha slenzù mi cum hom bon parlente e sprologaore. Nè gnian guardé ch'aon vogiù mandar un preve nè un de quigij dalle centure insofranè che favella per gremego e in avogaro fiorentinesco, de quigij — saìvu? — che se domanda dottori.[1] Perqué se giè igi dottore, a ge son mi tre delle torre. Mo no saìvu ch'aum mo piasere de tegnire el nostro naturale derto in piè e dertamen per la natura, chiamentre mé ch'a | [3ᵛ] serom vivi, smissianto la lengua a nostro muò e no alla fiorentinesca. A vuo' dir de mi che inchina da mo a no cambiarae la mia lengua con dosento fiorentinesche, nè no torae de esser nassù in l'Egitto de Betheleme, dum nassè Missier Jesumdio, per no esser pavan. Mo no saveravegio an mi zà s'a volesse favellare fiorentinescho? Favellarè sì fieramen ch'a dissè che foesse pruopiamen un pulitan de Talia nasù a Rubin. Mo ascolté Bonsegnore, 'Io mi asseamo contadino dela villa che habitamo e stassamo sul Pavan e io mi se

---

[1] 'domandare' (to call, to name) was a Tuscanism whose popularity was then spreading, according to *GDLI*, *s.v.*, no. 7; Colussi, *s.v.*

rebutamo alla vostra de vu Segnoria.' Ve par mo per la vostra chara fe che 'l parerae mé ch'a fosse nasù sul Pavan? Po' l'è un gran cagare. Ve par mo che sarae an mi esserge s'a volesse? Mo a no vuogio — a vuogio andare cum a v'ho zà ditto cum el me naturale in pè derto e dertamen cum a digo.

3) Mo dime un pocho: Missier Francesco Spetracha, mo no nascello in Fiorentinaria? Mo chanchar'è. Perqué 'l fo mal contento d'esserge nasù, che 'l vorae essere nasù sul Pavan, et ge vene a morire e stare e sì ge vosse essere sotterò. E sì no fu buffa ne cepelletta. E sì no guardé a partirse donde l'ira nasù e lagar parentò e misté, che saì pur el provierbio cha dise, 'Ligame le mane e i piè e butame de brigà d'i mie'.' El se giè partì e sì viene sul Pavan e lagè tutto e sì saea pure tutto quello che se pò saere. E perqué el fello mo? Mo per esser daspo' morto pavan. Adesché 'l no g'harà possù nasire, che 'l cognoscea che 'l nostro era el pì bel favellare e parlare del mondo e pì bel paese. Po l'è cum a dige alla vostra de vu Magnificentia: che no g'è de miegio de bon Pavan. Po mosignore Tenore che vene oltra 'l mare de Turcaria per far Pava chi sul Pavan, che prima fu 'l Pavan cha Pava? Ei nuostri antessori viechij vosse che se ge metesse lome de femena perché | [4^r] la stesse sottomittò al Pavan e la va mo a un aotro moio. Mo adesch'a 'l poì fare, ala conzerì che l'è peccò de sto puovero Pavan.

4) Po no favellare de sto Pavan. Mo no ge ven chiamentre me le cesille che se parte dalla Colecuta e chiamentre mé dal choato del sole per vegnir chi sul Pavan e per vegnir a far i suo'[2] furti cum gnu in le nuostre cha senza paura cum se le foesse desmestegè e canta tuta la doman per fargne apiasere. E sì no guarda ch'a vegnire chive sul Pavan le habbi da passare tanti mari e tante salbegure. Mo le quagie che ven an elle d'ivelo e ven a ingrassarse chive sul Pavan per dargne ben da magniare a gnu Pavani? Pavan? Mo i betuzzi, paruzole, coarussi, rossignati, turdi, spinchi, e tanta altra fatta d'osiegij che ven dalla terra toescha e passa tante montagnie e tante nieve e per vegnire mo onve? Mo sul Pavan. A far mo que? A ingrassarse.

5) Pavan an? Mo no se pò gnian andar a Roma chi ven dalla volta de Terviso ch'i no passa sul Pavan. Pavan an? Mo se no fosse lomé i bagni de Abano che ge n'è tanti altri de megiori che ge ven tutto el mondo de giuhomeni folestieri muorti amalè cum le

---

[2] MS sue.

casse al culo e torna via arsanè del Pavan. Pavan an? Mo di' che [se] supia fare negun bel ballo chi no fa la Pavana che a fazzon gnu sul Pavan. Pavan an? Mo che agere g'è, Christo da Loreto! Cun un è amalò e chinamentre de quigi dale Venesie cum g'è ben inmelè e amalè e che i se ge fa portare, a dige, senza bagni nè meesine de fatto i guarisse chive su sto Pavan.

6) Pavan an? Mo quel pan che ge nasse an? On che se fa pan da frate de quel sboffetto o pan schaffetto che con te 'l | [4^v] magni le groste borre inchinamentre mé in cielo — che ge perderae un spezzaprie — miegio che nibie o braciegi. Che l'è ben poltron chi no ne magna quatro a far collation. Mo quel vin sgarbozzo an? On[3] che dise, 'Bivime', che salta in tel migiollo, vin porpio da resussitar muorti amalè, che chi haesse cento ferìe el no gie farae male. Vin da far pair prie. On nascelo sto vin? Mo sul Pavan. Vin Pavan an? Mo no gie nase de tutta fatta legumi del mondo? De fava mo no favellare: che non se può fare che no se g'in magne quatro scuelle alla filla chi scomenza. Pezuolli, po fasuolli, mare biata, che chiama verze imbraghè da mille migia. Mo cesere mo, mo lente, bisi mo, panizzo mo. Mo biave po, come è megio, sorgo, spelta, segalla, orzo, scandella, venna, e vezza. Mo herbame mo? Verze, verzuoti, capuzzi, herbete, latuge, persimboli, e radichi. Mo ceolle e scalogne, agio, e puori che farae magnar un mezo morto. Cogombari e zuche e molon, rave[4] e ravaniegi, pestenege e carotte. Mo furti mo. Po, de furti no favellare. Mo pumi musuotti, pumi ruzini, pumi piuolli, pumi calaman, pumi dulzani, pumi russi, pumi burti e buoni, pumi cielà che è bianchi e russi cum è un velù de sea. Po piri quanti? Piri ranzi, piri moscatiegij, piri zuchuolli, piri da San Piero, piri invernise, piri strangolapreve. Mo nose e noselle po. Che besogna dire? Inchinamentre mé le ciese e spini in sto paese fa furto. Le roe fa more, i spini | [5r] nigri brombiolli, e i bianchi sbrogiaculli, che è pur an igi furti buoni per i boari. Mo sì che in ti fuossi no ge ven utilitè? No giè mosche? I vuol essere per niente igi si i no sa far delle scardole che soto le bronze rostie a g'in magnarae i muorti. I no sa far an de le rane? Che in l'agresto se g'in porae dar a un Pappa. Che pensanto con le è bone, a se me desconise el cuore, ch'a no posso far ch'a no spue. E un è sti fossè e un è ste rane? Mo sul Pavan.

---

[3] 'On' is set off by slashes as if to indicate the copyist's uncertainty; compare VR 36, XI 66 vin.

[4] Unclear if 'ravi' or 'rave'.

7) Pavan an? Mo de arbore? Mo no favellare. Mo on fu vezù mé i pì biegi pollari? I pì bie' salgari? I pì bie' rovere, upij, ulmi, frussene, carpene? Mo de bestiame? Po on è i pì bie' buo e vacche? Mo chi cancharo è mo quel cancaro sì pover hom[5] che n'abbi 'na bella vacca in cha? Mo piegore e castron? Ge n'è mo? Po no favellare. Mo cavagi e cavalle, mo puorci e scrove, mo cavre e bichi? Cancharo ge n'è de grandi, a digo, sì biegi con sipia al mondo e de la megiore naia e de la maore del mondo. Mo aseni[6] e asenon grandi? Mo che vuogio pì star a frapare de tanta altra fatta de anemali? In collusion a cherzo verasiamen che quando Domenedio fe el deslubio e che l'arsunè in la barca de Loe de tutte le biestie del roerso mondo e cum el le descargè e le cavè fuora, el cavè tutto el bestiame chi sul Pavan.

8) Pavan an? Mo favelon mo de femene ch'è miegio cha bestie. Per certo el ge è pur le belle femene a comenzando de sotto in su e dai piè. Pota mo che bie' piazon largi e firmi! Guardé che le zotte o i scataron, andando con le va | [5ᵛ] descolze, ge fazza male. Sì, in lo cullo! El vol esser ben scataron che no se intorza e zopa che no se sfregole. E po quelle belle gambe grosse cum quel lacheto pasù che [persenari][7] — a digo dal grosso — ge perderae. E quelle cossonazze! Haìvu mé vezù, la vostra Silentia, de quigi fusti e ramonazzi de nogara frissia da morbezzo, che è gruossi cum è un atraverso, che tra così al biancho? Mo ben così è le so cossonazze e così dure in tel pizegare. Va' po pì in su — quelle so belle neghe bianche e reonde sprecisamen cum è un purco ben grasso quando l'è pellò da frescho. Che cum te 'l vi, te no te può tegnire de no ge dare a man averta — così — una schiappeza. Mo quello che è po dal'altro lò dananzo, infra le gambe un sommesso [in su], quel che pensanto me se desconisse el cuore, e per rebelienzia dela vostra Spettabilitè, che è pur sì cum preve, a no 'l vuogio dire. A digo mo quello che me tira El cuore de dire. Se l'è ben quello don fina vu vegnanto al mondo El basissi. Lagonlo pur stare, che la n'è tropo segura a favellarve, che an l'hom se porae incordare con fa i

---

[5] MS hon.

[6] The final vowel is clearly 'i' despite the apparently feminine gender, perhaps by the raising influence of the preceding nasal.

[7] A blank space occurs here where in the other manuscripts the word 'persenari' (haypresses) occurs, possibly indicating that the copyist was unfamiliar with the term.

cavagi. E po quella panza reonda, panza puorpio da portar tri puti in un portò, cum quelle tetonazze che se ge puolle asconder el cao in migola in mezo. Mo tette? Verasiamen da bergola da late, cum quelle spalazze che portarae ogno gran carga, che dise, 'Cargame s'te me se cargare, ch'a porterò o in spalla, o da sacco, o imbigolò'. Cum quelle brazze e quelle man, puorpio brazze da faiga e man da | [6ʳ] baìlle, da no se stancare a cargare cento barelle al dì, cum quel voltonazzo reondo norìo, bianco e rosso, che ge perderae fette de persuto inverzelò e ravi di qui bianchi e russi quando giè ben lavè. E po que giochij de sole inrazè che tra de ponta che passarae le muragie de Pava. Christo da Loreto, mo giè pur biegi. Le è pur a bel fatto tutte belle le nostre femene. E on nasselе ste belle femene? Mo sul Pavan.

9) Pavan an? Mo no favellare mo del Pavan? In collusion a crezo verasiamen che 'l supia El paraiso taresto e tanto pì bello e megiore cum la su no si ge magna e chialo sì. Spettabel missier lo Sgardenale saì zo che ven a dir Pavan? Tanto vol dir Pavan cum dir, 'Va al Pan'. Senza pan no se pò vivere e chi vol Pan vagi sul Pavan. Pavan an? L'andarae male se 'l no ge fosse 'l Pavan e piezo se 'l no ge fosse Pan. E sti cogiombari de sti sletran vol favellare per gramego o in fiorentinesco e va cercanto megior pan cha de formento. E perzondena a i lagarè baiare a so muò et sì favelerè alle nostre devise, che è le pì belle del mondo, da bon Pavan.

10) La vostra Silientia spaternitè magnificentia serenitè lustrissima, piasantove mo a vu cum a diga, me ascoltarà mi e mi dirè, piasantove a vu. Nè gnan guardè ch'a vuogia star a frapare nè dire nè sbagiafare dela vostra schiatta zenia e narration, cum ha fatto quigi sletran da Pava in le so rengaure, che tante i ve n'ha fatto che, se die m'ai', a doì esser bell'è stuffò e cum disse questù le ve die' esser cazù dal cullo perquè, cum a saì, crezanto laldarve i ve disea contra. Perquè i dise ch'a si de schiata vegnù de Romagnarolaria de Roma. Alla fe i ve ha | [6ᵛ] do un bel laldo. Mo no l'è gnan la pezor zenia de Romagnarolli. Mo no ègij brisigiegi o Pulitan da Rubin? Da igi ai spagnaruolli el ge è pocha differentia. Mo no giaonte proè in ste guerre sgagaborde e muzaruolle? Mo no fu mé romagnarollo che haesse mo nè fe nè lianza. Mo no ègi tutti a bel fatto biastemaori? A fagi de Dio e di sancti cum se i gi haesse fatto cum un cortellazzo, e ge tragij el cancaro cum i lo tresse in un salgaro. Cope fiorini! Te par mo ch'i ve habi do un bel laldo? A dige mo mi, che no sum sletran cum giè igi, ch'a si dale Venesie, venetian d'i buoni e d'i maore.

14) L'è pur un piasere vivo e snaturale a[9] sentir borir un braccho e cazar fuora una salvegina d'un macchion, e ti verla e lassarge el to levriero drio et ella muzanto farte correr don la va, e ti criare e dire, 'A poltron, a traitore, a ribaldo, a poltron, pigiela!'. E verre che 'l to can la pigie e ti zonzerge adosso e rivarla d'ammazzare e basar el can e alzarlo per tornarge le buelle a so | [8ᵛ] luogo. E po chiamare i compagni e dirge, 'L'è morta, l'è morta!' quanto se pò mé de ose. E sonare el corno fazante allegrezza, merdolagie m'in cullo. E po arrivare i compagni e dirge cum l'è andà, e un dire haver vezù El tutto e che 'l bracco la borì ben. E che te gie 'l lassissi con rason e che l'è bon levriero quel to, e che te fussi presto a zonzerge adosso, et che te si bon Cazaore. E ti dirge, 'G'in fosse pur de gianimali, s'i fosse ben lion!'. Te te senti frello che la camisa non te tocha el cullo, e 'l t'è arviso de haverlo in t'un cain de late nomè[10] monta. Te tre un salto, te te fregoli le man, te guardi el to can, e te vi che gialtri dise, 'L'è stò quello.' Te guardi po l'anemale se l'è de i viegi. È mo questo un bel piasere vivo? E no le merdolagie, che no è bone da spendere.

15) Orbentena chi la intende, chi no la intende. A se che vu, bonsignore, a la intendì, la vostra spaternitè. E sì a se che andé per la carezà. Crezime a mi che, alla fe haì un gran celebrio, e che asi un gran pizol hom da ben, e si a fosse altramen a ve 'l dirae mi. Perqué que me fa a mi? intendìvu? A no so dire se nomé cum la è, intendìvu? A si vu an sliberale bon compagno maregale. A no si gnian di proviersi, de sti ostinè spisimusi che no se sa mé de que vuogia i supia. Intendìvu? De sti altieri che vol star sempre de sora da tutti e sottomitare tutti, che[11] i no cre che ge supia altri al mondo. Alla fe che a me piasí e per questo a ve vuogio de bon ben, a dige sì cum da frello. Andé pur drio per sta carezà cum a fé, la vostra rebellientia e magnificentia. E governé pur ben le vostre piegore, che a seon gnu del Pavan. Perqué a si nostro pegoraro e pastore e nostro | [9ʳ] veschoo e Pappa che ha lubertè, cum disse esum Dio, de fare e desfare e, in collusion, de volzer la torta a ostro mo. E perzondena gnu poveritti a ve hon pì desirò che no fe né cavalla magra, secca, e restia l'herba nova. E haon fatto per esinanza che mi a son vegnù per lome de tutti a legrarme de la

---

MS e.

MS noma.

MS chi.

11) Mo chi cancaro no sa che ca Cornaro è la maor ca che supi'al mondo? Mo no ge n'è da per tutto? Alla fe, no trognanto, così cum no g'è el megior legno al mondo del Cornaro, a digo, pì tegnente e pì fremo e che duri pì, così cha Cornaro se pò ben dire che la sipia de Cornaro frema. Mo di che se farì una bona gugia nè una bona chaechia se la no è de Cornaro? Mo dente da molin? Sì, se masenarae doman se i dente da molin no fosse de Cornaro. Mo se no fosse cha Cornaro, che è adesso Parona de Pava e del Pavan, cum stasson gnu? C'haon speranza che gn'agiè. Basta ch'a si da cha Cornaro e dela[8] [terra] ch'è parona de Pava e del Pavan. Puzela mo da agio questa? N'è 'l mo assé? El n'è zà altra terra al mondo che supia Parona del Pavan: Roma de Romagnarolaria no zà, Franza de Franzosaria | [7ʳ] no zà, Spagna de Spagnaria no zà, Rubin no zà, Collocuta no zà, terra toescha no zà. Siché Bonsignore missier lo sgardenale, a si vu dela terra che è delle Venesie, parona de Pava e del Pavan, che no ge n'è zà de tante un'altra. E igi dise ch'a si da Roma romagnarollo. O chancaro i sbreghe!

12) Mo a me fagi squasi cagar da riso quando che i dise ch'a si un grand'homo. No ge vigi, morbo i magne? A sivu ben pizol'homo, i no 'l sa dire. A si un gran pizol e no un grand'homo. Haì ben una gran cosa per pizol ch'a si, i no 'l sa dire. Mo a 'l dirè ben mi. Haì per certo un gran cuore per quel ch'a e intendù. Mo disime un po' per la vostra cara fe e da frello, ch'a no ve tegno — se die m'ai' — altramen, chi chancaro serave quel cancaro de quelù che fosse a cavallo e che veesse un cengiaro abavò che gie vegnesse incontra e che no se tolesse da un lò e muzare? Mi inchina da mo a me torae via, e s'a fosse a pè ch'a no poesse muzare, a me roegarae su n'albaro. E vu, missier lo Bonsignore, a desmontè zó da Cavallo e sì l'andé pur tal fià a incontrare e a frontare, a digo, da prodohomo e sì l'amazè. Te parsela mo che questa se tegna al baille? No fé, alla fe, che la n'è troppo segura. La ve porae an butar male e cum a fosse morto, assasse roinò del mondo. E sì harissi scapò su quella bromba, che vossevu mé pì far de Cengiari nè de vescoè? Mi così pover'hom cum a sum, a no torae d'esser morto e esser Papa. Che Pappa, Pappa, la merda — perdoneme. Ampò a digo ch'a no torae a esser signore del Roerso mondo. A ve vuogio dare alla vostra | [7ᵛ] Rebelientia un consiegio

---

[8] MS 'delo' with the final vowel malformed.

che quigi sletran da Pava no ve l'harà sapù dare.
sentio an mi dele so rengaure asé cum el me paron
fatte? Mo ligevela al deo, che la è de importanza: ch
viver poltron cha morir valenthomo. Siché no guardè
cuore, e cum ve vien un cengiaro incontra, tireve da u

13) Haìvu imparò — disime da compagno re
rengaure me tanto? Se die m'ai' no, ch'a creza. Po
aigi tal ponto che Stotene nè Sinica no se 'l pense m
dire ch'a si sgardenale e ch'a dir sgardenale el ven a
ten su le porte del paraiso che gnu a i chiamomo ca
ghia igi mé vezù El paraiso nè le porte nè quigi che i
che le ten su, che se chiama canchari, a vorae che
magnesse mi. E se no le ha vezù, a vorae che
magnesse igi. Dhe, cancharo i magne matti, adesch'
cancaro. A si el sgardenale cum a dirè mi, e no
essegij cavò giochij. A stasse fresco s'a fosse co
sgardenale cum a dirè mi, e cum a slainerè, i dorae
al capelletto rosso e tante intrè. *Proficiate vobise d*
an esser Papa e ch'a dessan vegnir tutti a verve a
cum una morise al Collo da Can. Sgardenale an?
sletran. Saìvu zo che ven a dire sgardenale? Cum
signore rico che se dà a sto mondo piasere. E cum
tutti a moron), se ben vu non haì fato massa be
andé de lungo in Paraiso. E se la porta è passà, a'l
intré per ogni via e per ogni buso. E quello ven
che sgardena e no un cancharo che ten su l'us
magne igi e le so letre, mati spertegé. N'èlla mo
se la intendo pì de igi, sgardenale an? L'è pur b
Inchinadamo, se die m'ai', ch'a torae a no m
fromento e esserge, a sarae propio cum a s
compagno e mi vostro. Gnan mi a no farae mé
le muragie cum ha zà fato tal sgardenale che è z
che no haea cuore de spendergi, g'in fosse pu
ben i spendessan! Nè a no crezo mé ch'a i de
statoe intagiè nè in quelle parpagiolle che ha q
le chiama merdolagie. Al mancho se spende
monea. De', cancharo alle merdolagie e a l'a
m'è deviso che sipia un favelar coi morti a fave
A no torae inchina da mo d'esserge stampò su
e non gie esser pì se lomé in stampa. Se die
piasere no la intende a haver piasere de muorti.
vivi coi vivi.

vostra vegnua. Tochéme la man, che a supie el ben vegnù e 'l ben trovò. A vuogio ch'a me faze no so che leze e stratuti nuovi, che è ben de rason. Madequidem, in bona fe, sì:

16) La prima: che a ogno cazaore o osellaore che [va] per piasere e no per guagno a cazzare o osellare possa andar la domenega senza aldir messa e no sipia peccò perqué a saì che in quel'hora l'è el bello del piasere per pì rason, e chi perde quel'hora la no torna mé pì in drio.

17) Le do: che negun dela villa supia ubrigò a zunare perqué, cum a saì, el faigare fa pair pri. E cum se ha paìo, chi no magna se ge sconisse El core e va a risego de spuar el polmon e morir da salivo che te ven in bocha. Te ve po in letto e te ne può dromire. E s'te e mogiere, per pararte la fame e farte vegnir sono, te fé quello che te no farissi che tu dormirissi. E se te n'e mugiere, gran fatto che de doman te no ge n'habbi una. E per no star otioso se fa po pezo, cum a saì, intendìvu?

18) Le tre: che de tempo de taiar i frominti ne supia peccò a lavorare la festa. Perqué da un'hora a l'altra pò vegnire una fraza de tempesta e roinargi del mondo. A biastemon po a muò can. E chi no biastemarae? Disíme per la vostra cara fe. A scovegnon an robare s'a vogion vivere e a sto mo a fazon du pecchè, e si n'haon la colpa l'è pur così, n'è vera?

19) Le quatro: che se posse magnare la doman innanzo messa per poer stare po col cuore | [9^v] a missier Jesumdio che l'è el cancaro quando se ha fame e che 'l se è alla giesia, l'è pur forza havere el cuore a cha a magnare. E se harom magnò, harom el cuore ivelo a missier Jesomdio e no a cha al Pan.

20) Le cinque: che per magnar no supia peccò de golla quando el se magna per che El sa bon se ben no s'ha fame. Perqué i vechij dise che quel che sa bon fa bon pro e fa sanitè, stagando sani se vive assé, vivendo assé se ven vechij, vegnando vechij se fa del ben, fazando del ben se va in paraiso. Siché no pò esser male nè peccò, perqué cum sarae peccò chi magnasse tossego sapiando che 'l fa male, così magnanto cossa che faza bon pro die esser merito, cum è a magnar de bon.

21) Le sie: ch'a fazè ch'ogni preve possa haver mogiere o ch'i supia castrè, perqué l'è el cancaro le frazilitè dela carne. Le dà qualche botta tanto fastidio che no se sa in che buso cazzarse e se giè ben previ, giè huomeni cum a son gnu e de quigi an pì maschi. Perqué i no ha femene, i va in tanta veregagia che cum i s'imbate la prima botta in t'una de le nuostre femene, che i le ingravia de fatto. E gnu poveritti a fazzon le spese a suo' figioli che 'l n'è zà ben

fatto, nè de rason. E se i serà castrè a no haron sta briga alle spalle. E se gi harà mugiere, i no serà sì rabiusi nè sempre sì in veregagia che le i tegnerà monzù. E se pur g'ingraviarà le nostre femene, a ingraviaron an gnu le sue, e se gnu faron le spese ai suo' putti, an igi le farà ai nuostri. E se saron su e su.

    22) Le sette: perqué l'è tanto gran cancaro le nemistè e malivolientie tra gnu containi dalle ville e i Citaini da Pava ch'a se magnessom del cuore e tutto 'l dì per questo a se tragagion. E se a fossom cossì gnu de fuora con giè igi, bao babao bao cope fiorini! a no ge duraravegi un'hora in le man. Mo patientia. I gne dise a gnu, 'Containi, villani, marassi, ragagni'. E gnu a ge digon a igi, 'Chagariegi, Can, usurari, magnasangue de' poveritti'. A vosson mo, che cum a e zà ditto a seon dal lò dessoto, che a conciessi sta differentia e che a fasse ch'a fosson una cosa medema. A vuogio perzontena che a ne faze sta leze: che ogn'hom da villa possa tore quatro mogiere e ogno femena da villa possa tuore quatro marì. Perqué cum quigi chagariegi da Pava vega così, e perché i tra alle nostre femene, tutti per poer haver quatro femene se farà dalla villa che 'l sta igi a farsege. E tutte le femene citaine, perqué el ge sa bon, per poere haver quatro marì, se farà da villa. E gnu scaparon su quelle brombette e a sto muò sarom una cosa medesma, nè ge sarà invidia nè nemistè perqué a serom tutti un parentò. E tutte le femene andarà piene e se impirà la leze de missier Jesomdio che dise, 'Crescì e moltipichè'. Guardè che harom mé pì paura de Turchi che ne impalle — sì — in lo cullo. Se verà se nomé cielo e femene gravie e puti e tosati. Perqué adesso el g'è tal una che cum un homo solo la no se pò ingraviare, che cum la ne harà quatro gran fatto che un no ge chatti la stralecha. A no se farà gnan negun becco e quel peccò, che no doerae esser peccò, d'andar dale femene d'altri, che tutti harà da far a cha soa. Sarallo mo questo un bel ben an? Quante costion che se fa per questo no se farae? Quanti vien amazè che sarae vivi? Quante | [10^r] belle pute poverete in Pava che n'ha muò de poerse mariare se mariarae? Che le va a farse ficchare monege in ti monestieri? Tutte sfigiollerave. Ge n'è mo che sta indarno che harae da fare. Che è maor peccò dele ociositè? E fuorsi che no gie n'è de belle? Le belle e le burte harae bon aviamento. Per un parente che si ha, se ne harae quatro. Ogn'hon harae fià e pì[12] potientia da cazzare i spagnaruolli e i

---

[12] Compare the present 'breath and more power' with the other manuscripts' 'quatro fiè pì potentia' (four times the power).

cavagi. E po quella panza reonda, panza puorpio da portar tri puti in un portò, cum quelle tetonazze che se ge puolle ascondere el cao in migola in mezo. Mo tette? Verasiamen da bergola da late, cum quelle spalazze che portarae ogno gran carga, che dise, 'Cargame s'te me se cargare, ch'a porterò o in spalla, o da sacco, o imbigolò'. Cum quelle brazze e quelle man, puorpio brazze da faiga e man da | [6^r] baìlle, da no se stancare a cargare cento barelle al dì, cum quel voltonazzo reondo norìo, bianco e rosso, che ge perderae fette de persuto inverzelò e ravi di qui bianchi e russi quando giè ben lavè. E po que giochij de sole inrazè che tra de ponta che passarae le muragie de Pava. Christo da Loreto, mo giè pur biegi. Le è pur a bel fatto tutte belle le nostre femene. E on nassele ste belle femene? Mo sul Pavan.

9) Pavan an? Mo no favellare mo del Pavan? In collusion a crezo verasiamen che 'l supia El paraiso taresto e tanto pì bello e megiore cum la su no si ge magna e chialo sì. Spettabel missier lo Sgardenale saì zo che ven a dir Pavan? Tanto vol dir Pavan cum dir, 'Va al Pan'. Senza pan no se pò vivere e chi vol Pan vagi sul Pavan. Pavan an? L'andarae male se 'l no ge fosse 'l Pavan e piezo se 'l no ge fosse Pan. E sti cogiombari de sti sletran vol favellare per gramego o in fiorentinesco e va cercanto megior pan cha de formento. E perzondena a i lagarè baiare a so muò et sì faverlerè alle nostre devise, che è le pì belle del mondo, da bon Pavan.

10) La vostra Silientia spaternitè magnificentia serenitè lustrissima, piasantove mo a vu cum a diga, me ascoltarà mi e mi dirè, piasantove a vu. Nè gnan guardè ch'a vuogia star a frapare nè dire nè sbagiafare dela vostra schiatta zenia e narration, cum ha fatto quigi sletran da Pava in le so rengaure, che tante i ve n'ha fatto che, se die m'ai', a doì esser bell'è stuffò e cum disse questù le ve die' esser cazù dal cullo perqué, cum a saì, crezanto laldarve i ve disea contra. Perqué i dise ch'a si de schiata vegnù de Romagnarolaria de Roma. Alla fe i ve ha | [6^v] do un bel laldo. Mo no l'è gnan la pezor zenia de Romagnarolli. Mo no ègij brisigiegi o Pulitan da Rubin? Da igi ai spagnaruolli el ge è pocha differenza. Mo no giaonte proè in ste guerre sgagaborde e muzaruolle? Mo no fu mé romagnarollo che haesse mo nè fe nè lianza. Mo no ègi tutti a bel fatto biastemaori? A fagi de Dio e di sancti cum se i gi haesse fatto cum un cortellazzo, e ge tragij el cancaro cum i lo tresse in un salgaro. Cope fiorini! Te par mo ch'i ve habi do un bel laldo? A dige mo mi, che no sum sletran cum giè igi, ch'a si dale Venesie, venetian d'i buoni e d'i maore.

11) Mo chi cancaro no sa che ca Cornaro è la maor ca che supi'al mondo? Mo no ge n'è da per tutto? Alla fe, no trognanto, così cum no g'è el megior legno al mondo del Cornaro, a digo, pì tegnente e pì fremo e che duri pì, così cha Cornaro se pò ben dire che la sipia de Cornaro frema. Mo di che se farì una bona gugia nè una bona chaechia se la no è de Cornaro? Mo dente da molin? Sì, se masenarae doman se i dente da molin no fosse de Cornaro. Mo se no fosse cha Cornaro, che è adesso Parona de Pava e del Pavan, cum stasson gnu? C'haon speranza che gn'agiè. Basta ch'a si da cha Cornaro e dela[8] [terra] ch'è parona de Pava e del Pavan. Puzela mo da agio questa? N'è 'l mo assé? El n'è zà altra terra al mondo che supia Parona del Pavan: Roma de Romagnarolaria no zà, Franza de Franzosaria | [7^r] no zà, Spagna de Spagnaria no zà, Rubin no zà, Collocuta no zà, terra toescha no zà. Siché Bonsignore missier lo sgardenale, a si vu dela terra che è delle Venesie, parona de Pava e del Pavan, che no ge n'è zà de tante un'altra. E igi dise ch'a si da Roma romagnarollo. O chancaro i sbreghe!

12) Mo a me fagi squasi cagar da riso quando che i dise ch'a si un grand'homo. No ge vigi, morbo i magne? A sivu ben pizol'homo, i no 'l sa dire. A si un gran pizol e no un grand'homo. Haì ben una gran cosa per pizol ch'a si, i no 'l sa dire. Mo a 'l dirè ben mi. Haì per certo un gran cuore per quel ch'a e intendù. Mo disime un po' per la vostra cara fe e da frello, ch'a no ve tegno — se die m'ai' — altramen, chi chancaro serave quel cancaro de quelù che fosse a cavallo e che veesse un cengiaro abavò che gie vegnesse incontra e che no se tolesse da un lò e muzare? Mi inchina da mo a me torae via, e s'a fosse a pè ch'a no poesse muzare, a me roegarae su n'albaro. E vu, missier lo Bonsignore, a desmontè zó da Cavallo e sì l'andé pur tal fià a incontrare e a frontare, a digo, da prodohomo e sì l'amazè. Te parsela mo che questa se tegna al baìlle? No fé, alla fe, che la n'è troppo segura. La ve porae an butar male e cum a fosse morto, assasse roinò del mondo. E sì harissi scapò su quella bromba, che vossevu mé pì far de Cengiari nè de vescoè? Mi così pover'hom cum a sum, a no torae d'esser morto e esser Papa. Che Pappa, Pappa, la merda — perdoneme. Ampò a digo ch'a no torae a esser signore del Roerso mondo. A ve vuogio dare alla vostra | [7^v] Rebelientia un consiegio

---

[8] MS 'delo' with the final vowel malformed.

che quigi sletran da Pava no ve l'harà sapù dare. Ampò hogie sentio an mi dele so rengaure asé cum el me paron che i ve ha fatte? Mo ligevela al deo, che la è de importanza: che l'è miegio viver poltron cha morir valenthomo. Siché no guardè al vostro gran cuore, e cum ve vien un cengiaro incontra, tireve da un lò.

13) Haìvu imparò — disime da compagno reale — in le so rengaure me tanto? Se die m'ai' no, ch'a creza. Po a g'insegnarae aigi tal ponto che Stotene nè Sinica no se 'l pense mé, i sa solamen dire ch'a si sgardenale e ch'a dir sgardenale el ven a dire quigi che ten su le porte del paraiso che gnu a i chiamomo canchari. Dhe, se ghia igi mé vezù El paraiso nè le porte nè quigi che i dise ch'a si vu che le ten su, che se chiama canchari, a vorae che 'l cancharo me magnesse mi. E se no le ha vezù, a vorae che 'l chancaro i magnesse igi. Dhe, cancharo i magne matti, adesch'i vol ch'a sie el cancaro. A si el sgardenale cum a dirè mi, e no el cancaro, che essegij cavò giochij. A stasse fresco s'a fosse coi dise igi. A si sgardenale cum a dirè mi, e cum a slainerè, i dorae pur cognoscerve al capelletto rosso e tante intrè. *Proficiate vobise domine*: possevu an esser Papa e ch'a dessan vegnir tutti a verve a Roma in gatolon cum una morise al Collo da Can. Sgardenale an? Dhe, morbo a i sletran. Saìvu zo che ven a dire sgardenale? Cum è a dirè: un gran signore rico che se dà a sto mondo piasere. E cum el muore (perché tutti a moron), se ben vu non haì fato massa ben tamentre, | [8ʳ] andé de lungo in Paraiso. E se la porta è passà, a'lla sgardenalé e sì intré per ogni via e per ogni buso. E quello ven a dir sgardenale, che sgardena e no un cancharo che ten su l'usso, che cancaro i magne igi e le so letre, mati spertegé. N'èlla mo così? Mo ben vivu se la intendo pì de igi, sgardenale an? L'è pur bella cosa esserge. Inchinadamo, se die m'ai', ch'a torae a no magnar mé pan de fromento e esserge, a sarae propio cum a si vu, assasse me compagno e mi vostro. Gnan mi a no farae mé mosine de dinari in le muragie cum ha zà fatto tal sgardenale che è zà sto chive a Pava, che no haea cuore de spendergi, g'in fosse pure, n'è vero? Cum ben i spendessan! Nè a no crezo mé ch'a i decipesson in prie de statoe intagiè nè in quelle parpagiolle che ha quelle figure su che i le chiama merdolagie. Al mancho se spendessele cum se fa la monea. De', cancharo alle merdolagie e a l'agio e alle ceole. El m'è deviso che sipia un favelar coi morti a favellar de qui bordiegi. A no torae inchina da mo d'esserge stampò su e esser stò Rolando e non gie esser pì se lomé in stampa. Se die m'ai' chi de elle ha piasere no la intende a haver piasere de muorti. Muorti coi muorti e vivi coi vivi.

14) L'è pur un piasere vivo e snaturale a[9] sentir borir un braccho e cazar fuora una salvegina d'un macchion, e ti verla e lassarge el to levriero drio et ella muzanto farte correr don la va, e ti criare e dire, 'A poltron, a traitore, a ribaldo, a poltron, pigiela!'. E verre che 'l to can la pigie e ti zonzerge adosso e rivarla d'ammazzare e basar el can e alzarlo per tornarge le buelle a so | [8ᵛ] luogo. E po chiamare i compagni e dirge, 'L'è morta, l'è morta!' quanto se pò mé de ose. E sonare el corno fazante allegrezza, merdolagie m'in cullo. E po arrivare i compagni e dirge cum l'è andà, e un dire haver vezù El tutto e che 'l bracco la borì ben. E che te gie 'l lassissi con rason e che l'è bon levriero quel to, e che te fussi presto a zonzerge adosso, et che te si bon Cazaore. E ti dirge, 'G'in fosse pur de gianimali, s'i fosse ben lion!'. Te te senti frello che la camisa non te tocha el cullo, e 'l t'è arviso de haverlo in t'un cain de late nomè[10] monta. Te tre un salto, te te fregoli le man, te guardi el to can, e te vi che gialtri dise, 'L'è stò quello.' Te guardi po l'anemale se l'è de i viegi. È mo questo un bel piasere vivo? E no le merdolagie, che no è bone da spendere.

15) Orbentena chi la intende, chi no la intende. A se che vu, bonsignore, a la intendì, la vostra spaternitè. E sì a se che andé per la carezà. Crezime a mi che, alla fe haì un gran celebrio, e che asi un gran pizol hom da ben, e si a fosse altramen a ve 'l dirae mi. Perqué que me fa a mi? intendìvu? A no so dire se nomé cum la è, intendìvu? A si vu an sliberale bon compagno maregale. A no si gnian di proviersi, de sti ostinè spisimusi che no se sa mé de que vuogia i supia. Intendìvu? De sti altieri che vol star sempre de sora da tutti e sottomitare tutti, che[11] i no cre che ge supia altri al mondo. Alla fe che a me piasí e per questo a ve vuogio de bon ben, a dige sì cum da frello. Andé pur drio per sta carezà cum a fé, la vostra rebellientia e magnificentia. E governé pur ben le vostre piegore, che a seon gnu del Pavan. Perqué a si nostro pegoraro e pastore e nostro | [9ʳ] veschoo e Pappa che ha luberté, cum disse Jesum Dio, de fare e desfare e, in collusion, de volzer la torta a vostro mo. E perzondena gnu poveritti a ve hon pì desirò che no fe mé cavalla magra, secca, e restia l'herba nova. E haon fatto per vesinanza che mi a son vegnù per lome de tutti a legrarme de la

---

[9] MS e.

[10] MS noma.

[11] MS chi.

vostra vegnua. Tochéme la man, che a supie el ben vegnù e 'l ben trovò. A vuogio ch'a me faze no so che leze e stratuti nuovi, che è ben de rason. Madequidem, in bona fe, sì:

16) La prima: che a ogno cazaore o osellaore che [va] per piasere e no per guagno a cazzare o osellare possa andar la domenega senza aldir messa e no sipia peccò perqué a saì che in quel'hora l'è el bello del piasere per pì rason, e chi perde quel'hora la no torna mé pì in drio.

17) Le do: che negun dela villa supia ubrigò a zunare perqué, cum a saì, el faigare fa pair pri. E cum se ha paìo, chi no magna se ge sconisse El core e va a risego de spuar el polmon e morir da salivo che te ven in bocha. Te ve po in letto e te ne può dromire. E s'te e mogiere, per pararte la fame e farte vegnir sono, te fé quello che te no farissi che tu dormirissi. E se te n'e mugiere, gran fatto che de doman te no ge n'habbi una. E per no star otioso se fa po pezo, cum a saì, intendìvu?

18) Le tre: che de tempo de taiar i frominti ne supia peccò a lavorare la festa. Perqué da un'hora a l'altra pò vegnire una fraza de tempesta e roinargi del mondo. A biastemon po a muò can. E chi no biastemarae? Disíme per la vostra cara fe. A scovegnon an robare s'a vogion vivere e a sto mo a fazon du pecchè, e si n'haon la colpa l'è pur così, n'è vera?

19) Le quatro: che se posse magnare la doman innanzo messa per poer stare po col cuore | [9ᵛ] a missier Jesumdio che l'è el cancaro quando se ha fame e che 'l se è alla giesia, l'è pur forza havere el cuore a cha a magnare. E se harom magnò, harom el cuore ivelo a missier Jesomdio e no a cha al Pan.

20) Le cinque: che per magnar no supia peccò de golla quando el se magna per che El sa bon se ben no s'ha fame. Perqué i vechij dise che quel che sa bon fa bon pro e fa sanitè, stagando sani se vive assé, vivendo assé se ven vechij, vegnando vechij se fa del ben, fazando del ben se va in paraiso. Siché no pò esser male nè peccò, perqué cum sarae peccò chi magnasse tossego sapiando che 'l fa male, così magnanto cossa che faza bon pro die esser merito, cum è a magnar de bon.

21) Le sie: ch'a fazè ch'ogni preve possa haver mogiere o ch'i supia castrè, perqué l'è el cancaro le frazilitè dela carne. Le dà qualche botta tanto fastidio che no se sa in che buso cazzarse e se giè ben previ, giè huomeni cum a son gnu e de quigi an pì maschi. Perqué i no ha femene, i va in tanta veregagia che cum i s'imbate la prima botta in t'una de le nuostre femene, che i le ingravia de fatto. E gnu poveritti a fazzon le spese a suo' figioli che 'l n'è zà ben

fatto, nè de rason. E se i serà castrè a no haron sta briga alle spalle. E se gi harà mugiere, i no serà sì rabiusi nè sempre sì in veregagia che le i tegnerà monzù. E se pur g'ingraviarà le nostre femene, a ingraviaron an gnu le sue, e se gnu faron le spese ai suo' putti, an igi le farà ai nuostri. E se saron su e su.

22) Le sette: perqué l'è tanto gran cancaro le nemistè e malivolientie tra gnu containi dalle ville e i Citaini da Pava ch'a se magnessom del cuore e tutto 'l dì per questo a se tragagion. E se a fossom cossì gnu de fuora con giè igi, bao babao bao cope fiorini! a no ge duraravegi un'hora in le man. Mo patientia. I gne dise a gnu, 'Containi, villani, marassi, ragagni'. E gnu a ge digon a igi, 'Chagariegi, Can, usurari, magnasangue de' poveritti'. A vosson mo, che cum a e zà ditto a seon dal lò dessoto, che a conciessi sta differentia e che a fasse ch'a fosson una cosa medema. A vuogio perzontena che a ne faze sta leze: che ogn'hom da villa possa tore quatro mogiere e ogno femena da villa possa tuore quatro marì. Perqué cum quigi chagariegi da Pava vega così, e perché i tra alle nostre femene, tutti per poer haver quatro femene se farà dalla villa che 'l sta igi a farsege. E tutte le femene citaine, perqué el ge sa bon, per poere haver quatro marì, se farà da villa. E gnu scaparon su quelle brombette e a sto muò sarom una cosa medesma, nè ge sarà invidia nè nemistè perqué a serom tutti un parentò. E tutte le femene andarà piene e se impirà la leze de missier Jesomdio che dise, 'Crescì e moltipichè'. Guardè che harom mé pì paura de Turchi che ne impalle — sì — in lo cullo. Se verà se nomé cielo e femene gravie e puti e tosati. Perqué adesso el g'è tal una che cum un homo solo la no se pò ingraviare, che cum la ne harà quatro gran fatto che un no ge chatti la stralecha. A no se farà gnan negun beccho e quel peccò, che no doerae esser peccò, d'andar dale femene d'altri, che tutti harà da far a cha soa. Sarallo mo questo un bel ben an? Quante costion che se fa per questo no se farae? Quanti vien amazè che sarae vivi? Quante | [10ʳ] belle pute poverete in Pava che n'ha muò de poerse mariare se mariarae? Che le va a farse ficchare monege in ti monestieri? Tutte sfigiollerave. Ge n'è mo che sta indarno che harae da fare. Che è maor peccò dele ociositè? E fuorsi che no gie n'è de belle? Le belle e le burte harae bon aviamento. Per un parente che si ha, se ne harae quatro. Ogn'hon harae fià e pì[12] potientia da cazzare i spagnaruolli e i

---

[12] Compare the present 'breath and more power' with the other manuscripts' 'quatro fiè pì potentia' (four times the power).

toeschi se i tornasse mé pì in sto paese. A no fasse mé (se die m'ai')[13] la pì bella leze ch'a far la leze coille del mondo, nèlla Caluorica nè la Teluorica. Félla missier lo sgardenale, che a vuo' m'ai' nomé tante benidission che ve serà dè. A mi que me fa a mi, intendìvu? A digo mo mi per vostro miegio, intendìvu cum a digo? Saìvu perché, intendìvu? A faze per vu, mo intendìvu? Che me fa a mi, intendìvu? Félla pure ch'a serì adorò da gnu come s'a fosse un santo. Se a no ve volesse ben, a no ve consiegiarae. Mo a saì ben quel ch'a digo, che 'l serà ben per vu. A porì dire, 'A vuo' così' che così serà. Senza gnu che valessevu? E sì a ve tegnerom tutti da Pare e da figiollo e da frello, che gnan altramen a no ve tegnon. Deme la man e prometti me che un'altra fià a vegnerè a tuore el spatafio. Die v'ai'.

---

[13] The closing parenthesis is missing in the manuscript.

Note on the text

The text above has been transcribed from Biblioteca Civica Verona, MS 1635-36 (Cl. Poligr., Ubic. 168.2, busta 55a/10). It is bound together with the *Historia di Phileto Veronese* (MS 1635), which occupies folios 1-49. *Sopra la caccia,* which now begins on folio 50, had its own numeration. The third numeration began with the *Intermedio d'una comedia de Ruzante. alla Pavana*, which occupied fols 1 and 2 (now 58 and 59) and continued with the oration, which occupies fol. 3^r (now 60^r) to fol. 10^r (67^r), with numbers written only up to fol. 6. The text is written in a regular hand with few corrections. The S of 'Sprolico' is separate from the rest of the word and appears to have been added. Corrections are: par. 6: *che con*; par. 9 *a i lagarè* (*i lagarè*). Square brackets mark several omissions that have been reconstructed through comparison with the other manuscripts.

La oration de Ruzante al Cardinal Cornaro

BMV, Ital. XI 66

1) Perqué l'è el cancaro a cazarse don non se de e don no è honesto, e mo mi che a son mi — mo a son com disse questù hom compìo — a guardo ben com'a fazzo. E perzontena, Rebelissimo Missier lo Sgardenale, a n'he vogiù vegnire a farve sto sprolicho a Pava. Perqué? Mo perqué qui cancari de quij sbagiafaore e de quij chagariegi sletran l'harae habù per male. Che com dise el provierbio, 'Non bene conveniente zodie co samaritai'. Che ven a dire che no sta ben donzie' con mariè. Mo perqué? Mo perqué cussì com i donziegi cercha de far bichi i mariè, cussì i citaini ne trogna e ne deleza nu puoveri containi dale ville. E perzontena a muzon pì da egi cha no fa le celege dal falchetto. E questo è mo che a non son vegnù a Pava.

2) Mo a son vegnù chialò chive quencena chialondena in sta villa per poer ben dire e slainare la me rason, per lome de tutto el taratuorio pavan che me ha aslenzù mi com hom bon parlente e sprologaore. Nè gnian guardé che haom vogiù mandare un preve nè uno de quigi dale centure insophranè che favella per gramego o in avogaro fiorentinesco, de quigi — saìu? — che se chiama doctore perqué se gi è igi do tore[1] a ge son mi tre dele torre. Mo no saì? Haom mo piasere de tegnire el nostro naturale derto in pè e dertamen per la natura chiamentre che a serom vivi, smisianto la lengua a nostro muò e no ala fiorentinesca. E mo a vuo' dir de mi inchindamo a no chambierae la me lengua con dusento fiorentinesche. Nè no torae de essere nassù in l'Agito de Betheleme, don nascè missier Jesum Dio, per non esser nassù sul Pavan. Mo no saveravegio[2] an mi si a volesse favelare fiorentinesco? Favelarè, a dige, sì fieramen che a dissè che a foesse puorpio inpolitan[3] de Talia nassù a Robin. Mo ascolté bon segnore: 'Io mi a seamo contadino dela villa che abitamo e staxamo sul

---

[1] A space makes a clear division into two words.

[2] Compare VR 36 saravigio, VR 1636 saveravegio, *Teatro* saveravege.

[3] Perhaps an error by the copyist or perhaps an attempt to reflect or satirize a Neapolitan pronunciation.

Pavano e io mi se rebutamo ala vostra de vu Segnoria.' Ve par mo per la vostra chara fe che a parerae mé che a foesse nassù sul Pavan? Poh, l'è un gran cagare. Ve par mo che a sarae an mi esserge se a volesse? Mo a no vuogio — a vuogio andare cho a v'he zà ditto con el me naturale in pè derto e dertamen cho a dige.

3) Mo dime un puo': missier Francesco Spetrarcha, mo no nascelo in Fiorentinaria? Mo cancar'è e perqué el fo malcontento a esserge nassù, che 'l vorae essere nassù in sul Pavan, el ge vene a stare e ge morì e ge volse essere soterò, e no fo buffa nè capeleta. E sì no guardè a partirse don l'iera nassù e lagare parentò e amistè, che saì pure che 'l se dise, 'Ligame le man e i piè e mittime de brigà d'i mie'.' El se partì e vene in sul Pavan e lagè tuto e sì saea pure quello che se pò saere. E perqué el felo mo? Mo per essere daspo' morto pavan dasché el non g'haea possù nascere, che 'l cognoscea che 'l nostro giera pì bel favelare del mondo e pì bel paese. Poh, l'è mo cho a dige a la vostra Magnificentia: ch'a no ge è de miegio de bon pavan. Poh mo, segnor Tenore che vene oltra el mare de Turcharia per far Pava chi sul Pavan, che da prima fo el Pavan de Pava? E i nuostri antessore viegi volse che 'l mettesse lome a Pava da femena perqué la staesse sempre sotto el Pavan e che 'l Pavan tegnisse sodomitù Pava e la va mo a un altro muò, madasché el poì fare, ala concerì, che l'è peccò de sto puovero Pavan.

4) Pavan an? Poh no favelom | [123ʳ] del Pavan. Mo no ge ven chiamentre mé le cesiole che se parte de là de Colecuta e chiamentre de là del choato del sole per vegnirge chive in sul Pavan a farge i suo' furti con nu in le nostre cha senza paura com se le foesse desmestegè e canta tutta la doman per farge apiasere. E sì no guarda che a vegnir chive in sul Pavan le habia da passare tanti mare e tante sabelgaure. Mo le quagie? Che ven an elle de ivelo e ven a ingrassarse chive per darge ben da magnare a nu Pavani. Pavan an? Mo i betuci? Paruzole? Coarussi? Rosignati? Turdi? Spinchi? E tanta altra fata de osiegi che ven da la terra Toescha? E passa tante montagne e per vegnir onve? Mo sul Pavan. A far mo che? Mo a ingrassarse.

5) Pavan an? Mo no se po gnian andare a Roma chi ven da la volta de Terviso ch'i no va in sul Pavan. Pavan an? Mo se no foesse se lomé i bagni d'Abano cha g'è tanti altri megiore cha ge ven tut'el dì gi huomeni folestieri mezi muorti amalè, con le casse al culo e torna via arsanè del Pavan. Pavan an? Mo di che se sepa far nigun bel ballo chi no fa la Pavana cho a fazon nu sul Pavan. Pavan an? Mo che agiere g'è, Christo da Loreto! Com un è amalò e

tramentre de quigi da le Veniesie com giè ben impocolè e amalè e che i se ge fa portare, a dige, senza bagni nè mesine de fatto i guarisse chive in su sto Pavan.

7) Pavan an? Mo quel pan che ge nasce an? On che se ge fa pan da frare de quel buffetto e pan schafetto che com te 'l magni le croste bore inchiamentre mé in cielo, che ge perderae un spezzaprie, miegio che nibie o braciegi? Che l'è ben poltron chi no in magna quatro a far colation. Mo quel vin sgarbozo an? Vin che dise 'Bivime, bivime', che 'l salta intel mogiuolo, vin puorpio da resuscitare i muorti amalè che chi haesse cento ferì el no ge farae male. Vin da far pair prie. On nascelo sto vin? Mo sul Pavan. Pavan an? Mo no ge nasce po de tutta fatta legume del mondo? De fava non favelare, che 'l no se pò far che no seg'in magne quatro scuelle ala fila chi scomenza. Pezuoli po? Fasuoli — Mare Biata — che chiama verze imbragè da mille mii. Mo cesere mo? Mo lente? Bisi mo? Panizo mo? Mo biave po? Cum è megio, sorgo, spelta, segala, orzo, scandela, vena e vezza. Mo herbame mo? verze, verzuoti, capuci, herbette, latuge, parasimboli e radichio. Mo ceole? Scalogne? Agio e puori? Farae magnar a un mezo morto. E cogombari? Zuche? Molon? Ravi? Ravanegi? Pastenagie? E carote? Mo furti po? Mo de furti no favellare. Pumi musiti. Pumi ruzene. Pumi piola. Pumi calaman. Pumi dolzani. Pumi russi. Pumi burti e buoni. Pumi cielà che è bianchi e russi com è un velù de sea. Po piri quanti? Piri ranci. Piri moscatiegi. Piri zuchuoli. Piri da San Piero. Piri invernicè. Piri strangola preve. Mo nose e nosele. Mo che besogna dire? Inchinamentre mé le ciese e i spini in sto paese fa furto. Le roe fa more e i spini nigri fa brombiuoli e i bianchi sbrogiaculi che è pur an egi furti e buoni per i boaruoli. Mo sì che in ti fossè no ge ven utilitè? No zà, mosche, i vo' essere per niente igi? Sì, i no sa far dele scardole che sotto le bronce roste a g'in magnerae i muorti. E i no sa fare an dele rane? Che in gresta se g'in porae dar a un papa. Che a pensanto com le è buone el se me desconisse el cuore che a no posso far ch'a no spue. E on è sti fossè? E on è ste rane? Mo sul Pavan.

7) Pavan an? | [123ᵛ] Mo de erbore po? Po mo no favellare. Fo vezù mo mé i pì biegi polari? I pì bie' salgari? I pì bie' rovere? Ulmi? Upij? Frasene? E carpene? Mo de bestiame po? On è i pì bie' buò? Vache? Mo chi cancaro è mo quel cancaro sì poveron che non habia una bella vacha in cha? Mo piegore? E castron? Ge n'è mo? Poh mo no favelare. Mo cavagi? E cavale? Mo puorci e scroe? Mo cavere e Bichi? Cancaro el ge n'è de grandi e — dige — sì biegi com supia al mondo. E de la megior nagia e maore del

mondo. Mo asene e asenon grande? Poh mo che vuogio pì stare a frapare de tanta altra fatta de anemale? In conlusion a cherzo verasiamen che quando Domenedio fè el deslubio e che l'arsunè in l'archa de Loe de tutte le biestie del roverso mondo e com el descargè l'archa e che le cavè fuora el cavè tutto el bistiame chi in sul Pavan.

8) Pavan an? Mo favelom mo de le femene, che è megio cha biestie. Per certo el g'è pur de bele femene comenzanto de sotto in su e da i piè. Pota mo — che bie' piazon largi e frimi! Guarda che le zope o i scataron, andagando com le va descolze, ge fazza male. Sì in lo culo! El vo ben essere scataron che non se intuorza o zopa che no se sfregole. E po quelle belle gambe grosse con quel lachetto passù che persenari — a dige dal lò grosso — ge perderae. E quelle cossonace! Havìu mé vezù, la vostra Selincia, qui biegi fusti o ramonaci de nogare, de quigi che ha la scorza vitia, gualiva, fricia da morbezo, che è grossa come un atraverso, che tra cossì al bianco? Mo ben cussì è le suo' cossonace e cussì dure intel picegare. Ma[4] po pì in su — quelle suo' belle nege bianche e reonde precisamen com è un porco ben grasso quando l'è pelò da fresco. Che com tu le vi, te no te può tegnire de no ge dare, da amore, a man averta — cussì — una schiapeza. Mo quello ch'è po da l'altro lò dananzo, in fra le gambe, un somesso in su, quello che pensantose me se desconisse el cuore, e per rebelincia de la vostra Spetabilità, che è pure sì com preve, a no 'l vuogio dire — a dige mo quello che me tira el cuore de dire. Sì ben l'è quello don fina vu vignanto al mondo el basessi. Lagonte[5] pure stare, che la n'è troppo segura a favelarne, che an l'homo se porae incordare com fa i cavagi. E po quella panza reonda, panza puorpio da portare tri puti in tun portò, cum quelle tetonace che te ge porissi ascondere el cao in migola mezo. Mo tette? Verasiamen da bregola da latte, cum quelle spalace da portar ogno gran carga, che dise, 'Cargame s'tu me se cargare, che a porterè o in spala o da saco o in bigolon'. Cum quelle brace e quelle man, pruoprio brace da faiga e man da baìle che non se stracarae a cargare cento barele al dì. Cum quel voltonazo reondo vorio,[6] bianco e rosso, che ge perderae fette de

---

[4] An 'M' is clearly legible, see also *Teatro*; compare VR 36, VR 1636 Va.

[5] The 't' appears to have been corrected by the copyist from an original 'l', compare *Teatro* 'Lagonte' and VR 36, 1636 'Lagonlo'.

[6] Compare VR 36, 1636 'norio' (='nutrito', nourished); possibly misunderstood by copyist as 'vorio' (='avorio', ivory), as in the Petrarchan tradition.

persutto inverzelò. O ravi de qui bianchi e russi quando giè ben lavè. E po qui vogi de sole in razè che tra de ponta che paserae le muragie de Pava e gi anchuzene. Christo da Loreto, mo giè pur biegi. Le è pur a bel fatto tutte belle le nostre femene. E on nascele ste belle femene? Mo in sul Pavan.

9) Pavan an? Po mo no favelare mo | [124^r] del Pavan. In colusion a cherzo verasiamen che 'l supia el paraiso terestro e tanto pì bello e megiore chom che là su no se magna e chialò sì. Spetabele messiere lo sgardenale, saviu zo che vol dire Pavan? Tanto vol dire Pavan, com dire, 'Va al pan': senza pan non se po vivere e chi vol vivere vage al pan, e chi vol pan vage in sul Pavan. Pavan an? L'andarae male se no ge foesse pan, e pezo se 'l no ge foesse el Pavan. Pavan an: e sti cogombari de sti sletran vol favelare per gramego o in fiorentinescho, e va cercanto megior pan cha de fromento. E perzondena a i lagerè bagiare a so muò e sì a favelerè a le nostre devise che è le pì belle del mondo, da bon Pavan.

10) La vostra selentia, spaternitè, Magnefecintia e Serenitè Lostrissima, piasantove mo a vu — cho a dige — me ascolterà mo mi e mi a dirè piasantove a vu. Nè gnian guardé che a vuogia stare a frappare nè a dire nè a sbagiafare de la vostra schiata zenia e raration[7] com ha fatto quegi sletran da Pava in le suo' rengaure, che tante i ve n'ha fatte che, se die m'ai', a dové essere bell'e stufò. E, com disse questù, le ve de' essere cazù dal culo perché, com a sai, con tanto laldarve i ve disea contra perqué i dise che a si de schiata vegnù de Romagnolaria da Roma. A la fe i ve ha dò un bel laldo. Mo no g'è gnian la pezor zenia de romagnaruoli. Mo no ègi sbrisigiegi? O politani da Robin? Da igi a spagnaruoli el g'è puocha deferintia. Mo no gi haonte provè in ste guerre e muzarole? No fo mé romagnaruolo che haesse fe nè lianza. Mo no ègi tucti a bel fatto biastemaore? A fagi de Dio e de sancti com se gi haesse fatti con un cortelazo. A ge tragegi el cancaro com si 'l traesse in tun salgaro. Coppe fiorin: te par mo che i v'ha dò un bel laldo? A dige mo mi, ch'a no son sletran com gi è igi, che a si da le Veniesie, vinitian d'i buoni e d'i maore.

11) Mo chi cancaro no sa che cha Cornaro è la maor cha del mondo? Mo no ge n'è per tutto? A la fe, no trognando, cusì com no g'è megior legno al mondo del cornaro, a dige, pì tegnente,

---

[7] The preceding three words are run together as one.

pì fremo e che dure pì. Cossì è cha cornaro la pì frema e che se mantegne pì cha tutte le altre. Cherzi che 'l se po ben dire che cha Cornaro sipia de Cornaro frema. Mo di che se face una bona chaegia se la no è de Cornaro? Nè na bona gugia? Mo dente da molin? Sì, se masenerae doman s'i dente da molin no foesse de Cornaro. Mo si no foesse cha Cornaro che è adesso parona del Pavan, com stassom nu? Che haom speranza che n'aiè. Basta che si da cha cornaro e de la terra che è parona del Pavan e de Pava: n'è 'l mo assé? Pucela mo d'agio questa? El no g'è zà altra terra al mondo che supia parona del Pavan? Roma de Romagnolaria no zà. Spagna de spagnaria no zà. Franza de franzosaria no zà. Robin no zà. Colecuta no zà. Terra Thoesca no zà. Siché, bon Segnore massier lo sgardenale, a si vu de la terra che è le Veniesie parona de Pava e del Pavan, che 'l no ge n'è zà de tante neguna altra. E igi dise che si da Roma romagnaruolo, cancaro i brege.

12) Mo a me fagi ben po quaso cagare da riso quando che i dise che a si grande homo. Mo no ve veegi, morbo i magne? A si vu ben pizolo homo. I no 'l sa dire. A si un gran pizolo e no grand'homo. Haì ben | [124ᵛ] una gra cosa per pizolo che a si, che i no 'l sa dire. Mo a 'l dirè ben mi. Haì per certo un gran cuore, per quello che a he intendù. Mo dime un puo' per la vostra chara fe, e da frelo, che a no ve tegno — se die m'aj' — gnian altramen. Chi cancharo sarae quel cancaro de quelù che foesse a cavalo e che 'l veesse un cengiaro abavò che ge vegnisse in contra che non se tolesse da un lò e muzare? Mi inchina da mo a me torae via, e se foesse a pè che a no poesse muzare, a me roegerae su un erbore. E vu, massier lo bon segnore, a desmonté zó da cavallo e sì l'andé pure tal botta a frontare, a dige, da pordhomo e sì l'amacé. Te parse mo che questa se tegne al baìle? No fé, a la fe: la no è troppo segura — la ve porae an butar male. E com a fosse morto vu, a sarissi deruinò del mondo. E si haesse schappà su quella bromba, che vosseu mo pì fare de cingiari nè de vescovè? Mi, cussì pover'hom co a son, a no torae de esser morto e essere stò papa. Che papa, la merda — perdoneme. An po a dige che a no torae de essere Segnore del roerso mondo. A ve vuogio dare a la vostra rebelintia un consegio che quigi sletran da Pava no ve l'harà sapù dare. Ampò egi sentio an mi con el me paron assé de le suo' rengaure che i ve ha fatto? Mo ligevelo al deo, che l'è de importantia. Che l'è megio vivere poltron cha morire valenthomo. Siché no guardé al vostro gran cuore, e com un cengiaro ve ven

incontro andé da un altro lò.

13) Havìu[8] imparò — disìme da compagno reale — in le so rengarij anchora mé tanto? Se die m'ai' no, ch'a cherza. Poh, a ge insegnerae a igi tal ponto che Stotene nè Sinica no se 'l pensé mé. I sa se lomé dire che a si sgardenale e che a dir sgardenale el ven a dire quegi che ten su le porte del paraiso, che nu ai chiamon canchari. E se gi a mé vezù igi paraiso, nè le porte, nè quigi che i dise cha a si vu che le ten su che se chiama canchari, a vorae che 'l cancharo me magnasse mi e se i no l'ha vezù, a vorae che 'l cancharo i magnasse igi. De', cancharo i magne, matti, a dasché i vuo' che vu a sie el cancharo. A si sgardenale e no el cancharo, che haessegi cavò giuogi. A staesse fresco se a foesse cho i dise igi. A si sgardenale cho a ve dirè mi. E com a ve slainerè, i doerae pur cognoscerve al capeleto rosso, e a tante intrè. *Proficiata vobesse domine*: posseu an essere papa e che a desson tutti vegnir a veerve a Roma in gatolom con una morise al collo da chan. Sgardenale, an? De', morbo ai sletran. Saivu zo che ven a dire Sgardenale al nostro muò Pavan? Mo a ve 'l dirè. Tanto ven a dire Sgardenale, com a dirè, un gran segnore richo che se dà a sto mondo piasere. E com el muore (perqué tutti a moron), se ben vu a no haì fatto massa ben, Tamentre andé de longo in paraiso. E se la porta è passà, ala sgardené e intrè entro per ogna via e per ogno buso. E quello ven a dire sgardenale — che sgardena, e no Un cancharo che ten su l'usso, che cancharo i magne igi e le so letre, matti spertegè. N'è la mo cussì? Mo ben, viu mo s'a la intendo pì de igi? Sgardenale an? L'è pur bella cosa esserge. Inchina damò, se die m'ai', che mi a torae a no magnare mé pan de fromento e esserge. A sarae puorpio cho a si vu, a sasse me compagno e mi vostro. Gnian mi no farae mé mosine de dinari in le muragie chom ha fatto tal sgardenale che è stà zà chive | [125ʳ] in sul Pavan. Che no harae cuore de spendergi? Gin foesse pure, n'è vero? Com ben ai spendesson! Nè a[9] no cherzo mé che a i decipesson in pri de statoe intagè nè in quelle parpagiuole che ha quelle fegure su, che se chiama merdolagie. Almanco se spendessele com se fa la monea. Do',

---

[8] Although the form *-ivu* is more common for the second person plural with postcliticized subject pronoun (compare 'saivu' below in this paragraph), the form here appears to be the rarer but also attested *-viu* (there is no jot over the first upright and compare *Teatro*), although overwriting from the loop of the *g* of 'cengiaro' makes this difficult to discern.

[9] MS an.

cancharo ale Merdolagie. E al agio e ale ceole. El m'è deviso che 'l supia un favelare cun muorti, a favelare de quij bordiegi. A no torae inchindamo de essere stampò e essere stò Rolando e no ge essere pì se lo mé in stampa. Se die m'ai' che chi de elle ha piasere no la intende a haver piasere de muortj. Muorti cum muorti e vivi con vivi.

14) L'è pur na bella cosa e un bel piasere vivo e snaturale,[10] a sentir borire a un bracho a chazar fuora una salvesina de un machion, e ti veerla e lassarge el to levriero drio e ella muzanto, ti forte corere don la va, e ti criare e dire, 'Ah poltron, ah traitore, ah ribaldo, ah poltron, pigiala!'. E veere che 'l to chan la pige e ti azonzerge adosso e rivarla d'amazare e basar el to chan e alzarlo per tornarge le buele al so luogo. E po chiamar i compagni e dire, 'L'è morto, l'è morto!' quanto se po mé de ose. E sonar el corno fazanto alegreza, merdolagie m'in culo. E po arivare i compagni e dirge chom la è andà, e vu a dire haver vezù el tutto e che el bracho l'a borì ben. E che te ge 'l lassiessi cum rason e che l'è bon levriero quel to, e che ti ge fussi presto azonzerge adosso e che te si bon cazaore. E ti dire, 'G'in foesse pure de gi anemale, s'i foesse ben lion!'. Te te sinti frelo che la camisa no te tocca el culo, che 'l t'è deviso d'haverlo in t'un cain de late nomé monto. Te tre un salto. Te te frigoli le man. Te guardi el can e Te vi' che gialtri dise, 'L'è stò quello'. Te guardi po l'anemale che è d'i vegi. È mo questo un piaser vivo? E no le merdolagie, che no è buone da spendere.

15) Horbentena chi la intende e chi no la intende. A se che vu, bonsegnore, la intendì, la vostra spaternitè. E sì a se che andè per charezà. Cherzime a mi, a la fe, che haì gran celibrio e che a si un gran pizolo homo da ben, e se 'l foesse altramen a ve 'l dirae mi. Perqué? Que me fa a mi? Intendìu? E[11] no se dire selomé com la è, intendìu? A si an slibrale bon compagno marigare. A no si gnan de sti perviosi, de sti stinè spisemusi che no se sa mé de que vuogia i supia. Intendìu? De sti altieri che vo stare sempre de sora de tutti e sottomitare tutti, che i no chre che ge supia altri al mondo. A la fe che a me piasí e per questo a ve vuoge de bon ben, a dige sì com da frelo. Andé pur drio per sta charezà com a fé, la vostra rebelincia e magnificintia. E governé pur ben le vostre piegore, che

---

[10] Compare *Teatro* 'naturale' but a prefixed 's' is clearly visible.

[11] Clearly 'E' but compare *Teatro*, VR 36, 1636 'A'.

a seom nu del Pavan. Perqué a si nostro pegoraro e pastore e nostro visio[12] de papa, che haì luberté, com disse Jesum Dio, de fare e desfare. E, in colusion, de volzere le torte a vostro muò. E perzontena nu poveriti a v'haom[13] desirò pì cha non fè mé cavalla magra, secha, e rostìa l'erba nuova. E haom fatto per visinanza che mi a son vegnù per lome de tutti a alegrarme de la vostra vegnua. Tochéme la man, che a supie el ben vegnù e 'l ben trovò. A vogion che a ne face no se que leze e stratuti nuovi, che è ben de rason. Madequidem, in bona fe, sì.

16) La prima: che agno chazaore o oselaore che va per piasere e no per guagno a chaza o a oselare posse andare la domenega senza aldir messa e no supia peccò perqué, com a saì, in quella hora | [125^v] l'è el bello del piasere per pì rason, e chi perde quella hora la no torna mé pì in drio.[14]

17) Le do: che negun de villa supia ubrigò a zunare perqué, com a saì, el faigare fa paire pri. E com se ha paì, chi no magna se ge desconisse el cuore e va a risego de morire e de spuare el polmon da salivo che te ven in bocca. Te ve po in leto e te no può dromire. E s'te e mogiere, per pararte la fame e farte vegnir sono, te fé quello che te no farissi, che te dromirissi. E se te n'e mogiere, gran fato che de doman te no ge'n habi una. E per no stare ocioso se fa piezo, com a saì, intendìu?

18) Le tre: che dal tempo de tagiare el fromento no supia pechò a laorare la festa. Perqué da una hora al'altra po vegnire una sfraza de tempesta e deroinarge del mondo. A biastemon po a muò cani. E chi no biastemerae? Disíme per la nostra[15] cara fe? E scoegnon po an robare se a vogiom vivere. E a sto muò a fazom du pechè e sì no haon la colpa. La è pur cussì.

19) Le quatro: che 'l se posse magnare la doman ananzo messa, per poere po pì stare cho el cuore a massier Jesum Dio, che l'è el cancharo quando se ha fame, e che se è al gesiò, l'è pur forza haver el cuore a cha al magnare. E se haron magnò, harom[16] el cuore ivelo a massier Jesum Dio e no a cha al pan.

---

[12] Possibly 'visco', as *Teatro*.

[13] A following 'pi' (perhaps an anticipation error) is crossed out; compare *Teatro* pur.

[14] A small *x*-like flourish occurs in the right margin at the end of each point.

[15] Clearly 'nostra'; compare *Teatro*, VR 36, VR 1636 vostra.

[16] Possibly 'haron', obscured by blot.

20) Le cinque: che per magniare no supia peccò de gola quando el se magna perqué el sa bon, se ben el non se ha fame, perqué i miegi dise che quel che sa bon fa bon pro. Fazanto bon pro, el fa sanitè, stagento san se vive assé, vivanto assé se ven viegi, vegnanto viegi se fa del ben. E fazanto del ben se va in paraiso. Siché el no pol essere male nè peccò, perché cussì com[17] el serae pechò[18] chi magnasse tosego sapianto che 'l fa male, cussì magnanto chosa che faza bon pro de' essere mierito, com è a magnare de bon.

21) Le sie: che a facè che agno preve possa haver mogiere o che i supia castrè, perqué l'è el cancharo la fragilitè dela carne. La dà qualche botta tanto fastubio che no se sa in che buso cazarse, e se giè ben preve giè huomenj co a seon nu e de quigi an pì maschi. E perqué i n'ha femene, i va in tanta veregagia che com i se imbatte in una dele nuostre femene ala prima botta i l'ha ingravià de fatto. E nu poveriti a fazon le spese a' suo' figiuoli, che 'l n'è zà de rason. E se i serà chastrè a no harom sta briga ale spalle. E se gi harà mogiere, i no serà sì rabiusi nè sempre sì in veregagia che ele i tignerà monzù. E se pur g'ingravierà le nostre femene, a ingravieron an nu le suo', e se nu faron le spese ai suo' puti an igi le farà ai nuostri. E sì a saron su e su.

22) Le[19] sette: perqué l'è tanto gran cancharo de nemistè e malivolintia tra nu containi dale ville e i citaini de Pava che a se magnesson del chuore e tutto el dì per questo a se tragagion. E se a foessam cussì nu de sora con giè igi, bao babao bao cope fiorin! a no ge dureravegi una hora in le man. Mo pasincia. I ge dise a nu, 'Containi, vilani, marassi, ragani'. E nu a ge digomo a igi, 'Cagariegi, Can oselari,[20] magna sangue de' poveriti'. A vosson mo, che com a ve he zà ditto a seon da lò de sotto, che conciessi ste defferincie e che a fasse che a foesson una cosa miesema. A vogion perzontena che a ne facè sta leza: Che ognohom de villa possa tuor quatro mogiere, e ogno femena de villa possa tuore quatro marì. Perqué com quegi | [126ʳ] cagariegi da Pava vega cussì — perqué i tra ale nostre femene — tutti per poer havere quatro femene se farà

---

[17] Compare *Teatro* an.

[18] Heavily overwritten.

[19] MS la.

[20] Compare *Teatro* 'osolari' but the 'e' is clearly visible; the word is smaller than surrounding text.

de villa, che 'l sta a igi a farsege. E tutte le citaine, perqué el ge sa bon, per poere haver quatro huomeni se farà de villa e nu scaperon su quelle brombette e a sto muò a sarom una cosa miesima, nè no ge sarae pì invilia nè nimistè perqué a fassom tutti un parentò e tutte le femene andarà[21] pine e se impirà la leza de massier Jesum Dio che dise, 'Cressì e smultiplichè'. Guardé che harom mé pì paura de Turchi che ne impale — sì — in lo culo. Se veerà selomé cielo e femene gravie e puti e tosati, e perqué adesso el ge n'è tal una che com un homo solo la non pò ingravearse con la n'harà quatro, gran fatto che uno no ge chate la stralecha. A no se farà gnian nessun becco e quel pecchò che no doerae esser peccò de andare dale femene d'altri, che tutti harae da fare a cha so. Saralo mo questo un bel ben an? Quante costion se fa per questo che no se farae? E quanti ven amacè che sarae vivi? Quante belle pute poverete in Pava che no ha muò da poerse mariare se marierave? Che le se va a far fichare monege inti monestieri? Tutte sfigiolerae; ge n'è mo che sta indarno che harae da fare? Che è mazor pecchò che la uciosità? E fuorsi che no ge n'è de belle? Le belle e le burte harae bon inviamento. Per un parente che se ha se 'n harae quatro, ogn'hom harae quatro fiè pì potintia da cazare i spagnaruoli e Thoischi se i tornasse mé pì in sto paese. A no fessi, se die m'ai', la pì bella leza. Che a farè la leza tutta zoile del mondo, Nè la saluoricha nì la teluoricha. Féla missier lo sgardenale, che da bio mé vu de[22] tante benesion che ve sera de. A mi que me fa a mi, intendìu? A dige mo mi per vostro megio: intendìu cho a dige? Saì perqué, intendìu? A fazo pre vu, me intendìu? Que me fa a mi, intendìu? Féla pure che a sarì adorò da nu com se a foesse un sancto. S'a no ve volesse ben, a no ve consegerae. Mo a se ben quello che a dige, che 'l serà ben pre vu. A porì dire, 'A vuo' cussì' che cussì serà. Senza mi che valessevu e sì ve tegneson tutti da pare, da figiuolo, e da frelo, che gnian altramen a no ve tegnom. Deme la man e prometime che un'altra fià a vignerè a tuore el spatafio. Die vaj'.

---

[21] MS 'andae' is clearly a copyist's error; compare *Teatro*, VR 36, 1636.

[22] Compare VR 1636 'che a vuo mai nome' (since would I ever want at least), VR 36 'che, dabiu m'ai'' (because, may bod help me).

Note on the text

The text above has been transcribed from BMV Ital. XI 66; it begins on fol. 122^v (which bears the erroneous modern numeration 123 in pencil) and concludes on fol. 126^r. Erosion at the top of the sheet has rendered the title virtually illegible; that given here depends upon the Zorzi edition. Numerous corrections are evident, as is the case with the other Beolco works in XI 66. The corrections appear to be in the same hand as the main text, but are so small as to render difficult or even impossible a definitive assessment. The corrections are here listed by paragraph, with the underlying form if visible in parentheses, interlinear additions between single slashes, and marginal additions between double slashes: par. 1 *bichi* (*bechi*), *no* (*non*); par. 2 *inchindamo* (*inchinadamo*), *staxamo* (*stasamo?*), *ala* (*ala alu*); par. 3 *nuostri* (*nustri*), *femena* (*femina?*), //*altro*//, *madasché* (*modasche?*); par. 4 *Poh* (*Po*), //*favelom*// (compare Zorzi *favelè*); par. 5 /*mezi*/; par. 6 *vena e* (*vena*), *Farae* (*Farae i*), *buoni* (*boni*), *niente* (illeg.); par. 7 *vezù mo* (*vezù me?*), *Mo asene* (*Mo i asene*), *l'archa e che* (*l'archa e* illeg.); par. 8 *cuore* (*cuor?*), *Lagonte* (*Lagonle*; compare VR. 36 and VR 1636 *Lagonlo*), *inverzelo* (*inverzeloo*), *bel fatto* (*bel fatto belle*); par. 9 *se po* (*se po magnare*), *vivere* (*vivere* illeg.); par. 10 *ha fatto* (*ha fatto egi*); par. 11 *dire* /*che*/; par. 12 *a no* (*a* illeg.) ; par. 13 *ogna* (illeg.; compare Zorzi *ogne*, VR 36, VR 1636 *ogni*), *puorpio* (*purpio*), //*chive*// (compare Zorzi *chi*, VR 36 *chive*, VR 1636 *chive a Pava*), *haver* (*havere*); par. 14 *a sentir* (*a sentir a*), *m'in* (*me'n?*); par. 15 *chareza* (*careza*); *fe che* /*a*/, *v'haom* (*v'haom pi?*), *stratuti* (*stratutti*); par. 16 *o a oselare* (*xaselare*); par. 19 *E se* (illeg. *se*), *harom* (*haron?*); par. 20 *pecho* (illeg.); par. 21 *sera* /*chastre*/; par. 22 *malivolintia* (*malivolencia*); *com a* /*ve*/, *tuore* (blotted final vowel), *nostr*/*e*/, *Perque* (*perche*), *tosati* /*e*/, *benesion* (*beniesiom?*).

Bibliography

Primary Sources

Archival Sources

Padua, ASP, *Estimo 1518*

Padua, ASP, Archivio Notarile

Padua, Archivio della Curia Vescovile, *Acta Capitularia*

Venice, ASV, Archivio Grimani Santa Maria Formosa

Venice, ASV, Senato, *Secreta*

Manuscript Sources

Brno, Státní Oblastní Archiv, Collalto Archive, Rambaldo, Antonio, Conti di Collalto, *Genealogia Rectae, imperturbataeque Lineae Excellentissimi Principis Antonij Rambaldi Collalti Comitis Collalti Comitis ab anno aesti 930 usque ad annum 1729 Sive a Rambaldo primo usque ad Vinciguerram Sextum Antonij Rambaldi filium Primogenitum*

Padua, BCP, C.M. 894, *Albero genealogico della Nobile Veneta Famiglia dei Mocenigo dall'anno 1195 all'anno 1773*

Padua, BCP, B.P. 55, Buzzacarini, G.F., *Storia d'Italia dal 1463 al 1520*

Padua, BCP, B.P. 3159, da Corte (Cortivo), Zuan Antonio, *Historia di Padova, 1509-1530 (Diario degli avvenimenti padovani dal 13 giugno 1509 al 12 ottobre 1529)*

Padua, BCP, B.P. 143, Dorighello, Francesco, *Notizie storiche delli collegii d'artisti e medici in Padova*

Padua, BCP, B.P. 801 V, Lazara, Giovanni, ed., *Memorie di famiglie nobili di Padova descritte nel Collegio dell'arte della lana e di famiglie nobili applicate all'esercizio di banchiere e cambista, raccolte dal c. Giovanni Lazara*

Venice, ASV, Marco Barbaro, *Origini e discendenze delle famiglie patrizie* (holograph copy)

Printed Sources

Ariosto, Ludovico, *Commedie*, ed. by Angela Casella, Gabriella Ronchi, and Elena Varasi, Vol. IV of *Tutte le opere*, ed. by Cesare Segre (Milan: Mondadori, 1974)

——, *Orlando furioso: secondo la princeps del 1516*, ed. Marco Dorigatti (Florence: Olschki, 2006)

Bembo, Pietro, *Della Historia vinitiana di M. Pietro Bembo Card. Volgarmente scritt: Libri XII* (Venice: Gualtero Scotto, 1552)

——, *Lettere*, ed. by Ernesto Travi, Collezione di opere inedite o rare 143, 4 vols (Bologna: Commissione per i testi di lingua, 1987-93)

Beolco, Angelo Il Ruzante, *La Pastoral, la Prima Oratione, Una lettera giocosa*, ed. and trans. by Giorgio Padoan (Padua: Antenore, 1978)

——, *Teatro*, ed. and trans. by Ludovico Zorzi (Turin: Einaudi, 1967)

Berni, Francesco, *Opere*, ed. by Eugenio Camerini, 2nd edn (Milan: Sonzogno, 1874)

Giustinian, Sebastian, *Four Years at the Court of Henry VIII: Selection of Despatches Written by the Venetian Ambassador, Sebastian Giustinian, and Addressed to the Signory of Venice, January 12th 1515, to July 26th 1519*, ed. and trans. by Rawdon Brown, 2 vols (London: Smith, Elder and Co., 1854; reprint New York: AMS, 1970)

Mantuanus, Baptista, *The Eclogues of Baptista Mantuanus*, ed. by Wilfred P. Mustard (Baltimore: Johns Hopkins University Press, 1911)

[Michiel, Marcantonio], *The Anonimo: Notes on Pictures and Works of Art in Italy Made by an Anonymous Writer in the Sixteenth Century*, ed. by George C. Williamson, trans. by Paolo Mussi (London: Bell and Sons, 1903)

Sanuto, Marino (Sanudo, Marin), *I diarii*, ed. by Rinaldo Fulin and others, 58 vols (Venice: Visentini, 1879-1902)

Speroni, Sperone, *Apologia dei Dialoghi*, in *Opere di M. Sperone Speroni degli Alvarotti tratte da' mss. originali*, 5 vols (Venice: Domenico Occhi, 1740)

Secondary Sources

Ballarin, Alessandro, 'L'Évêque Jacopo Pesaro présenté à saint Pierre par le pape Alexandre VI', cat. no. 40, in *Le siècle de Titien: L'âge d'or de la peinture à Venise*, exhibition at the Grand Palais (Paris: Éditions de la Réunion des musées nationaux, 1993), pp. 316-23

Baratto, Mario, 'L'esordio del Ruzante', in *Tre studi sul teatro* (Vicenza: Neri Pozza, 1968), pp. 11-68

Battaglia, Salvatore, Giorgio Bàrberi Squarotti, and others, *Grande dizionario della lingua italiana*, 21 vols (Turin: UTET, 1961-2003)

Beltrami, Daniele, *La penetrazione economica veneziana in terraferma: Forze di lavoro e proprietà fondiaria* (Venice and Rome: Istituto per la collaborazione culturale, 1961)

Berthold, Peter, *Bird Migration: A General Survey*, trans. by Hans-Günther Bauer and Tricia Tomlinson (Oxford: Oxford University Press, 1993)

Biadego, Giuseppe, *Catalogo descrittivo dei manoscritti della Biblioteca Comunale di Verona* (Verona: Civelli, 1892)

——, 'Notizie', in Ludovico Corfino, *Istoria di Phileto veronese*, ed. by G. Biadego (Livorno: Giusti, 1899), pp. ix-xx

Bonardi, Antonio, 'I padovani ribelli alla repubblica di Venezia (a. 1509-1530), studio storico con appendice di documenti inediti', *Miscellanea di storia veneta a cura della Deputazione veneta di storia patria*, 2nd ser., 8 (1902), 303-612

Borsellino, Nino, 'La datazione dell'*Anconitana*', in *Rozzi e Intronati: Esperienze e forme di teatro dal 'Decameron' al 'Candelaio'*, 2nd edn (Rome: Bulzoni, 1976), pp. 163-75

Boschi, Ruggiero, 'L'architettura della villa nel Veneto del Cinquecento', in Pegorari, pp. 169-92

Briquet, C.M., *Les filigranes: Dictionnaire historique des marques du papier dès leur apparition vers 1282 jusqu'en 1600, avec 39 figures dans le texte et 16,112 facsimiles de filigrane*, 4 vols (Paris: Picard; Geneva: Julien, 1907)

Brown, Patricia Fortini, *Venice and Antiquity: The Venetian Sense of the Past* (New Haven: Yale University Press, 1996)

Burgkmair, Hans, and others, *The Triumph of Maximilian I*, trans. and ed. by Stanley Appelbaum (New York: Dover, 1964)

Calendoli, Giovanni, *Ruzante* (Venice: Corbo e Fiore, 1985)

Calore, Andrea, 'Giovanni Foscari, un amico veneziano di Angelo Beolco', in *III Convegno Internazionale di Studi sul Ruzante*, ed. by Giovanni Calendoli (Padua: Società Cooperativa Tipografica, 1993), pp. 21-27

Carroll, Linda L., 'Dating *The Woman from Ancona*: Venice and Ruzante's Theater after Cambrai', *Sixteenth Century Journal*, 31 (2000), 963-85

——, '"Fools of the Dukes of Ferrara"': Dosso, Ruzante, and Changing Este Alliances', *MLN*, 18 (2003), 60-84

——, '"I have a good set of tools": The Shared Interests of Peasants and Patricians in Beolco's *Lettera giocosa*', *Theatre, Opera and Performance in Italy from the Fifteenth Century to the Present: Essays in Honour of Richard Andrews*, ed. by Brian

Richardson, Simon Gilson, and Catherine Keen, Occasional Papers 6 (Egham: Society for Italian Studies, 2004), pp. 83-98

———, *Language and Dialect in Ruzante and Goldoni* (Ravenna: Longo, 1981)

———, 'Linguistic Correlates of Emotion in Ruzante', *The Eleventh LACUS Forum 1984*, ed. by Robert A. Hall, Jr. (Columbia, South Carolina: Hornbeam Press, 1985), pp. 377-91

———, 'A Newly-Discovered *Charles V with Dog*', *Ateneo Veneto*, 3rd ser., 4 (2005), 43-77

———, 'A Nontheistic Paradise in Renaissance Padua', *Sixteenth Century Journal*, 34 (1993), 881-98

———, 'The Peasant as Imperialist: An Unpublished *Canzone* in Ruzantine Style', *Italica*, 70 (1993), 197-211

———, 'Ruzante's Early Adaptations from More and Erasmus', *Italica*, 66 (1989), 29-34

———, 'The Shepherd Meets the Cowherd: Ruzante's *Pastoral*, the Empire and Venice', *Annuario dell'Istituto Romeno di Cultura e Ricerca Umanistica*, 4 (2002), 288-97

———, 'Venetian Attitudes toward the Young Charles: Carnival, Commerce, and *Compagnie della Calza*', in *Young Charles V 1500-1531*, ed. by Alain Saint-Saëns (New Orleans: University Press of the South, 2000), pp. 13-52

Casella, Angela, Gabriella Ronchi, and Elena Varasi, 'Presentazione', in Ariosto, *Commedie*, pp. ix-xlix

Cattini, Marco, 'L'agricoltura nella piana bresciana al tempo del Gallo: strutture fondiali, forme di conduzione e tecniche colturali', in Pegorari, pp. 25-43

Cestaro, Benvenuto, 'Il canonicato padovano di Messer Pietro Bembo', *Atti e memorie della R.e Accademia di Scienze, Lettere, ed Arti in Padova*, 45 (1929), 1-30

Colussi, Giorgio, *Glossario degli antichi volgari italiani* (Helsinki: G. Colussi, 1982-)

Concina, Ennio, *La macchina territoriale: La progettazone della difesa nel Cinquecento veneto* (Bari: Laterza, 1983)

Cozzi, Gaetano, 'Stato e chiesa: vicende di un confronto secolare', in G. Cozzi and others, *Venezia e la Roma dei papi* (Milan: Electa, 1987)

——, and Michael Knapton, *Storia della Repubblica di Venezia dalla Guerra di Chioggia alla Riconquista della terraferma* (Turin: UTET, 1986)

Cristofari, Maria, *Il Codice Marciano It. XI, 66* (Padua: CEDAM, 1937)

Cruciani, Fabrizio, *Il Teatro del Campidoglio e le feste romane del 1513* (Milan: Polifilo, 1968)

Cummings, Anthony M., *The Maecenas and the Madrigalist: Patrons, Patronage, and the Origins of the Italian Madrigal* (Philadelphia: American Philosophical Society, 2004)

——, 'Music and Theatre in Leo X's Rome', in *'Uno gentile et subtile ingenio': Studies in Renaissance Music in Honour of Bonnie Blackburn*, ed. by M. Jennifer Bloxam and Gioia Filocamo, in collaboration with Herbert Kellman and Leofranc Holford-Strevens (Turnhout: Brepols, Centre d'Études Supérieures de la Renaissance, 2008)

Dandelet, Thomas James, *Spanish Rome, 1500-1700* (New Haven: Yale University Press, 2001)

D'Elia, Anthony, *The Renaissance of Marriage in the Fifteenth Century* (Cambridge: Harvard University Press, 2004)

del Torre, Giuseppe, *Venezia e la terraferma dopo la guerra di Cambrai: Fiscalità e amministrazione (1515-1530)* (Milan: Franco Angeli, 1986)

Del Vita, Alessandro, *L'Aretino: 'Uomo libero per grazia di Dio'* (Arezzo: Edizioni Rinascimento, 1954)

De Ventura, Paolo, 'Il prologo-"sprolico" di Ruzante: un passe-par-tout per il "roesso mondo"', *Studi medievali e moderni*, 1 (2003), 151-70

Di Maria, Salvatore, 'Blame-by-praise Irony in the *Ecatommiti* of Giraldi Cinzio', *Quaderni d'Italianistica*, 6 (1985), 178-92

Dionisotti, Carlo, 'La testimonianza del Brucioli', in *Machiavellerie*, Einaudi paperbacks 113 (Turin: Einaudi, 1980), pp. 193-226

Dizionario biografico degli italiani, directed by Alberto Ghisalberti (Rome: Istituto dell'Enciclopedia Italiana, 1960-)

Dondi Dall'Orologio, Francesco Scipione, *Dissertazioni sopra l'istoria ecclesiastica padovana*, 9 vols (Padua: Stamperia del Seminario, 1802-17)

—————, *Serie cronologico-istorica dei canonici di Padova* (Padova: Nella Stamperia del Seminario, 1805)

Dykema, Peter A., and Heiko Oberman, eds, *Anticlericalism in Late Medieval and Early Modern Europe* (Leiden: Brill, 1993)

Earle, Peter, 'The Commercial Development of Ancona, 1479-1551', *Economic History Review*, 2nd ser., 22 (1969), 28-44

Edlin, Herbert, *The Tree Key* (New York: Charles Scribner's Sons, 1978)

Fasullo, Franco, 'Livelli e livellari del monastero di Praglia tra '400 e '500: Primi risultati di una ricerca', in *S. Benedetto e otto secoli (XII-XIX) di vita monastica nel padovano* (Padua: Antenore, 1980), pp. 113-49

Favaretto, Lorena, *L'istituzione informale: Il Territorio padovano dal Quattrocento al Cinquecento* (Milan: Unicopli, 1998)

——, 'La richiesta di uguaglianza tra città e contado nell'opera di Ruzante: La storia e la rappresentazione teatrale', in Schiavon, pp. 43-68

Ferguson, Ronnie, *The Theatre of Angelo Beolco (Ruzante). Text, Context, and Performance* (Ravenna: Longo, 2000)

Ferrari, Ciro, 'I pascoli di Pozzo Moretto', *Archivio Veneto-Tridentino*, 3 (1923), 142-68

Ferrari, G., 'La legislazione veneziana sui beni comunali', *Nuovo Archivio Veneto*, 36 (1918), 5-64

Ferroni, Giulio, *Il testo e la scena* (Rome: Bulzoni, 1980)

Finlay, Robert, *Politics in Renaissance Venice* (New Brunswick: Rutgers University Press, 1980)

——, 'Crisis and Crusade in the Mediterranean: Venice, Portugal, and the Cape Route to India (1498-1509)', *Studi Veneziani*, n.s. 28 (1994), 45-90

——, 'Fabius Maximus in Venice: Doge Andrea Gritti, the War of Cambrai, and the Rise of Habsburg Hegemony, 1509-1530', *Renaissance Quarterly*, 53 (2000), 988-1031

Freedman, Paul, *Images of the Medieval Peasant* (Stanford: Stanford University Press, 1999)

Giannetto, Nella, *Bernardo Bembo umanista e politico veneziano*, Civiltà veneziana, Saggi 34 (Florence: Olschki, 1985)

Gibbons, Felton, *Dosso and Battista Dossi: Court Painters at Ferrara* (Princeton: Princeton University Press, 1968)

Gilbert, Felix, *The Pope, His Banker, and Venice* (Cambridge: Harvard University Press, 1980)

Gloria, Andrea, *Il territorio padovano*, 4 vols (Padua: Prosperini, 1862)

Grafton, Anthony, 'Ah, Wilderness' [rev. of Wood], *New York Review of Books*, 41, n. 17 (1994), 46

Grubb, James S., *Firstborn of Venice: Vicenza in the Early Renaissance State* (Baltimore: Johns Hopkins University Press, 1988)

Halberstadt-Freud, H.C., 'Electra in Bondage: On Symbiosis and the Symbiotic Illusion between Mother and Daughter and the Consequences for the Oedipus Complex', *Free Associations*, 17 (1989), 58-89

Hughes, Diane Owen, 'Earrings for Circumcision: Distinction and Purification in the Italian Renaissance City', in *Persons in Groups: Social Behavior as Identity Formation in Medieval and Renaissance Europe*, ed. by Richard C. Trexler (Binghamton, N.Y.: Medieval and Renaissance Texts and Studies, 1985), pp. 155-77

Humphrey, Peter, *Lorenzo Lotto* (New Haven: Yale University Press, 1997)

Kaplan, Paul H.D., '"Io son fatta villanella": Girolama Corsi Ramos and the Anti-pastoral', *Miscellanea Marciana*, 18 (2003), 81-97

Kellenbenz, Hermann, 'La vendita del diritto castigliano sulle Molucche', in *Venezia e la Spagna* (Milan: Electa, 1988), pp. 121-42

King, Margaret L., *Venetian Humanism in an Age of Patrician Dominance* (Princeton: Princeton University Press, 1986)

Klaniczay, Tibor, *La crisi del Rinascimento e il Manierismo*, trans. by Riccardo Scrivano (1970; Rome: Bulzoni, 1973)

Knecht, R.J., *Renaissance Warrior and Patron: The Reign of Francis I* (Cambridge: Cambridge University Press, 1994)

Kohl, Benjamin G., *Padua under the Carrara, 1318-1405* (Baltimore: Johns Hopkins University Press, 1998)

Labalme, Patricia H., and Laura Sanguineti White, eds, trans. by Linda L. Carroll, *Venice, Città Excelentissima: Selections from the Renaissance Diaries of Marin Sanudo* (Baltimore: Johns Hopkins University Press, 2008)

Lane, Frederic C., 'The Funded Debt of the Venetian Republic, 1262-1482', in *Venice and History*, pp. 87-98

———, 'News on the Rialto', in *Studies in Venetian Social and Economic History*, ed. by Benjamin G. Kohl and Reinhold C. Mueller (London: Variorum, 1987), pp. 1-8

———, 'Venetian Bankers, 1496-1533', in *Venice and History*, pp. 69-86

———, 'Venetian Shipping during the Commercial Revolution', in *Venice and History*, pp. 3-24

———, *Venice. A Maritime Republic* (Johns Hopkins University Press, 1973)

———, *Venice and History* (Baltimore: Johns Hopkins University Press, 1966)

Laurenza, Domenico, *De Figura Umana: Fisiognomica, anatomia e arte in Leonardo* (Florence: Olschki, 2001)

Lawner, Lynne, 'Introduction', in Giulio Romano, Marcantonio Raimondi, Pietro Aretino, and Count Jean-Frederic-Maximilien de Waldeck, *I Modi: The Sixteen Pleasures: An Erotic Album of the Italian Renaissance*, edited, translated from the Italian, and with a commentary by Lynne Lawner (Evanston, IL: Northwestern University Press, 1988), 1-56

Lazzarini, Vittorio, 'Beni carraresi e proprietari veneziani', in *Studi in onore di Gino Luzzatto*, 2 vols (Milan: Giuffrè, 1949), I, 274-88

———, 'L'industria della carta nel padovano durante la dominazione carrarese', in *Scritti di paleografia e diplomatica* (Venice: Ferrari, 1938), pp. 47-61

―――, 'Possessi e feudi veneziani nel Ferrarese', in *Miscellanea in onore di Roberto Cessi*, 2 vols (Rome: Edizioni di storia e letteratura, 1958), I, 213-232

Lewis, Carolyn Kolb, *The Villa Giustinian at Roncade* (New York and London: Garland, 1977)

Ling, Lesley A., 'La presenza fondiaria veneziana nel padovano (secoli XIII-XIV)', *Istituzioni, società e potere nella Marca Trevigiana e Veronese: Sulle tracce di G.B. Verci*, ed. by Gherardo Ortalli and Michael Knapton (Roma: Istituto Storico Italiano per il Medio Evo, 1988), pp. 305-20

Logan, Oliver, *The Venetian Upper Clergy in the 16th and Early 17th Centuries: A Study in Religious Culture* (Lewiston, NY: Edwin Mellen Press, 1996)

Looney, Dennis, rev. of Ariosto, *Orlando furioso: secondo la princeps*, *Renaissance Quarterly*, 60 (2007), 1313-15

Lovarini, Emilio, 'Aggiunte e conclusioni sulle danze e le canzoni popolari nel Veneto', in *Studi*, pp. 200-31

―――, 'Notizie sui parenti e sulla vita del Ruzzante', in *Studi*, pp. 3-60

―――, 'Per l'edizione critica del Ruzzante', in *Studi*, pp. 109-63

―――, 'Premessa alle traduzioni', in *Studi*, pp. 355-62

―――, 'Ruzzante a Venezia', in *Studi*, pp. 81-107

―――, *Studi sul Ruzzante e la letteratura pavana*, ed. by Gianfranco Folena (Padua: Antenore, 1965)

―――, ed., *Antichi testi di letteratura pavana*, Scelta di curiosità letterarie inedite o rare, 248 (Bologna: Romagnoli Dall'Acqua, 1894)

Lowe, K.J.P., *Church and Politics in Renaissance Italy: The Life and Career of Cardinal Francesco Soderini, 1453-1524* (Cambridge: Cambridge University Press, 1993)

Mallett, M.E., 'Venezia e la politica italiana: 1454-1530', in Tenenti and Tucci, pp. 245-310

——, and J.R. Hale, *The Military Organization of a Renaissance State: Venice c. 1400 to 1617* (Cambridge: Cambridge University Press, 1984)

Mathew, K.S., *Indo-Portuguese Trade and the Fuggers of Germany* (New Delhi: Manohar, 1997)

Menegazzo, Emilio, 'Alvise Cornaro: un veneziano del Cinquecento nella terraferma padovana', in *Storia della cultura veneta*, III, *Dal primo Quattrocento al Concilio di Trento* (Vicenza: Neri Pozza, 1986), part 2, 513-38

——, 'Ricerche intorno alla vita e all'ambiente del Ruzante e di Alvise Cornaro', *Italia medioevale e umanistica*, 7 (1964), 180-220

——, 'Stato economico-sociale del Padovano all'epoca del Ruzante', in *La poesia rusticana nel Rinascimento: Atti del Convegno, Rome 10-13 October 1968*, Accademia Nazionale dei Lincei, Anno CCCLXVI-1969, Quaderno N. 129 (Rome: Accademia Nazionale dei Lincei, 1969), pp. 145-69

Molà, Luca, *The Silk Industry of Renaissance Venice* (Baltimore: Johns Hopkins University Press, 2000)

Moncallero, Giuseppe Lorenzo, *Il cardinale Bernardo Dovizi da Bibbiena umanista e diplomatico* (Florence: Olschki, 1953)

——, 'La politica di Leone X e di Francesco I nella progettata crociata contro i turchi e nella lotta per la successione imperiale', *Rinascimento*, 8 (1957), 61-109

Monga, Luigi, *'In the Very Heart of Man': The Life and Poetry of Carlo Porta* (Gainesville: University of South Florida Press; Tampa: University Presses of Florida, 1986)

Muir, Edward, *Civic Ritual in Renaissance Venice* (Princeton: Princeton University Press, 1981)

Oliveira Barata, José, 'Sulla cultura del Ruzante', *Atti dell'Istituto Veneto di Scienze, Lettere, ed Arti*, Classe di scienze morali, lettere ed arti, 131 (1972-73), 101-37

Olivieri, Achille, 'Capitale mercantile e committenza nella Venezia del Sansovino', in *Investimenti e civiltà urbana: Secoli XIII-XVIII*, ed. by Annalisa Guarducci (Florence: Le Monnier, 1991), pp. 531-69

——, *Riforma ed eresia a Vicenza nel Cinquecento* (Rome: Herder, 1992)

Paccagnella, Ivano, 'Ruzante e i testi teatrali veneti del primo Cinquecento. Alcune questioni filologiche e di metodo', in Schiavon, pp. 164-92

Padoan, Giorgio, 'Nota ai testi', in Angelo Beolco Il Ruzante, *La Pastoral, la Prima Oratione, Una lettera giocosa*, pp. 29-57

Pagels, Elaine, *Adam, Eve, and the Serpent* (New York: Vintage Books, 1988)

Pegorari, Maurizio, ed., *Agostino Gallo nella cultura del Cinquecento: Atti del Convegno, Brescia, 23-24 ottobre 1987* (Brescia: Edizioni del Moretto, 1988)

Pellegrini, Giovanni Battista, 'Postille etimologiche a voci giuridiche alto-medievali', in *Studi di dialettologia e filologia veneta* (Pisa: Pacini, 1977), pp. 273-86

Polano, Sergio ed., *L'architettura militare veneta del Cinquecento* (Milan: Electa, 1988)

Reynolds, Anne, 'Francesco Berni (1497?-1535), An Introductory Biography' and 'Giovan Matteo Giberti (1495-1543), Papal Servant and Political Strategist', in *Renaissance Humanism at the Court of Clement VII: Francesco Berni's 'Dialogue Against Poets' in Context. Studies, with an Edition and Translation by Anne Reynolds* (New York and London: Garland, 1997), pp. 35-57, 59-85

Richardson, Brian, *Print Culture in Renaissance Italy: The Editor and the Vernacular Text 1470-1600* (Cambridge: Cambridge University Press, 1994)

Rigobello, Bruno, *Lendinara Estense*, Vol. II of *Storia antica di Lendinara* (Lendinara: Tipografia lendinarese, 1977)

———, 'Modi di intervento del capitale veneziano nel polesine e l'insediamento agricolo dei Loredan, dei Corner, dei Badoer, e dei Grimani', in *Palladio e palladianesimo in Polesine* (Rovigo: Minelliana, 1984), pp. 21-35

Rodriguez-Salgado, M.J., 'Terracotta and Iron: Mantuan Politics (ca. 1450-ca. 1550)', in *La corte di Mantova nell'età di Andrea Mantegna/The Court of Mantua in the Age of Mantegna: 1450-1550: Atti del convegno (Londra, 8 marzo 1992/Mantova 28 marzo, 1992)*, ed. by Cesare Mozzarelli, Roberto Oreski, and Leandro Ventura (Rome: Bulzoni, 1997), pp. 15-59

Romei, Danilo, 'Introduzione', in Pietro Aretino, *Scritti di Pietro Aretino nel Codice Marciano It. XI 66 (=6730)*, ed. by D. Romei (Florence: Cesati, 1987), pp. 9-35

Rossi, G.B., *Flora popolare agordina* (Florence: Francolini, 1964)

Ruggiero, Guido, *The Boundaries of Eros: Sex Crime and Sexuality in Renaissance Venice* (Oxford: Oxford University Press, 1985)

Rylands, Philip, *Palma Vecchio* (Cambridge: Cambridge University Press, 1992)

Sabbatino, Pasquale, *La scienza della scrittura: dal progetto del Bembo al manuale* (Florence : Olschki, 1988)

Sambin, Paolo, 'Altre testimonianze (1525-1540) di Angelo Beolco', *Italia medioevale e umanistica*, 7 (1964), 221-47

———, 'Lazzaro e Giovanni Francesco Beolco, nonno e padre del Ruzante', *Italia medioevale e umanistica*, 7 (1964), 133-79

Scarabello, Giovanni, *Carceri e carcerati a Venezia nell'età moderna* (Rome: Istituto della Enciclopedia Italiana, 1979)

Schiavon, Chiara, ed., *'In lengua grossa, in lengua sutile': Studi su Angelo Beolco, il Ruzante* (Padua: Esedra, 2005)

Seidel Menchi, Silvana, 'Characteristics of Italian Anticlericalism', in Dykema and Oberman, pp. 271-81

Seneca, Federico, *Venezia e Papa Giulio II* (Padua: Liviana, 1962)

Setton, Kenneth M., *The Sixteenth Century to the Reign of Julius III*, Vol. III of *The Papacy and the Levant (1204-1571)*, Memoirs of the American Philosophical Society Vol. CLXI (Philadelphia: The American Philosophical Society, 1984)

Stella, Aldo, 'Bonifiche benedettine e precapitalismo veneto tra Cinquecento e Seicento', in *S. Benedetto e otto secoli (XII-XIX) di vita monastica nel padovano* (Padua: Antenore, 1980), pp. 171-93

Tanner, Marie, *The Last Descendant of Aeneas: The Hapsburgs and the Mythic Image of the Emperor* (New Haven: Yale University Press, 1993)

Tenenti, Alberto, and Ugo Tucci, eds, *Il Rinascimento: Società ed Economia*, Vol. V, *Storia di Venezia dalle origini alla caduta della Serenissima*, 8 vols (Rome: Istituto della Enciclopedia Italiana, 1992-98)

Tierney, Brian, *Religion, Law, and the Growth of Constitutional Thought, 1150-1650* (Cambridge: Cambridge University Press, 1982)

———, *Foundations of the Conciliar Theory* (Cambridge: Cambridge University Press, 1955)

Turner, Frederick, '"Hyperion to a Satyr": Criticism and Anti-structure in the Work of Victor Turner', in *Victor Turner and the Construction of Cultural Criticism*, ed. by Kathleen M. Ashley (Bloomington: Indiana University Press, 1990), pp. 47-62

Varanini, Gian Maria, 'Proprietà fondiaria e agricoltura', in Tenenti and Tucci, pp. 807-79

Ventura, Angelo, 'Considerazioni sull'agricoltura veneta e sull'accumulazione originaria del capitale nei secoli XVI e XVII', in *Agricoltura e sviluppo del capitalismo: Atti del convegno organizzato dall'Istituto Gramsci* (Rome 1968) (Rome: Editori Riuniti, 1970), pp. 519-60

Verstegen, Ian F., 'Francesco Maria and the Duchy of Urbino, Between Rome and Venice', in *Patronage and Dynasty: The Rise of the Della Rovere in Renaissance Italy*, ed. by Ian F. Verstegen (Kirksville, MO: Truman State University Press, 2007), pp. 141-60

Viggiano, Alfredo, *Governanti e governati: Legittimità del potere ed esercizio dell'autorità sovrana nello Stato veneto della prima età moderna* (Treviso: Fondazione Benetton, Canova, 1993)

Virgili, Antonio, *Francesco Berni* (Florence: Le Monnier, 1881)

Wendriner, Richard, 'Un codice di Ruzante nella Comunale di Verona', *Giornale storico della letteratura italiana*, 16 (1890), 436-37

―――, *Die paduanische Mundart bei Ruzante* (Breslau: Koebner, 1889)

Wood, Christopher S., *Albrecht Altdorfer and the Origins of Landscape* (Chicago: University of Chicago Press, 1993)

Zamperetti, Sergio, *I piccoli principi: Signorie locali, feudi e comunità soggette nello Stato regionale veneto dall'espansione territoriale ai primi del '600* (Venice: Il Cardo, 1991)

Zorzi, Ludovico, 'Nota al testo', in Beolco, *Teatro*, pp. 1604-36

―――, 'Note alla *Prima Orazione*', in Beolco, *Teatro*, pp. 1552-67

Index

Because citations of *I diarii* of Marino Sanuto occur on virtually every page, they are not included in the index.

Abano 26, 43-44, 45, 59, 82-83, 105, 116
Adria 44
Aeneid 51
Africa 40-42, 69
Agnadello, battle of 6, 7, 11, 19, 23
Alessi, Stefano 67
Alexander VI 20; *see also* papacy
Alexandria 10, 17, 50; *see also* Egypt
Alvarotto family 28, 30, 71
Alvarotto, Alvarotto 10, 11
Alvarotto, Conte 10
Alvarotto, Francesco 10, 11, 38
Alvarotto, Giacomo 10, 11, 30, 70-71
Alvarotto, Marc'Aurelio 10, 28
Alvarotto, Paolo 70
Ancona 39, 43
Antenor 30, 40, 51, 57, 58, 63, 80-81, 104, 116
Aquinas, Thomas 52
Aragon, house of 50
Aragona, Eleanora d' 69
Aretino, Pietro 53 n., 59, 59 n., 67 n.
Ariosto, Ludovico 69, 69 n.
Aristotle 52, 65, 90-91, 109, 121
Arquà 5, 39
Asia 16, 40-42
Asolo 7, 9, 12, 14, 19, 32, 35, 39, 57, 57 n., 73, 78-79
asses 84-85, 106, 118
Assumption, feast of 30
Augustine of Hippo 48
Austria 58

Badoer, Agnesina 17
Badoer, Francesco 45
Bandello, Matteo 34, 35
Baratto, Mario 36
Barbaro, Marco 20 n.

Barozzi, Pietro 8, 23
Bassano 17
Becichemo, Marino 30, 32, 56
Beltrami, Daniele 16, 17 n., 45 n.
Bembo, Bernardo 39, 46
Bembo, Pietro 9, 10, 11 n., 39, 44, 45, 45 n., 46 n., 54 n., 67 n.
benefices 11, 17, 23, 24, 25, 52, 67 n., 71, 90-91, 120
Beolco family 38, 64
Beolco, Angelo (Ruzante)
    Anconitana (*The Woman from Ancona/The Anconitan Play*) 7, 54 n., 66, 68
    Betia 6, 35, 47, 47 n., 48 n., 49 n., 51, 54, 54 n., 57, 65, 72
    Bilora (*Weasel*) 7, 53
    Dialogo facetissimo 6, 54 n.
    Fiorina 7
    Intermedio d'una comedia de Ruzante alla Pavana 39, 43 n., 68-69, 114
    Lettera all'Alvarotto 7, 47 n., 66, 68, 70, 70 n., 114
    Lettera giocosa (*Playful Letter*) 43
    Moscheta 7, 43 n., 56 n., 62 n., 63, 68; see also *Intermedio d'una comedia de Ruzante alla Pavana*
    Pastoral 6, 14, 29, 36, 40 n.
    Piovana (*The Girl from Piove*) 7, 11 n., 45
    prologues 56 n.
    Reduce (*The Veteran*) 6, 65
    Seconda Oratione 6, 34, 40, 40 n.
    Sopra la caccia see Lettera all'Alvarotto
    Vaccaria (*The Cow Comedy*) 7, 33 n.
    Vita humana see Lettera all'Alvarotto
    works in manuscripts 65-73
    anti-Florentine polemic 38, 39, 49, 51, 57, 59, 60, 64, 69, 72, 78-79, 86-87, 92-93, 103, 107, 109, 115, 119, 122
    emperor in works 47
    France, king of, in works 47
    performances 6, 7, 14, 26, 27, 28, 31, 32, 34, 35, 36, 45, 56, 57, 61, 62, 63-64, 65, 69-70, 72-73, 78-79, 103
    social programme 48, 65
    soldier 33, 33 n.
    theatre group 10, 26
    and Alvise Cornaro (Alvise Righi) 6, 25, 34, 51, 63, 74
    and Marco Cornaro 7, 31, 35, 36, 52, 56, 64, 86-87, 90-91, 107, 118, 120

  and mother 5
  and war 65
Beolco, Gian Giacomo 6, 9
Beolco, Gian Francesco 5, 6, 9, 38
Beolco, Imperio 6
Beolco, Lazzaro 5, 9
Beolco, Melchiorre 6
Beolco, Paola 6
Bergamo 11
Berni, Francesco 34, 35, 53 n., 70, 70 n.
Berthold, Peter 40
Bethlehem 39, 78-79, 103, 115
Biadego, Giuseppe 65, 69, 69 n., 70 n.
Bibbiena *see* Dovizi
birds 42, 58, 65, 80-81, 104, 116
boar 51, 64, 90-91, 120
Boccaccio, Giovanni 14
Boiardo, Matteo Maria 34
Bolani family 11
Bolani, Troian 11
Bologna 10
  University of 41
Bonardi, Antonio 5 n., 10, 22 n.
Boni, Valerio 23, 24
Borgia family 47
Borgia, Lucrezia 69
Borsellino, Nino 35 n.
Boschi, Ruggiero 46 n.
Brancaforte, Elio 41 n.
bread 82-83, 86-87, 92-93, 105, 107, 109, 117, 119, 121
Brescia 11, 20, 21, 23, 27, 28, 33
Briquet, C.M. 71 n.
Brisighella 29, 31, 49, 86-87, 107, 119
Brown, Patricia Fortini 40
Brown, Rawdon 9, 16, 28, 40 n.
Burgkmair, Hans 41, 56
Buzzacarini, G.F. 49

Cajetan *see* Vio, Tommaso de
Calendoli, Giovanni 57 n.
Calicut *see* Colecut
Calmo, Andrea 68

Calore, Andrea 17
Cambrai *see* League of Cambrai
    Peace of 47
Camillus, Furius 30
Campofregoso, Janus da 26, 33, 34
Capello family 15, 17, 18
Capello, Antonio 15, 18
Capello, Antonio qu. Batista 15 n.
Capello, Polo 13, 15, 17, 19, 20, 21, 59
Carnival 6, 32, 33, 69
Carrara family 17, 20, 27
Carroll, Linda L. 5 n., 6, 7 n., 16, 20, 22, 23 n., 24 n., 25 n., 26, 28, 32, 33, 38, 47, 48, 49, 49 n., 52, 52 n., 54, 59, 64, 65, 67 n.
Casella, Angela 69 n.
Castellesi, Adriano 23, 50
Caterina Corner 9, 19, 39
Cattini, Marco 46
Cestaro, Benvenuto 15 n., 17
Charles V (Charles I of Spain) 7, 13, 14, 16, 25, 27, 29, 30, 32, 33, 34, 50-51, 52, 57, 58, 64, 70 n.
Chigi, Agostino 33
China 40
Chrysostom, John 48
Cibo, Innocenzo 22, 24, 56-57, 59, 59 n., 69, 69 n., 70, 70 n., 71
Cicero 64
Clement VII (Giulio de' Medici) 53 n., 71
Colacut (Colecut, Colicut) 16, 28, 40-42, 50, 57, 80-81, 104, 116
Collalto family 18, 44
Collalto, Antonio di 18
Collalto, Toso da 33
Colussi, Giorgio 60, 103 n.
compagnie della Calza
    Immortali 24, 24 n., 25, 26, 27, 28, 45-46, 64
    Ortolani 24 n., 27, 28, 45-46, 48, 64
Concina, Ennio 15 n., 19
Contarini family 27
Contarini, Alvise 25
Contarini, Ambrosio 25
Contarini, Francesco 27, 40
Contarini, Marco 25
Contarini, Zacaria 37
Corfino, Girolamo 69

Corfino, Ludovico 66, 69, 70, 114
Cornaro, Alvise (Alvise Righi) 6, 25, 28, 51, 63, 66, 67, 68, 74
Cornaro, Giacomo (Giacomo Righi) 25
Cornaro, Marco 8, 9, 13, 15, 19, 25, 34, 67 n.
    as bishop of Padua 7-9, 12, 24, 25, 35, 38, 53, 54, 64, 65, 67, 70, 90-91, 94-95, 110, 120, 123
    as bishop of Verona 24, 30, 32, 34, 70
    episcopal entry 30, 31, 32, 43, 53, 56, 73
    and farming 45, 47
    and papacy 8, 10, 11, 12, 39, 44, 49, 51, 52, 54, 60-61
    and priesthood 60
    and prostitutes 48
    in Venice 15, 17, 19, 22, 23, 24
Corner family 8-9, 16, 17, 20, 22, 26, 32, 50, 53 n., 56, 57, 59, 62, 66-67, 67 n., 74, 88-89, 108, 120
Corner, Caterina *see* Caterina Corner
Corner, Francesco 13, 16, 25, 27, 29, 34, 50, 61
Corner, Jacomo 25, 50, 59
Corner, Marco *see* Cornaro, Marco
Corner, Zorzi 9, 15, 19, 20, 21, 22, 23, 25, 29, 30, 31, 44, 48, 50
Corner, Zuan 8, 19, 20, 26, 27, 67
Cosaza, Zuan 26, 28
cows 47, 59, 65, 68, 84-85, 106, 117
Cozzi, Gaetano 8, 15 n., 17
Cremona 69
Cristofari, Maria 53 n., 66, 71
Cruciani, Fabrizio 39, 48, 59 n.
Cummings, Anthony M. 23 n., 53 n., 69 n., 71 n.
Cyprus 9

da Corte (Cortivo), Zuan Antonio 8 n., 11 n., 14, 15 n., 26, 27, 29, 30, 31, 31 n., 32, 49, 55
dalla Vedova, Gaspare *see* di la Vedoa, Gaspare
dal Verme family 17, 19
Damascus 10, 50; *see also* Syria
Dandelet, Thomas James 47
Dandolo family 8,
D'Elia, Anthony 54
de la Tour d'Auvergne, Madeleine 22, 23
della Rovere, Francesco Maria 23, 39, 50, 59
della Scala family 17
della Torre, Girolamo 38

della Torre, Marc'Antonio 38
del Torre, Giuseppe 18, 19, 20 n., 22, 22 n., 46 n.
Del Vita, Alessandro 59 n.
Denmark 58
De Ventura, Paolo 56 n.
Diacceto, Jacopo da 71
di la Vedoa, Gaspare 43, 66-67
di la Vedoa, Hironimo 43, 66-67
Di Maria, Salvatore 59
Dionisotti, Carlo 71, 71 n.
doctors 31, 61, 62, 78-79, 98-99, 103, 115, 124
dogs 52, 53, 55, 63, 64, 92-93, 96-97, 98-99, 109, 111, 122, 124
Dolce, Vincenzo 31
Dolfin, Dolfin 35, 46, 70
Dolfin, Nicolò 14
Donà, Alessandro 33, 33 n.
Donado (Donà), Alvise 25
Donà, Francesco 43
Dondi Dall'Orologio, Francesco Scipione 8, 11 n., 22, 31
Dorighello, Francesco 9
Dossi, Dosso 47, 69 n., 70
Dottori, Anton Francesco de' 38
Dovizi, Bernardo (il Bibbiena) 44
Dykema, Peter A. 54

Earle, Peter 39
earrings 69-70
Edlin, Herbert 46
Egypt 9, 17, 39, 78-79, 103, 115; *see also* Alexandria
England 12, 15, 23, 28, 58; *see also* Henry VIII
equality 48, 55, 65
Erasmus 40, 52, 71
Este 28
Este, Alfonso I d' 11, 26, 29, 30, 43-44, 59, 70-71
Este, Cardinal Ippolito II d' 44

Fasullo, Franco 17 n., 22 n.
Favaretto, Lorena 13 n., 36, 37, 37 n., 55
Feltre 22
Ferdinand of Aragon 10, 12, 19
Ferdinand of Austria 33, 50, 58
Ferguson, Ronnie 52 n., 59 n.

Ferrara 6, 18, 19, 22, 29, 30, 69, 69 n., 70;
    see also Este, Alfonso I d'
Ferrarese (territory) 24, 27, 32, 55, 64
Ferrari, Ciro 46
Ferrari, G. 46 n.
Ferroni, Giulio 39
Ficino, Marsilio 55
Finlay, Robert 9, 16, 19, 20 n., 46 n.
Flanders 16, 28; *see also* galleys, Flanders or Western
Florence 10, 22, 24, 39, 70, 70 n., 71, 80-81, 104, 116; *see also* Beolco, Angelo, anti-Florentine polemic; *entries under* Medici
Foscari, Francesco 18, 19
Fragnito, Gigliola 23
France 12, 16, 21, 23, 29, 30, 33, 40, 40 n., 41 n., 44, 47, 50, 52, 58, 62, 64, 88-89, 108, 120; *see also* Francis I; Beolco, Angelo, France, king of, in works
Francis I 13, 14, 29, 30, 32, 51, 52
Frangipani, Cristoforo 43
Frederick III 41
Freedman, Paul 55
free will 48, 52
Friuli 15, 26
fruit 82-83, 105, 117
Fugger family 41-42

Gaismair, Michael 33
galleys, Flanders or Western 9, 16, 25, 48, 57
Gara della Rovere, Sisto 8
German merchants 40-42, 43
Germany 27, 30, 48, 50, 58, 80-81, 89-90, 100-01, 104, 112, 116, 120, 125
Giannetto, Nella 10, 39
Gibbons, Felton 69 n.
Giberti, Giovan Matteo 34
Gilbert, Felix 8, 9, 15, 19, 20 n.
Giorgione 24, 64
Giotto 9
Giuntine press 71
Giustinian family 22, 24 n.
Giustinian, Andrea qu. Unfredo 14
Giustinian, Antonio 14, 21

Giustinian, Bernardo 18, 19
Giustinian, Hironimo qu. Antonio 15, 17, 21
Giustinian, Hironimo qu. Unfredo 8, 14, 32, 35
Giustinian, Marin 49
Giustinian, Sebastian 23, 49
Gloria, Andrea 9, 17, 18, 19, 25
goats 47, 84-85, 106, 117-18
Gonzaga family 10
Gonzaga, Federico II 25, 26, 45, 67 n., 74
Gonzaga, Gianfrancesco 18
Grafton, Anthony 47
grain 43, 45, 82-83, 96-97, 105, 111, 117, 123
Grimani family 24 n.
Grimani, Antonio 11, 27, 29, 30, 32, 46
Grimani, Domenico 11, 30, 38, 49, 52, 53, 92-93, 109, 122
Grimani, Francesco 28
Grimani, Pietro 28
Gritti, Andrea 15, 19, 21, 22 n., 29, 32
Grubb, James S. 9, 20, 46
Gullino, Giuseppe 9 n., 19, 20

Habsburg, house of 50, 51; *see also* Charles V, Ferdinand of
    Austria, Maximilian I
Halberstadt-Freud, H.C. 38
Hale, J.R. 15 n.
hat dance *see pavana*
hawks 78-79, 103, 115
Henry VIII 49; *see also* England
Hercules 47
Hesiod 69
Holy Roman Emperor 6, 11, 15, 20, 26, 27, 29, 32, 33, 47, 50, 64;
    see also Maximilian I, Charles V
homosexuality 53, 53 n., 66
horses 48, 86-87, 90-91, 96-97, 107, 111, 117, 118, 120, 123
Hughes, Diane Owen 69 n.
humanism, humanists 18-19, 49, 53 n., 54
Humphrey, Peter 69 n.
hunting 51, 52, 54, 55, 94-95, 96-97, 110, 111, 122

Immortali *see compagnie della Calza*
imperialists 6, 10, 13, 21, 22, 25, 28, 44, 58, 64, 65, 69, 71
India 16, 40-42

INDEX

Italia *see* Talia

Jerusalem 38
Jesus Christ 39, 48, 63, 78-79, 82-83, 86-87, 94-95, 100-01, 103, 105, 107, 111, 112, 115, 117, 119, 123, 125
Jews 78-79, 103, 115
Julius II (Giuliano della Rovere) 7, 8, 10, 11, 19, 20, 21, 50, 51; *see also* papacy

Kaplan, Paul H.D. 55
Kellenbenz, Hermann 16, 41 n.
King, Margaret L. 19
Klaniczay, Tibor 52
Knapton, Michael 15 n., 17
Knecht, R.J. 14 n., 58
Kohl, Benjamin G. 9

Labalme, Patricia H. 24 n.
Lane, Frederic C. 15, 16, 18, 20 n., 22, 46 n.
Lang, Apollonia 43
Lang, Matteo 10, 43-44
Laurenza, Domenico 38
Lawner, Lynne 53 n.
laws 54, 55, 57, 59, 62, 88-89, 96-101, 108, 111-13
Lazara, Giovanni 6, 11 n.
Lazzarini, Vittorio 17 n., 22 n., 45 n.
League of Cambrai 6, 7, 10, 20, 21, 50
    war of 6, 15, 18, 19, 20, 21, 28, 29, 33, 33 n., 37, 43, 64, 71
League of Cognac 6, 33
    war of 6, 33, 34
Legnago 15 n., 18, 46
Leipzig, University of 41
Leo X (Giovanni de' Medici) 8, 9, 10, 11, 22, 29, 30, 39, 50, 51, 53 n., 54, 64, 69, 71; *see also* papacy
    foreign policy 10, 11, 12, 13, 23, 29, 30, 31, 39-40, 41-42, 43-44, 49, 50, 57, 58, 59
Leonardo da Vinci 38
Lewis, Carolyn Kolb 17
Liguria 30
Ling, Lesley A. 17
Lisbon 41; *see also* Portugal
Logan, Oliver 23, 54

Lombardy 29, 34
London 28, 49; *see also* England
Looney, Dennis 62
Loredan family 22 n.
Loredan, Bernardo 13
Loredan, Zuan Francesco 22, 25
Loredan, Leonardo 9, 21, 30
Loredan, Lorenzo 15, 21, 22
Loredan, Marc'Antonio 25, 26
Loreto (Loreo) 43-44, 48, 48 n., 82-83, 86-87, 105, 107, 117, 119
Lotto, Lorenzo 69 n.
Lovarini, Emilio 5 n., 11 n., 24, 38, 64, 65-66, 67, 68, 70, 70 n., 71 n.
Lowe, K.J.P. 71 n.
Lucian of Samosata 71
Luther, Martin 29, 48, 52
Luvigliano 32

Magellan, Ferdinand 16
Magno, Andrea 14, 29, 30, 32
Magno, Stefano 14, 29, 36
Mallett, Michael E. 15 n., 19
Mantua 18, 24
Mantuanus, Baptista 47
Marcello, Cristoforo 23
Marcello, Valerio 27
Marignano, battle of 12, 59
marriage 55, 61, 63, 96-96, 98-99, 111-13, 124-25
Martinengo family 18, 23, 25
Martinengo, Cesare 34
Martinengo, Marc'Antonio 27, 28, 33
Mathew, K.S. 41, 41 n.
Maximilian I 6, 10, 12, 14, 17, 21, 22, 23, 41, 44, 50-51, 58, 64; *see also* Habsburg, house of ; Holy Roman Emperor
Medici family 10, 39, 53 n., 57, 59, 70
Medici, Alessandro de' 70, 70 n.
Medici, Giovanni de' *see* Leo X
Medici, Giuliano de' 10, 11
Medici, Giulio de' *see* Clement VII
Medici, Lorenzo de' (Il Magnifico) 10, 59
Medici, Lorenzo di Piero di Lorenzo 22, 40, 43, 71

INDEX

Menegazzo, Emilio 5 n., 6, 17 n., 22 n., 33 n., 36, 47, 51, 51 n., 54, 66
Mercadelli, Andrea 11
Michiel, Marcantonio 24
Milan 12, 29, 32, 41 n.
Mirano 46
Mocenigo family 18, 18 n.
Mocenigo, Alvise 18, 27
Mocenigo, Bianca 18
Mocenigo, Lucia 18
Mocenigo, Lunardo 15, 18, 29
Mocenigo, Tommaso 18, 19
Molà, Luca 10, 50
Moncallero, Giuseppe Lorenzo 14 n.
Monga, Luigi 38
Montagnana 5, 6, 9, 11
More, Thomas 49, 49 n., 71
Morello, Giacomo 66, 67
Moro, Cristoforo 26
Moro, Gabriel 25, 26
Morosini family 9
Muir, Edward 24 n., 40
Mullo, Jeronymo dal 31

Naldo family 49; *see also* Brisighella
Naldo, Babon di 29; *see also* Brisighella
Naples 13, 14n., 20, 27, 39-40, 69, 78-79, 88-89, 104, 108, 115, 119
natural 52, 63, 78-79, 80-81, 94-95, 104, 110, 115, 116, 122
Noah 47, 57, 84-85, 106, 118
Nogarola family 25

Oberman, Heiko 54
Oliveira Barata, José 56
Olivieri, Achille 37
Origen 48, 52
Orsato, Gaspare 13
Orsini, Alfonsina 23
Ortolani *see compagnie della Calza*

Paccagnella, Ivano 35
Padoan, Giorgio 5 n., 14, 66, 67

Padua 5, 6, 7, 10, 11, 14, 15, 17, 18, 19, 20, 20 n., 21, 22, 24, 25, 26, 27, 29, 31, 34, 35, 37, 50, 57, 78-79, 100-01, 103, 112, 115, 124-25
    bishopric of 7, 8, 12, 25, 29, 30, 31, 32, 36, 51, 54
    cathedral canons 14, 30, 35, 36, 37
    civil government 8, 30, 37, 44
    defence of 6, 17, 30, 49
    Estimo 13, 36, 57, 70
    University of 5, 9, 13, 15, 20, 21, 25, 30, 36, 37, 38, 43, 56, 57, 63, 78-79, 88-89, 90-91, 98-99, 103, 108, 115, 119, 120, 121, 124-25
    Venetian governors of 8, 9, 18, 19, 21, 25, 26, 29, 30, 44-45, 48, 50, 56, 90-91, 120
    walls of 28, 32, 48, 86-87, 107, 119
    and Antenor 30, 40, 51, 57, 80-81, 104, 116
    and Corner 9, 19
    and manuscript copies 66-67
Pagels, Elaine 48
papacy 7, 15, 17, 19, 22, 23, 30, 33, 41, 49, 50, 60-61, 62, 69, 71, 84-85, 90-91, 106, 117
Papal States 49; *see also* Romagna; Bologna
papalisti 8, 11, 15, 30, 50, 57
Pavan 5, 6, 24, 26, 27, 30, 36, 37, 38, 39, 40, 45, 46, 50, 57, 82-83, 90-91, 104, 105, 117, 120
    dialect of 73-74, 80-81, 104, 116
    earthly paradise 48, 86-87, 107, 119
    fertility of 47, 65
    possible or intended performances in 6, 53, 53 n., 54, 64
    and Antenor 80-81, 104, 116
    and soldiers 49
    and *visinanza* 53, 78-79, 103, 115
pavana (hat dance) 24, 59, 82-83, 105, 117
Pavia 29, 33 n., 34
peasants 24, 36, 39, 40, 45-46, 47, 50, 52, 53, 54-55, 56, 57, 57 n., 58, 59, 62, 64, 65, 78-79, 98-99, 103, 112, 115, 123-25
Pelagius 52
Pellegrini, Giovanni Battista 48, 60
Peripatetics 52
Pernumia 5, 6, 11, 38
Pesaro, Alessandro 28
Pesaro, Francesco 13
Pesaro, Hironimo 28, 29

Pesaro, Jacopo 23, 50, 60
Pesaro, Piero 28, 33, 59
Petrarca 6, 39, 60, 80-81, 104, 116
Petrucci, F. 59 n., 70 n.
pigs 84-85, 106, 117
Piove di Sacco 9, 11, 48
Pisani family 16, 17, 22, 22 n.
Pisani, Alvise 14, 15, 20, 22, 24, 25
Pisani, Francesco 20, 22, 24, 67
Pisani, Zorzi 15, 20
Pisani, Zuan 24
Platonism 55
Polano, Sergio 6
Polesine 18
Polo, Marco 59
Portugal 16, 28, 39, 40-42, 46, 57, 58; *see also* Lisbon
Praglia, abbey of 30
priests 60-61, 63, 64, 78-79, 84-85, 98-99, 103, 105, 111, 115, 117, 124-25
Priuli, Alvise 30
Priuli, Ferigo 26
Priuli, Francesco 26

Querella contra Madonna Trucignicignacola (The Case against Lady Trucignicignacola) 68
Querini, Piero 26, 43-45
Querini, Stefano 26, 45

Rambaldo, Antonio 18
rams 59, 84-85, 106, 117
Reynolds, Anne 34, 70 n.
Richardson, Brian 14
Rigobello, Bruno 22, 70
Rodriguez-Salgado, M.J. 27
Roland 53, 92-93, 109, 122
Romagna 29, 49, 59, 88-89, 90-91, 108, 119, 120
Rome 24, 25, 30, 32, 34, 40, 43, 49, 57, 58, 62, 69, 70, 71, 82-83, 88-89, 90-91, 92-93, 105, 108, 109, 117, 119, 120, 121
Romei, Danilo 53 n., 66
Ronchi, Gabriella 69 n.
Rossi, G.B. 46
Ruggiero, Guido 53 n.

Ruzante *see* Beolco, Angelo
Rylands, Philip 26, 45

Sabbatino, Pasquale 38
Salamon, Michiel 15, 21
Salviati, Giovanni 22, 24, 56-57, 59, 70, 70 n.
Samaritans 78-79, 103, 115
Sambin, Paolo 5, 5 n., 9, 33 n., 38
Sanguineti White, Laura 24 n.
Sanseverino, Pier Antonio da 27
Sanseverino, Roberto da 33
Sanudo, Marin (Marino Sanuto) 12, 37, 53, 59
Scaligero *see* della Scala
Scarabello, Giovanni 10
Scardeone, Bernardino 31
Scrovegni, Enrico 9, 50
Scrovegni, Giovanna 9
Seidel Menchi, Silvana 54
Selim the Grim 12, 13, 27, 64
Seneca 52, 90-91, 109, 121
Seneca, Federico 19, 21
Setton, Kenneth M. 8, 12, 14 n., 15 n., 29, 40, 50, 51
sheep 47
silk 50
Sirmione 28
soldiers 29, 31, 32, 33, 40, 49, 56, 65, 70, 86-87, 100-01, 107, 112, 119, 125
Spain 10, 11, 12, 13, 16, 19, 23, 29, 30, 40, 44, 50, 55, 57, 58, 62, 69-70, 88-89, 100-01, 108, 112, 119, 120, 125
sparrows 78-79, 103, 115
Speroni, Sperone 6, 40
starlings 40
Stella, Aldo 45 n.
Stoics 52
Suleiman 27, 64
swallows 40, 57, 58, 80-81, 104, 116
Swiss 11, 12, 41
Syria 9, 39; *see also* Damascus

Talia 104
Tanner, Marie 47, 51
Tierney, Brian 54

trees 46-47, 62, 84-85, 88-89, 106, 108, 117, 120
Trevisan family 17, 22 n.
Trevisan, Andrea 15, 19, 21
Trevisan, Bortolo 22
Trevisan, Domenego 15, 19, 21, 22, 22 n., 25, 26, 30
Trevisan, Pietro 25
Treviso 20, 20 n., 21, 29, 43, 82-83, 105, 117
Turks 9, 12, 16, 23, 39, 40, 45, 55, 64, 80-81, 100-01, 104, 112, 116, 125
Turner, Victor 7
Tuscan language 60, 68, 78-79, 103, 115; *see also* Beolco, Angelo, anti-Florentine polemic
Tuscany 30, 39, 53 n.

Urbino 22, 39-40, 78-79, 88-89, 104, 108, 115, 120

Valois, house of 64; *see also* Francis I; France
Varanini, Gian Maria 15, 17, 17 n., 18, 19, 21, 22 n., 45 n.
Varasi, Elena 69 n.
vegetables 45, 58, 61, 82-83, 105, 117
Vendramin family 15
Vendramin, Luca 15
Venice 5, 6, 7, 8, 9, 10, 19, 20, 22, 25, 26, 35, 37, 40, 46, 58, 68, 73, 82-83, 103, 105, 117
    Venetian isles (*le Veniesie*) 88-89, 90-91, 108, 119, 120
    and England 23, 48
    and Ferrara 11, 18, 19, 22, 24
    and France 13, 14, 16, 21, 29, 33, 43-44, 55, 58
    and galleys *see* galleys, Flanders or Western
    and Holy Roman Empire 14, 15, 16, 21, 26, 27, 29, 33, 41, 43-44, 50, 51, 57, 58, 64
    and Milan 41 n.
    and Ottoman Empire (Turkey) 40, 45
    and Padua 17, 18, 19
    and papacy 11, 12, 15, 16, 21, 22, 23, 26, 27, 29, 30, 31, 32, 33, 33 n., 39, 43, 49, 51, 57, 58
    and Portugal 41
    and printing 4, 67, 71
    and Spain 13, 16, 19, 58
Ventura, Angelo 15, 15 n., 45 n.
Verità, Girolamo 70
Verona 17, 19, 24, 32, 33, 34, 47, 69, 70, 71, 71 n., 73

Verstegen, Ian F. 40
Vicenza 5, 26, 32, 33, 70, 71
Vicoaro, Giacomo 33, 33 n., 34
Vienna, University of 41
Viggiano, Alfredo 46
Vio, Tommaso de (Cajetan) 48, 52
Virgili, Antonio 34, 67 n., 70 n.

war 65
Welser family 42
Wendriner, Richard 66, 67, 102
wine 82-83, 105, 117
women 47, 48, 55, 60-61, 62, 70, 84-85, 86-87, 100-01, 106, 107, 112, 118-19, 124-25
wood 46-48, 50, 51, 57, 60, 88-89, 108, 120
Wood, Christopher S. 47

Zabarella, Francesco 54
Zacaroto family 26
Zacaroto, Giacomo 26
Zago, R. 14 n.
Zamperetti, Sergio 15 n., 37
Zorzi, Ludovico 31 n., 38, 51 n., 66, 67
Zorzi, Marino 30, 37

MHRA Critical Texts

This series aims to provide affordable critical editions of lesser-known literary texts that are not in print or are difficult to obtain. The texts will be taken from the following languages: English, French, German, Italian, Portuguese, Russian, and Spanish. Titles will be selected by members of the distinguished Editorial Board and edited by leading academics. The aim is to produce scholarly editions rather than teaching texts, but the potential for crossover to undergraduate reading lists is recognized. The books will appeal both to academic libraries and individual scholars.

Malcolm Cook
Chairman, Editorial Board

Editorial Board

Professor John Batchelor (English)
Professor Malcolm Cook (French) (*Chairman*)
Professor Ritchie Robertson (Germanic)
Professor Derek Flitter (Spanish)
Professor Brian Richardson (Italian)
Dr Stephen Parkinson (Portuguese)
Professor David Gillespie (Slavonic)

Published titles

1. *Odilon Redon, 'Écrits'* (edited by Claire Moran, 2005)

2. *Les Paraboles Maistre Alain en Françoys* (edited by Tony Hunt, 2005)

3. *Letzte Chancen: Vier Einakter von Marie von Ebner-Eschenbach* (edited by Susanne Kord, 2005)

4. *Macht des Weibes: Zwei historische Tragödien von Marie von Ebner-Eschenbach* (edited by Susanne Kord, 2005)

5. *A Critical Edition of 'La tribu indienne; ou, Édouard et Stellina' by Lucien Bonaparte* (edited by Cecilia Feilla, 2006)

6. *Dante Alighieri, 'Four Political Letters'* (translated and with a commentary by Claire E. Honess, 2007)

7. *'La Disme de Penitanche'* by Jehan de Journi (edited by Glynn Hesketh, 2006)

8. *'François II, roi de France'* by Charles-Jean-François Hénault (edited by Thomas Wynn, 2006)

10. *La Peyrouse dans l'Isle de Tahiti, ou le Danger des Présomptions: drame politique* (edited by John Dunmore, 2006)

11. *Casimir Britannicus. English Translations, Paraphrases, and Emulations of the Poetry of Maciej Kazimierz Sarbiewski* (edited by Krzysztof Fordoński and Piotr Urbański, 2008)

12. *'La Devineresse ou les faux enchantements'* by Jean Donneau de Visé and Thomas Corneille (edited by Julia Prest, 2007)

13. *'Phosphorus Hollunder'* und *'Der Posten der Frau'* von Louise von François (edited by Barbara Burns, 2008)

15. *Ovide du remede d'amours* (edited by Tony Hunt, 2008)

16. Angelo Beolco (il Ruzante), *'La prima oratione'* (edited by Linda L. Carroll, 2008)

Forthcoming titles

9. *Istoire de la Chastelaine du Vergier et de Tristan le Chevalier* (edited by Jean-François Kosta-Théfaine)

14. *Le Gouvernement present, ou éloge de son Eminence, satyre ou la Miliade* (edited by Paul Scott)

17. Richard Robinson, *'The Rewarde of Wickednesse'* (edited by Allyna E. Ward)

18. Henry Crabb Robinson, *'Essays on Kant, Schelling, and German Aesthetics'* (edited by James Vigus)

19. *A Sixteenth-Century Arthurian Romance: 'L'Hystoire de Giglan filz de messire Gauvain qui fut roy de Galles. Et de Geoffroi de Maience son compaignon'* (edited by Caroline A. Jewers)

For details of how to order please visit our website at www.criticaltexts.mhra.org.uk

www.ingramcontent.com/pod-product-compliance
Lightning Source LLC
Chambersburg PA
CBHW070550170426
43201CB00012B/1788